Paid
25¢

Silver Burdett & Ginn
SCIENCE

GEORGE G. MALLINSON
Distinguished Professor
of Science Education
Western Michigan University

JACQUELINE B. MALLINSON
Associate Professor of Science
Western Michigan University

WILLIAM L. SMALLWOOD
Head, Science Department
The Community School
Sun Valley, Idaho

CATHERINE VALENTINO
Former Director of Instruction
North Kingstown School Department
North Kingstown, Rhode Island

SILVER BURDETT & GINN
LEXINGTON, MA • MORRISTOWN, NJ
Atlanta, GA • Cincinnati, OH • Dallas, TX • Menlo Park, CA • Northfield, IL

THE SILVER BURDETT & GINN ELEMENTARY SCIENCE PROGRAM

Pupil Books Levels 1-6
Teacher Editions Levels K-6

Silver Burdett & Ginn

SCIENCE

Contents

The Adventure of Science .... A

Unit One
Discovering the Plant and Animal World 1

CHAPTER 1 Activities of Green Plants 2
CHAPTER 2 Animals Without a Backbone 26
CHAPTER 3 Animals With a Backbone 56
CHAPTER 4 Living Communities 80

Science in Careers 104
People in Science 105
Developing Skills 106

Unit Two
Discovering Matter and Energy 108

CHAPTER 5 Building Blocks of Matter 110
CHAPTER 6 Physical Changes in Matter 132
CHAPTER 7 Understanding Electricity 154
CHAPTER 8 Sources of Energy 180

Science in Careers 206
People in Science 207
Developing Skills 208

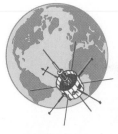

Unit Three
**Discovering the Earth
and Universe**................................. 210

CHAPTER 9 Changes in the Earth 212
CHAPTER 10 Cleaning Up the Earth 236
CHAPTER 11 Changes in the Weather 258
CHAPTER 12 Beyond the Solar System 282

Science in Careers 306
People in Science 307
Developing Skills 308

Unit Four
**Discovering
the Human Body**................................. 310

CHAPTER 13 Support and Movement of the Body 312
CHAPTER 14 Transport Systems of the Body 334

Science in Careers 358
People in Science 359
Developing Skills 360

Study Guide 362
Glossary 394
Index 404

The Adventure of Science

What Is Science?

Why can't insects grow to be the size of elephants? How is a firefly's light different from the light of an electric bulb? How do muscles move bones?

Science can help you find the answer to questions like these. Science is a way of asking and answering questions about the world. It is a way that human beings can learn about the world around them. Plants, animals, matter, energy, the earth, space, and weather are all part of the world around you.

What Will You Learn in Science?

Scientists have a method to learn how and why things happen. In science class you will learn to use this method. First you will ask a question. The students in the picture have asked a question. "How do materials differ in the way they heat?"

Next, you will gather information. The information may help answer your question. Some of this information will come from what you observe. Often, observations lead to a guess, or trial answer. This guess is called a hypothesis (hī poth' ə sis). After you form a hypothesis, you will test it to see if it is correct. This girl formed a hypothesis. *Soil and sand absorb heat faster than water because they are darker in color.* How do you think she can test her hypothesis?

You will study the results of your tests. Then you will come to the last step in the scientific method. You will try to draw conclusions. This means you will make statements based on what you have learned. What conclusions do you think the girl in the picture may draw?

c

How Is Science Important in My Life?

Long ago, science was not a part of everyday life. People could not explain many things that happened in the world. They made up myths, or stories, to explain these things. One myth was that lightning was a spear thrown by an angry god in the sky. Another myth was that comets caused disease and bad luck. Many years ago, it was hard to stay healthy. People did not understand that germs caused disease.

Today, people know more about lightning, comets, and disease. Many buildings have steel rods or wires on them. The rods or wires carry lightning safely into the ground. Pilots in special planes enter storm clouds to study lightning. Probes have been sent into space to find out more about comets. Thanks to science, many diseases now can be prevented or cured. What diseases are you protected against? Think of some times when you were ill. How did your treatment differ from that of a person in the past?

D

A Matter of Opinion

Scientists use certain thinking skills to solve problems. For example, scientists need to be able to look at common objects in new ways. Scientists must keep an open mind. They must consider all of the information before drawing conclusions. You will use thinking skills like these in this activity.

You are going to go on a science scavenger hunt. You will learn to think about and classify common objects in new ways. Number a piece of paper from 1 to 10. Read the list of groups below. Then look around your classroom for different types of matter. For each group, list as many kinds of matter as you can.

1. Matter that a magnet would attract
2. Matter that can be used to reduce friction
3. Matter that stretches
4. Matter that can be used as insulation
5. Matter that is waterproof
6. Matter that contains a mineral
7. Matter that is made from living things
8. Matter that can be a source of energy
9. Matter that can be used as a simple machine
10. Matter that would be useful in an emergency

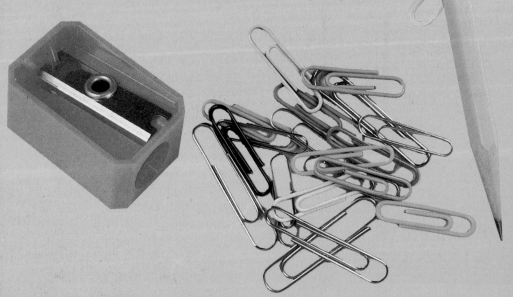

E

Mountain of the Mists

Deep in the jungles of South America there is a mysterious mountain. Its peak rises 2,700 m above the lush green forest floor. The mountain is hidden from the world below. Its forests and valleys have been lost in the clouds for millions of years. The mountain is called Cerro de la Neblina, or "Mountain of the Mists." Few people have tried to climb up through the cool mists at the top of it.

Until a few years ago, people knew more about Mars than they did about this mountain. Now, teams of scientists are exploring it. They are finding living things that have never been seen before on Earth. Would you predict that scientists would find dinosaurs or other extinct (ek stingkt') animals? Would you expect them to find an earthworm that is a foot long?

Mountain of the Mists

Scientists step from a helicopter onto the mountaintop. Their feet sink into spongy lichens and mosses. They see streams with water as dark as tea. They observe giant earthworms. They see frogs with legs longer than any seen before. Almost everywhere the scientists look they find plants found nowhere else on earth.

The scientists are surprised to find plants that look like artichokes on long stalks. These strange plants were named *Neblinaria*, after the mountain. The phrase "Find something new!" describes the excitement each person there feels. The pictures show some of the new plants and animals found on the mountain. What can you conclude about each of these plants and animals? How would you classify them?

Scientists on Mount Neblina work in teams. Each member of the team is an expert in one area of science. Some scientists study birds or insects. Others are experts in fungi or mosses. Some scientists classify the animals or plants. Scientists find that working together is exciting. One team member exclaimed, "To be on a trip with all these other scientists is like being a little kid again. You run around and catch frogs and bugs, only now you have somebody to tell you about them."*

Exploring the mountain is like going on a camping trip. Scientists must hike through the forests. They cannot carry heavy science equipment. They must make observations, keep records, and collect samples with just a few pieces of equipment. If you could carry just three pieces of science equipment as you explored, what would you take? How would you use each piece of equipment?

*From *Science 85* published by the American Association for the Advancement of Science. Used by permission.

Sometimes the scientists face problems. Mount Neblina is surrounded by rain forest. It has no roads. Scientists can reach the mountain only by helicopter. They find strong winds and frequent rains on the mountain. Scientists are unsure of what kinds of animals they will meet. What problems do scientists have to solve in order to explore the mountain? What dangers do you think scientists face on Mount Neblina?

In spite of the dangers, scientists continue to explore the mountain. One scientist explained why. He said, "No one's ever walked here before. No one's ever stood where I've been standing."*

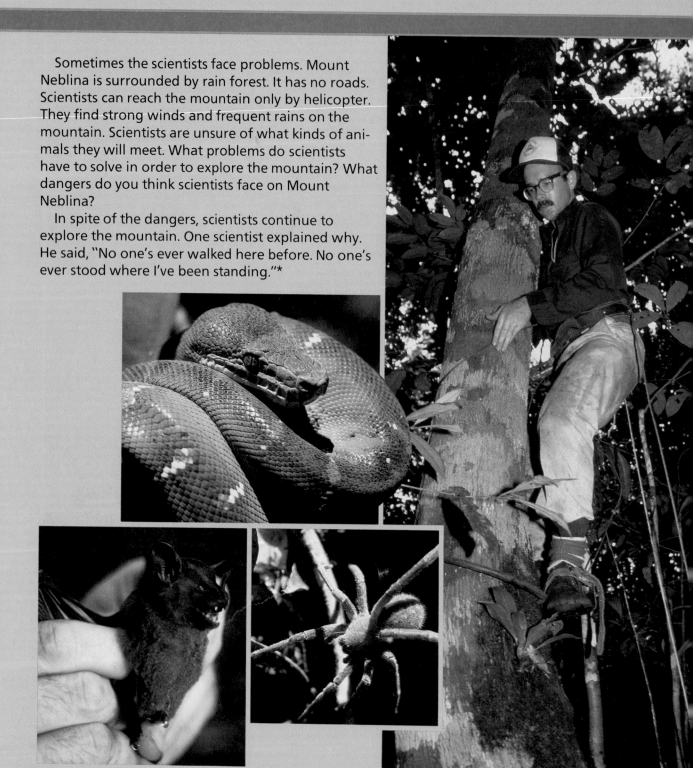

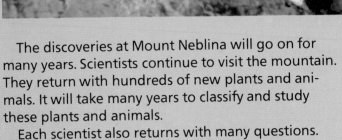

The discoveries at Mount Neblina will go on for many years. Scientists continue to visit the mountain. They return with hundreds of new plants and animals. It will take many years to classify and study these plants and animals.

Each scientist also returns with many questions. How do plants reproduce when there are few insects to carry pollen? Why do some frogs on the mountain hatch as tiny frogs instead of tadpoles? The scientists begin to answer these questions by forming hypotheses. What hypotheses would you form to answer these questions? What other questions would you ask? Scientists may answer these questions in the future. Could you be one of these scientists?

Unit One
Discovering the Plant and Animal World

Chapter 1–Activities of Green Plants This coneflower's bright colors attract insects to it. The insects help the plant to produce new plants of the same kind. This chapter will explain some activities of plants that help to keep them alive.

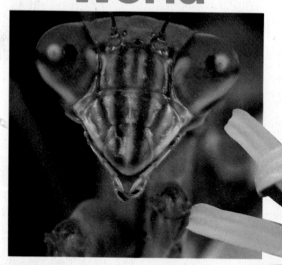

Chapter 2–Animals Without a Backbone You are looking at a close-up view of an insect called a praying mantis. The praying mantis and many other animals have no backbone.

Chapter 3—Animals With a Backbone
This gibbon belongs to a group of animals that includes mice and elephants. This chapter will compare some animals with a backbone.

Chapter 4—Living Communities
Clownfish, sea anemones, and coral live together in communities. These living things affect each other and the world around them.

1

Activities of Green Plants

In the spring the weather becomes warm, and green plants begin to grow. After a few weeks of growth, many plants produce beautifully colored flowers. The picture shows the stages in the opening of a daffodil flower. Flowers such as the daffodil do more than add beauty to the world. They are an important part of the plant. Without flowers many plants could not produce more of their kind.

Producing new plants is one important activity that green plants carry out. What are some other activities of green plants? How do the parts of green plants help them carry out these activities? You will find the answers to these questions in this chapter.

Plants and Animals Are Alike

What needs do all living things have?

All living things are alike in many ways. One way in which they are alike is that they are made up of cells. A **cell** is the basic unit of all living things. Cells are sometimes called the "building blocks of life." Some plants and animals are made up of only one cell. But most of the living things you are familiar with are made of millions of cells. The cells that make up most plants and animals can be compared with the bricks that make up a building. But, unlike bricks, most cells are very small. They cannot be seen without a microscope.

Most living things are made of many different kinds of cells. For example, the cells in your brain are quite different from those in your heart. The cells in the roots of a plant are different from those in the leaves or the stem.

Onion skin cells

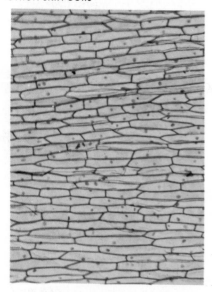

Bricks in a wall

Corn plants

Giraffe

Living things are alike in another way. All living things must satisfy certain needs in order to stay alive. All animals and plants need food, water, and air. However, plants and animals meet these needs in different ways. Green plants can make their own food, while animals must get food from plants or other animals. Are you more closely related to green plants or to animals? Why?

To satisfy their needs, living things must carry out life processes (pros'es iz). **Life processes** are the activities that keep living things alive. Some of the life processes carried out by all living things are listed in the chart below.

LIFE PROCESSES OF LIVING THINGS

Life process	What it means
Getting food	Green plants make their own food. People and other animals get food from plants and animals.
Releasing energy	Living things break down food to release energy stored in food.
Removing wastes	Living things get rid of waste materials.
Growing	Living things grow in size; they also replace old, worn cells by growing new cells.
Reproducing	Living things produce more living things of the same kind.

Transporting Materials

How do green plants transport the materials needed to make food?

You have learned some ways in which living things are alike. One way in which living things differ is in how they carry out some of the life processes. Most living things get food by eating plants and animals. But green plants do not eat food—they make it.

Green plants need three things to make food. They need (1) water, (2) carbon dioxide (kär'bən dī ok'sīd), and (3) light energy. How do green plants get these things? Food making usually takes place in the leaf cells of green plants. So the things needed to make food must be transported to these leaf cells by the roots, stems, and leaves.

Roots play an important role in transporting materials for food making. The picture shows small hairlike parts growing out from the sides of

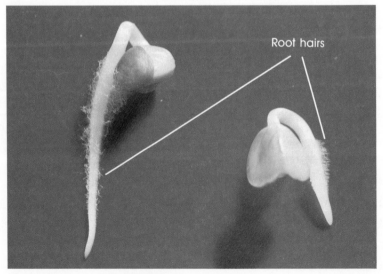

Root hairs

Root hairs on radish seedlings

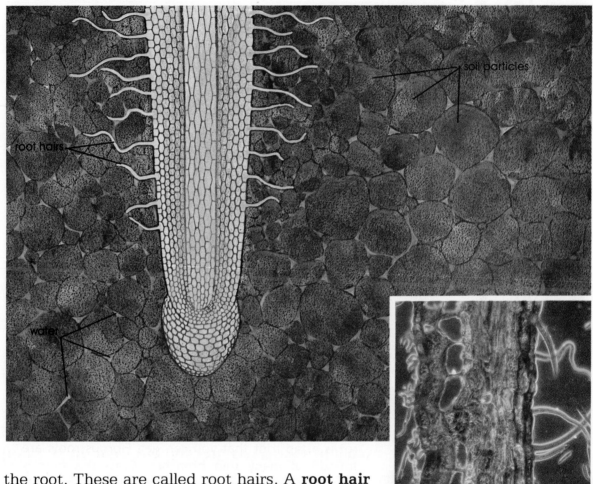

the root. These are called root hairs. A **root hair** is part of a single cell that grows from a root into the soil. Root hairs grow near the tips of roots. Almost all the water taken in by roots is taken in by the root hairs. The rest of the root helps to anchor the plant in the soil and to store food.

Root hairs under a microscope

The small root hairs enter spaces between bits of soil. The water in these spaces is taken in, or absorbed, by the root hairs. There are millions of root hairs on most plant roots. The more root hairs there are, the more water the root can absorb. The picture shows how root hairs look under a microscope.

How do roots help plants?

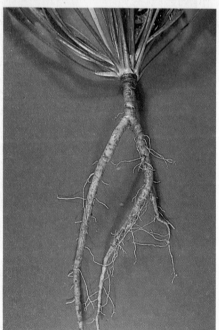

Materials 6 plants with roots attached / newspapers / drawing paper / colored pencils or markers

Procedure

A. With your teacher's help, collect six different kinds of plants, along with their roots. You might carefully pull up weeds from a vacant lot. Or, with permission from your parents, you might pull up some of their garden plants or potted houseplants.

B. Carefully shake most of the dirt off the roots of the plants. Spread the plants out on newspapers. Observe the roots of your plants.

1. Do you see many little roots or one main root?
2. Are the roots long or short? Are they thick or thin?
3. Make a drawing of each of your plants.

C. Look at the pictures on this page of a *tap root* and *fibrous roots.* A tap root is one long, thick main root that stores food for the plant. The tap root also forms some small roots that branch out to the sides. A carrot is a tap root that you can eat. Fibrous roots are formed of many thin branches. Grass has fibrous roots that grow over a large area. Compare the roots of your plants with the roots in the pictures.

4. How many of your plants have tap roots? Label any tap roots on your drawings.
5. How many of your plants have fibrous roots? Label any fibrous roots on your drawings.

Conclusion

1. Describe two kinds of roots.
2. Why do dandelions stay alive even when very little rain falls?
3. How do fibrous roots help a plant during heavy rains or winds?

From the roots, water is transported to the stem. The stem is the part of the plant between the roots and the leaves. The stem transports water and food to all parts of the plant through tubes.

The picture shows the inside of a stem. Notice that there are two kinds of tubes within the stem. Both kinds of tubes occur in bundles. One kind of tube transports water upward from the roots to the leaves. The other kind of tube transports food from the leaves downward to all parts of the plant. Look at the bundles of water-carrying tubes. In what direction does water move through the stem? Where does it go?

water-carrying tubes

food-carrying tubes

stem

Stem cross section

Do You Know?

You have probably heard of meat-eating animals. There are also meat-eating plants. Probably the most well-known of these plants is the Venus's-flytrap.

The Venus's-flytrap catches insects that land on its leaves. The surface of each leaf has sensitive hairs on the surface. Each leaf has a fold in the center. When an insect lands on a leaf, it touches the hairs. At once the plant's leaf folds in half and snaps shut, trapping the insect. Glands in the leaf then give off special juices. They digest the insect's body and the food is absorbed by the leaf. Then the leaf opens again, ready for the next victim.

A Venus's-flytrap traps insects to get minerals, especially nitrogen. All plants need minerals to perform life processes. As they absorb water from the soil, plants also take in minerals. But a Venus's-flytrap grows in bogs and swamps where the soil is poor in the minerals the plant needs. So this plant gets its supply of minerals from insects.

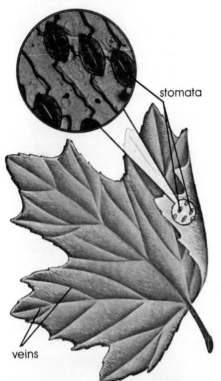

stomata

veins

The stem transports water and minerals from the roots to the leaves. Most leaves contain small, thin tubes called **veins** (vānz). The veins are much like the tubes in the stem. Some of the veins carry water to the leaves. Other veins carry food from the leaf cells down to the roots.

Besides water, leaf cells need carbon dioxide to make food. Carbon dioxide is one of the gases in air. How does air get into a leaf? The picture on the left shows the underside of a leaf as seen through a microscope. The small oval shapes are openings called **stomata** (stō′mə tə). Air enters a leaf through these stomata.

Light energy is the third thing needed for leaf cells to make food. Many leaves, like the one shown in the picture, are flat and broad. This allows light to reach the food-making cells inside the leaf.

Finding Out

Where are a plant's water-carrying tubes?

Put several drops of red food coloring into a jar three-fourths filled with water. Stir the water. Get a celery stalk with some leaves still on it. Cut about 3 cm off the bottom of the stalk. Place the stalk in the colored water and leave it in the jar overnight.

The next day examine the leaves. What has happened? Why did this happen? Take the stalk out of the water and cut off another 3 cm. Look at the bottom of the cut stalk. Where are the water-carrying tubes? How do you know?

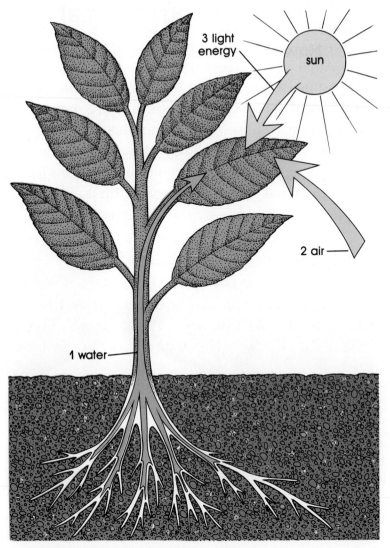

How a plant gets materials for food making

The drawing shows how a green plant gets the things it needs to make food.

1. Water enters the roots and moves through the stem to the leaf.
2. Air, containing carbon dioxide, enters the leaf through the stomata.
3. Sunlight striking the leaf provides the energy that leaf cells need to make food.

Food Making in a Leaf

How do green plants make food?

Imagine a factory in which bread is made. Flour, milk, and other materials are needed to make bread. These materials must first be transported to the factory. Then they must be mixed together to form dough. The dough is then baked in ovens. Heat energy is needed for baking. The product that is made by this process is bread.

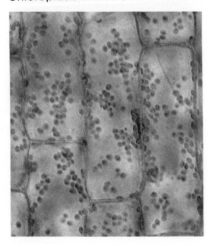

Chloroplasts in elodea leaf cells

The leaf of a green plant is much like a factory. Water and carbon dioxide are materials that must be transported to the leaf factory. Sunlight provides the energy to make the product. Food, in the form of sugar, is the product that is made. The process by which green plants make food is called **photosynthesis** (fō tə sin'thə sis).

To better understand photosynthesis, you should first know what the inside of a leaf is like. You can see chloroplasts (klôr'ə plasts) in the cells of this leaf. A **chloroplast** is a small green body in

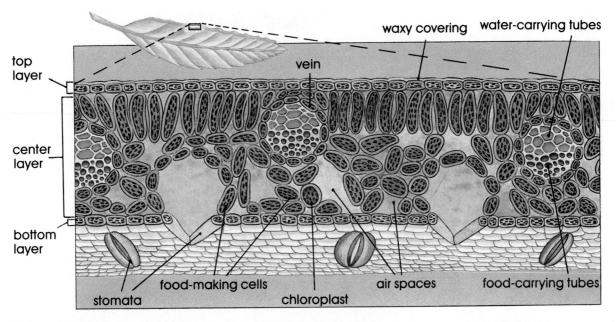

waxy covering   water-carrying tubes

top layer

vein

center layer

bottom layer

stomata   food-making cells   chloroplast   air spaces   food-carrying tubes

Leaf cross section

plant cells. The green color comes from a special material that is needed by the plant to make food. This material is called **chlorophyll** (klôr′ə fil).

The drawing shows how the cells inside a leaf would look under a microscope. Notice the waxy covering on the top and bottom. Beneath this covering is a single layer of cells. These cells help protect the leaf from damage. Usually these cells do not contain chloroplasts. Find these cells in the drawing. Notice the stomata in the bottom layer of these cells. As you learned, gases enter and leave the plant through these openings.

The food-making cells are in the middle part of the leaf. There are a great many chloroplasts in these cells. Around the food-making cells are air spaces. These air spaces are connected to stomata and allow carbon dioxide to reach the food-making cells. The vein contains cells that carry water to the food-making cells.

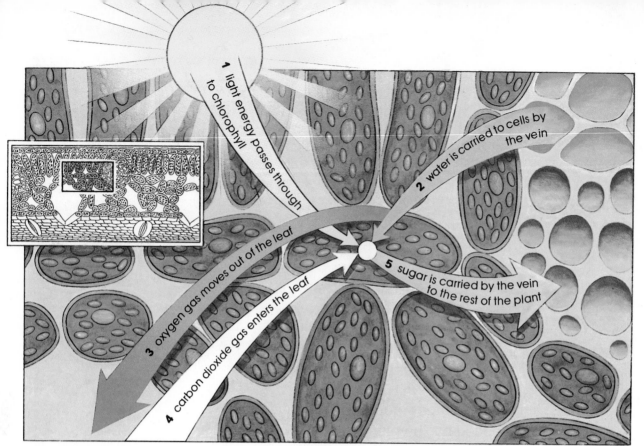

Food making in a leaf

You have seen how the food-making cells get the water and carbon dioxide they need to make food. Now you will see how food is made in these cells. Refer to this drawing as you read the steps.

1. Sunlight strikes the leaf and passes through to the cholorophyll in the food-making cells, where it is trapped.
2. Water is carried to the food-making cells by the vein.
3. The sun's energy is used to change water into two gases, hydrogen and oxygen (ok'sə jən). The oxygen gas, a waste product, moves out of the leaf through the stomata.
4. Carbon dioxide gas enters the leaf through the stomata and moves to the food-making cells.

The labels within the diagram read:

1 light energy passes through to chlorophyll

2 water is carried to cells by the vein

3 oxygen gas moves out of the leaf

4 carbon dioxide gas enters the leaf

5 sugar is carried by the vein to the rest of the plant

5. The hydrogen gas joins with carbon dioxide gas to make food, a type of sugar. The sugar is carried by the vein to the rest of the plant.

A way to show what happens during photosynthesis is:

water + carbon dioxide + energy $\longrightarrow$ sugar + oxygen
(from sunlight)

Most plants make more sugar than they need. This sugar is stored in the cells of the plant. Think about the fruits and vegetables you eat. Which of them taste sweet? These sweet-tasting plants contain much stored sugar.

Some of the extra sugar made by the plant is changed to starch. Starch is also stored in the cells of the plant. A white potato is an underground stem that contains large amounts of stored starch.

Sweet-tasting fruits and vegetables

White potatoes

SUGAR TRANSPORT

Using the Energy in Food

How do plants use the energy stored in food?

Living things need energy to carry out the life processes. They get energy from food. But the energy in food is stored energy. It must be released before it can be used by living things. **Respiration** (res pə rā′shən) is the process by which living things use oxygen to release energy in food. This process takes place in the cells of all living things.

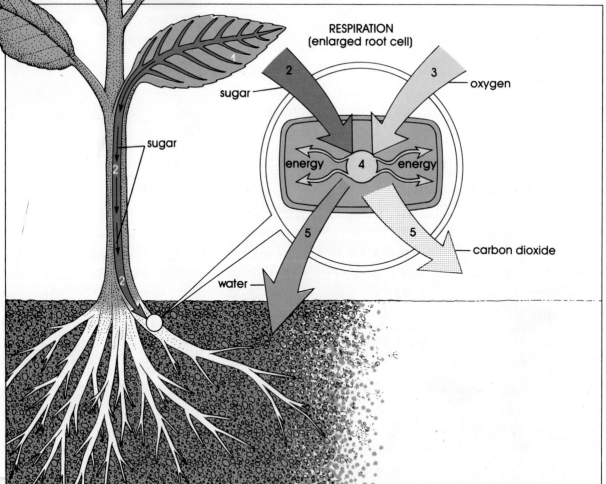

RESPIRATION
(enlarged root cell)

sugar

oxygen

energy   4   energy

carbon dioxide

water

Before cells can carry out respiration they must first have food. How do plants get the food needed for respiration? How do cells change sugar to energy? Refer to the drawing as you read the steps.

1. Sugar is made in the leaf.
2. It is carried by the veins in the leaf to the stem. Food-carrying tubes in the stem transport sugar to all parts of the stem and down to the roots.
3. The enlarged plant cell in the drawing shows oxygen entering the cell. The oxygen combines with sugar in the cell.
4. When oxygen and sugar combine, energy is released. The energy is used by the cell to carry out life processes.
5. Carbon dioxide and water are given off as waste products.

A way to show what happens during respiration is:

sugar + oxygen $\longrightarrow$ energy + carbon dioxide + water

The process of respiration is the opposite of the process of photosynthesis. Look at the chart. Compare the two processes.

COMPARISON OF PHOTOSYNTHESIS AND RESPIRATION

Photosynthesis	Respiration
Takes place only in cells with chlorophyll	Takes place in all cells
Food (sugar) is made	Food (sugar) is broken down
Sun's energy is stored in sugar	Energy stored in sugar is released
Carbon dioxide is taken in	Carbon dioxide is produced and given off
Water is taken in	Water is produced and given off
Oxygen is given off	Oxygen is used

Producing New Plants

How do flowers produce seeds?

Some of the energy released by plants during respiration is used for reproduction (rē prə-duk'shən). **Reproduction** is the process by which living things produce new living things of the same kind. Many green plants grow flowers. A flower is the reproductive part of a flowering plant.

Many flowers have three main parts. The drawing shows the parts of a typical flower. The main parts of the flower are the petals, the stamen (stā'mən), and the pistil. You will see the role that each part plays in reproduction.

Lily

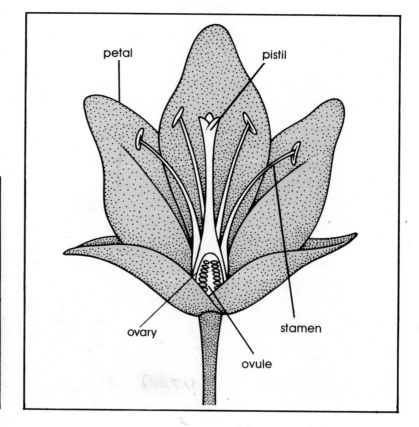

petal

pistil

ovary

ovule

stamen

The **petals** are the leaflike outer parts of a flower. They protect the inner reproductive parts. As you can see, petals are often brightly colored. Some petals have a sweet odor.

The other two parts of the flower are involved directly in reproduction. The **stamen** is the male reproductive part of a flower. The stamen is a long stalk with a sac at the top. How many stamens are shown in the drawing?

Stamens produce pollen (pol ′ən) grains. A **pollen grain** is a tiny body that contains the male reproductive cell. Millions of pollen grains form in the sac at the top of the stamen. If you rub the sac, colored dust will get on your skin. This dust is made up of pollen grains. The two pictures below show how different kinds of pollen grains look under a microscope.

The **pistil** is the female reproductive part. The bottom part of the pistil contains the ovary (ō′vər ē). The **ovary** is the part of the plant that contains ovules (ō′vyulz). An **ovule** is a small round body that contains the female reproductive cell. Identify the pistil in the drawing on page 18. Also find the ovules inside the ovary.

Sunflower pollen

Daylily pollen

How does a flower help a plant reproduce?

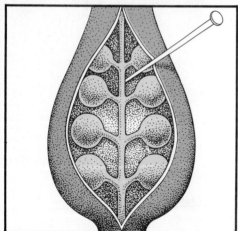

Materials 2 different kinds of flowers / hand lens / microscope / microscope slide / straight pin / sheet of paper

Procedure

A. Look at and compare two flowers. Identify the petals of each flower. Smell them.

   1. Which parts do the two flowers have in common?

   2. What are some differences between the two flowers?

B. Identify the stamens and the pistil of each flower. Use a hand lens to help you see the parts.

C. Choose one flower and carefully tear off any leafy parts around the petals. Then tear off the petals.

D. Gently remove one stamen and look at the top part with a hand lens. The powdery material is made up of many pollen grains. Shake some of the pollen grains onto a microscope slide. Look at the slide under a microscope.

   3. Draw some pollen grains.

E. Remove the rest of the stamens. Touch the end of the pistil.

   4. Describe how the pistil feels.

F. Place the pistil on a sheet of paper. Use a straight pin to pick apart the base of the pistil. The ovules are inside this base. Use a hand lens to look at the ovules.

   5. Draw what you see.

Conclusion

1. How do you think a flower's odor and color help it reproduce?

2. When pollen lands on a pistil, why doesn't it blow away in the wind?

3. How does it help the plant to have its ovules enclosed in the base of the flower?

For reproduction to take place, pollen grains must reach the top of the pistil. **Pollination** (pol ə-nā′shən) is the process by which pollen grains move from the stamen to the pistil. There are two main ways in which flowers are pollinated. One way is by insects. Another way is by the wind.

Most flowers are pollinated by insects. Some insects, such as the honeybee, are attracted to flowers that have a sweet odor and colorful petals. Honeybees feed on a sweet liquid produced by the flower. As the honeybee feeds, it brushes against pollen grains on the stamen. The pollen sticks to the bee. As it moves, the bee carries the pollen to the pistil.

Black birch tree

Other flowers are pollinated when the wind blows. The wind carries pollen grains from the stamen to the pistil. Plants that do not have a sweet odor and colorful petals are often pollinated in this way. Grasses and trees, such as those shown, are pollinated by the wind.

Grass (wheat)

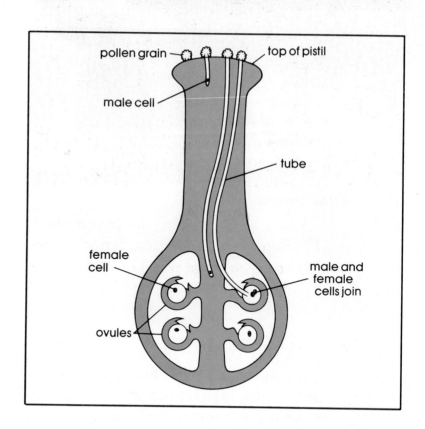

pollen grain
top of pistil
male cell
tube
female cell
male and female cells join
ovules

Bean seed cross section

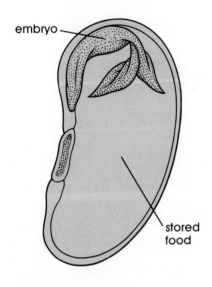

embryo
stored food

The drawing shows what happens when a pollen grain lands on the top of the pistil. The top of the pistil is sticky. So the pollen grain sticks to it. The pollen grain begins to grow a tube. The tube grows down through the pistil until it reaches an ovule. When it reaches an ovule, the male cell from the pollen grain combines with a female cell. The joining of male and female reproductive cells is called **fertilization** (fėr tə lə zā′shən).

The fertilized ovule becomes a **seed** containing a tiny young plant and stored food. The tiny young plant is called an **embryo** (em′brē ō). When conditions are right, the embryo begins to grow. The growth of a plant embryo from a seed is called **germination** (jėr mə nā′shən). As the embryo grows, it uses the food stored in the seed.

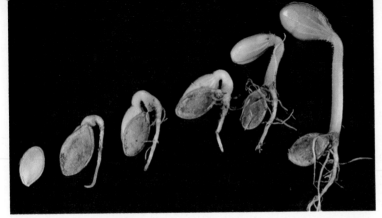
Germinating squash seeds

Once it reaches a certain size, the young plant will make its own food by photosynthesis. The picture shows seeds in different stages of germination.

Ideas to Remember

▶ The activities of living things that keep them alive are called life processes.
▶ The cell is the basic unit of living things.
▶ Photosynthesis is the process by which cells containing chlorophyll use water, carbon dioxide, and light energy to make food.
▶ Roots, stems, and leaves help supply food-making leaf cells with materials needed for photosynthesis.
▶ Respiration is the process by which living things use oxygen to release the energy in food.
▶ Reproduction is the process by which living things produce new living things of the same kind.
▶ A flower is the reproductive part of a plant.
▶ Seeds form from the fertilized ovule inside the pistil of a flower.

Reviewing the Chapter

SCIENCE WORDS

A. Write the letter of the term that best matches the definition. Not all the terms will be used.

1. Fertilized ovule containing tiny young plant and food
2. Green material needed by a plant to make food
3. Openings in a leaf through which air enters leaf
4. Part of a single cell that grows from a root into soil
5. Small green body in plant cells
6. Basic unit of living things
7. Tiny young plant in a seed
8. Thin tube in a leaf

    a. chloroplast
    b. embryo
    c. vein
    d. cell
    e. seed
    f. stamen
    g. stomata
    h. ovule
    i. root hair
    j. chlorophyll

B. Use all the terms below to complete the sentences.

fertilization   photosynthesis   reproduction   germination
life processes   pollination   respiration

The activities that keep living things alive are called __1__. Green plants make food by a process called __2__. They use oxygen to re-lease energy in food through the process of __3__. All living things produce new living things of the same kind by __4__. In a flower, pol-len grains are moved from the stamen to the pistil during __5__. The joining of male and female reproductive cells occurs during __6__. The growth of a plant embryo from a seed is called __7__.

UNDERSTANDING IDEAS

A. Write the terms that are *not* needed for photosynthesis to occur. Use the remain-ing terms to describe this process.

water   carbon dioxide
petal   food
stamen   chlorophyll

B. Write the terms that are *not* needed for respiration to occur. Use the remaining terms to describe this process.

light energy   sugar
carbon dioxide   seed
Pistal   oxygen

C. Write the correct term for each number in the diagrams.

pollen grain   ovule
stored food   pistil
embryo   stamen
seed   petal

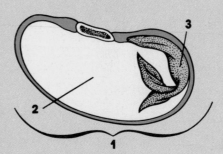

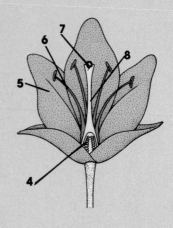

USING IDEAS

Plant reproduction can occur without seeds. Cut a leaf and the attached stem from a geranium, philodendron, or African violet plant. Put the stem end in a jar of water. Check the jar every few days for two weeks. What happens?

THINKING LIKE A SCIENTIST

Answer the following questions. You may be able to answer some of the questions just by thinking about them. To answer other questions you may have to do some research.

1. Life processes are activities that keep living things alive. Why is reproduction a life process?
2. Scientists do experiments to test their ideas. Suppose a scientist believed that the leaves of plants were the most important structure for absorbing water. How might the scientist test this idea?
3. Why do some plants need millions of pollen grains to reproduce? Would 1,000 pollen grains be enough?
4. Many green plants grow underwater. How do you think these plants are similar to green plants that grow on land? How might underwater plants be different from land plants?

Chapter 2

Animals Without a Backbone

The spider on this page is a great hunter. Did you know it can jump great distances? It can jump 40 times the length of its body. Can you see its four large eyes? It can see its insect victim from very far away.

In this chapter you will learn about all kinds of animals. Some of the animals are small, like the spider. Others are much larger than the spider. Some of these animals live in and near your home. Others live in oceans, in jungles, or on mountaintops.

You will find out about flying animals, floating animals, and creeping animals. You will learn how they look and where they live. This chapter will show you how they are different and how they are alike.

Classifying Living Things

How do scientists classify animals?

For a few minutes make a list of all the animals you can. How many animals did you think of? There are many different kinds of animals.

Did you think of a dog, a cat, and a horse? You probably did. The chances are you did not include a sponge, a clam, or an earthworm. But these are animals, too.

Think of a way to divide up your list of animals into groups. For example, you could group all large animals together and all small animals together. You could group all fast animals and all slow animals together. Putting animals into groups is one way to sort them out. Putting animals into groups makes them easier to study.

Scientists who study animals classify (klas′ə fī), or group, them. To **classify** is to arrange in

Gannet

Garden spider

28

Zebras, wildebeests, and springboks

groups by features that are alike. Scientists classify animals by structure (struk′chər). The structure of an animal is the kind of body parts it has and the way these parts are arranged. One structure scientists look for in classifying animals is the backbone. The backbone is made up of many small bones called **vertebrae** (vėr′tə brā). Vertebrae are linked together to form the backbone.

Some animals have a backbone and some do not. Scientists have classified all animals into two large groups. One group is made up of animals with a backbone. An animal with a backbone is called a **vertebrate** (vėr′tə brit). The other group is made up of animals without a backbone. An animal without a backbone is called an **invertebrate** (in vėr′tə brit). In this chapter you will learn about invertebrates. Which animals in these pictures have a backbone? Which do not have a backbone?

Chimpanzee mother with baby

Purple sea urchin

Sponges

What is a sponge and how does it look?

What do you think of when you hear the word *sponge*? You may think of a pink or blue pad used to clean the dishes. That kind of sponge is made by people. A sponge is also an animal. A **sponge** is an invertebrate that has many cells. Almost all sponges live in oceans. A few live in freshwater streams and lakes. The orange sponge in the picture lives in the Atlantic Ocean off the northeast coast of the United States.

Sponges do not have many of the parts we usually think of as animal parts. Most animals move about, but adult sponges stay in one place. They are found attached to rocks or other objects at the bottom of the ocean. In fact, for many years scientists thought sponges were plants. Why?

A sponge's body is simple. It contains many small holes called **pores.** Special cells line the inside of a sponge's body. Each of these cells has a

Orange sponge and close-up of pores

threadlike part that whips back and forth quickly to make water currents. Water carrying food and oxygen is drawn into the sponge through the pores.

As water flows into the sponge, food is filtered out. The sponge's cells digest the food. Oxygen is used to release the energy in the food. Water and waste materials pass out through the large opening at the top of the sponge, as shown in the drawing.

Sponges have many different shapes. Some are shaped like cups, some like fans, and others like vases. The shape of a sponge depends on its skeleton. The skeleton is the structure that supports the body of an animal.

The skeleton of some sponges is made up of hard material. But other sponges are made up of soft material. This soft skeleton is sometimes used in the home as a cleaning sponge or bath sponge. It is usually a light brown or yellowish color. It is not the same as the pink or blue sponge made by people. Are any sponges in your home from the soft skeleton of the animal?

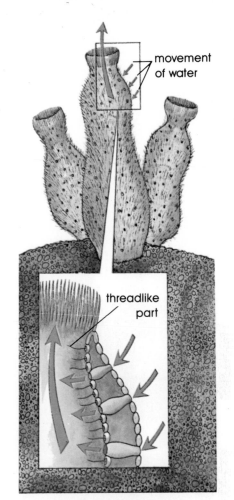

movement of water

threadlike part

What kind of sponge holds the most water?

Get a natural sponge and a manufactured sponge about the same size. Soak the natural sponge in water for 3 minutes. Carefully remove the sponge and squeeze out the water into a measuring cup. Record the amount of water that was in the sponge. Now do the same procedure with the manufactured sponge. Which sponge held the most water? Which sponge would be best to use when washing a car? Why?

Finding Out

Animals with Stinging Cells

What are animals with stinging cells, and how do they look?

The hydra, jellyfish, and sea anemone (ə nem'ə-nē) are also invertebrates. Like sponges, they do not have a backbone. Hydras live in freshwater ponds and streams. Most jellyfish and sea anemones live in oceans.

These animals are more complex than sponges. Their body is shaped like a hollow sac. The sac is open at one end. The hydra uses the opening in two ways. It is used for taking in food and for getting rid of wastes. The opening is surrounded by one or more rings of tentacles (ten'tə kəlz). A **tentacle** is a long, armlike part. The picture shows a hydra with six tentacles around the opening.

Hydras and jellyfish use their tentacles to catch small animals for food. Sea anemones catch food in the same way. The tentacles contain many stinging cells. A **stinging cell** is a special structure used to help capture food. How does a stinging cell help capture food? When a small animal

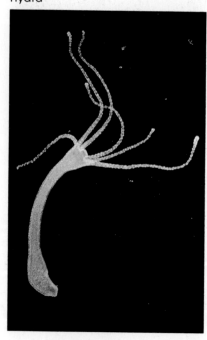

Hydra

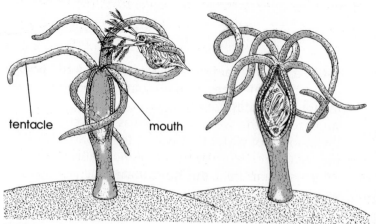

tentacle   mouth

HYDRA

comes close, the stinging cells explode. The explosion pushes tiny poisonous threads into the victim. These threads prevent the animal from moving. They may even kill it. The animal is then pushed into the mouth by the tentacles and swallowed. The drawing at the bottom of page 32 shows how the hydra captures and eats a tiny animal called a daphnia.

Sea anemone

Jellyfish

Have you ever walked along a beach? Perhaps you have seen a clear blob floating in the water. This blob was a jellyfish. Jellyfish may have also washed up on the beach. If you stepped on a jellyfish, it could have given you a painful sting.

The Portuguese man-of-war is an animal similar to the jellyfish. It has tentacles and stinging cells. This is one animal that can be dangerous to people. A swimmer can be tangled in the tentacles. The stinging cells can cause a painful injury to the swimmer.

Portuguese man-of-war

Worms

What are the three main groups of worms?

Scientists classify worms into three main groups. These groups are the flatworms, the roundworms, and the segmented (seg'mən təd) worms. The structure of worms is more complex than that of sponges. It is more complex than the structure of the animals with stinging cells.

The first group of worms is the flatworms. The flatworm is the simplest type of worm. Some live in streams and ponds. What is the shape of a flatworm's body?

A common flatworm found in fresh water is the **planarian** (plə nãr'ē ən). There are nerve cells in the head of the planarian. These cells act like a simple brain. Above this "brain" are two sense organs. An **organ** is a body part that does a certain job. These two sense organs are called eyespots. Eyespots can sense light. Can you find the eyespots on these planarians?

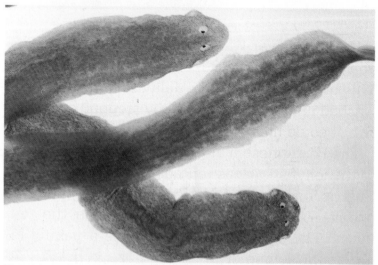

Planarians

Planarians have a very unusual ability. They can **regenerate** (ri jen′ə rāt), or regrow, body parts that are missing. For example, if a planarian's tail is cut off, it can grow a new tail. If its head is cut off, a new head will grow. If a cut is made down the center of the head, the two halves will form new heads. Look at the drawings of what these amazing animals can do.

Most flatworms are parasites. A **parasite** (par′ə-sīt) is an animal or plant that depends on and harms another animal or plant. The animal or plant on which a parasite depends is the **host.** A parasite depends on its host for food.

The tapeworm is an example of a flatworm that is a parasite. Tapeworms live in the digestive system of animals. A digestive (də jes′tiv) system is a group of body parts that breaks down food. A tapeworm does not have its own digestive system. The host animal does the eating and the digesting. The tapeworm takes in digested food through an opening in its body. It uses the host's food. The host loses weight and becomes weak.

REGENERATION IN A PLANARIAN

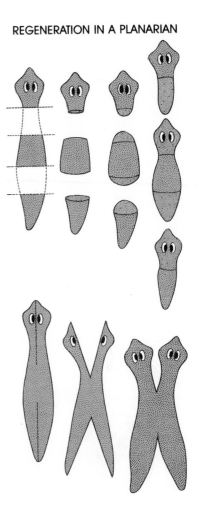

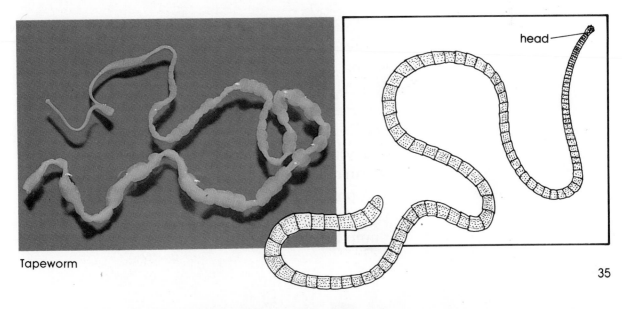

Tapeworm

head

The second group of worms is the roundworms. A **roundworm** is a worm that has a long tube-shaped body with a digestive system. The digestive system is made up of a tube that has an opening at each end. Food is taken in through the mouth opening. Wastes leave through the other opening. The drawing shows the two openings in the roundworm's body. Most roundworms live in soil, where they eat dead plant and animal matter. Other roundworms are parasites that live in host animals. Dogs must be treated to get rid of roundworms.

ROUNDWORM

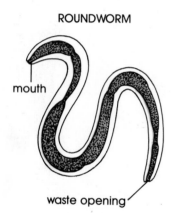

mouth

waste opening

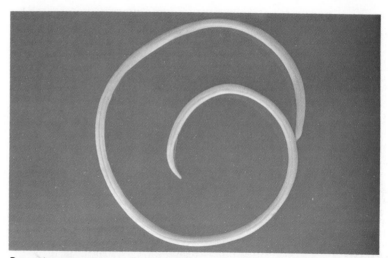

Roundworm

The third group of worms is the segmented worms. A **segmented worm** is a worm whose body is divided into segments, or sections. The segments look like a series of little rings. These segments are clearly shown in the picture of the worm on the next page.

Segmented worms are much more complex than flatworms or roundworms. A series of hearts pump blood through the worm's body. The blood travels in a system of closed tubes. Like round-worms, segmented worms have two body openings and a digestive system.

The earthworm is the best-known segmented worm. Earthworms live inside tunnels in wet soil. Their body structure allows them to move easily through soil. Each segment, except the first and last, has four pairs of bristles (bris′əlz). A **bristle** is a stiff, strong hair used for moving. You can see the bristles in the drawing of the earthworm. The earthworm also uses the bristles for clinging to the walls of the tunnels it lives in.

Earthworm

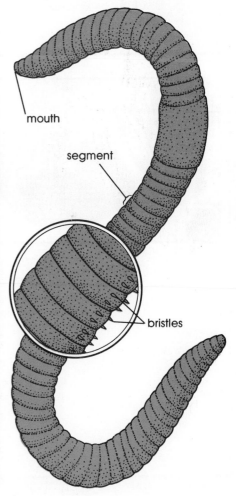

mouth

segment

bristles

How does an earthworm's body help it move?

Materials earthworm / metric ruler / hand lens / paper towel / pan or tray / pot with soil

Procedure

A. Carefully hold the earthworm in one hand. Use a metric ruler to measure the length of the earthworm's body.

   1. How long is the earthworm's body?

B. Use a hand lens to examine the earthworm. Count the number of body segments.

   2. How many segments does the earthworm have?

C. Find the mouth. Also find the light-colored swelling on the earthworm's body. It is located about ⅓ of the way down from the mouth. This swelling is used in reproduction.

D. Gently run your index finger over the segments. You should be able to feel bristles on the segments. Look at the bristles with a hand lens.

   3. Draw the earthworm. Label its parts.

E. Place the earthworm on a smooth surface. Watch it for a short time.

   4. Describe any movement that the worm makes.

F. Place a moist paper towel in a pan or tray. Place the earthworm on the towel and watch the worm move.

   5. How do the segments change?

G. Place the earthworm in a container of loose, moist soil. Use a hand lens to observe the worm.

   6. How did the earthworm behave in the soil?

Conclusion

1. Why did the earthworm move on the paper towel and not on the smooth surface?

2. In what way are the bristles on a worm like the cleats on football shoes?

Animals with Spiny Skin

What are echinoderms, and how do they look?

If you have ever been to the seashore, you may have seen some echinoderms (i kī'nə dẻrmz). An **echinoderm** is a spiny-skinned invertebrate that lives in the ocean. A spine is a sharp, pointy structure. The body of an echinoderm is hard and covered with spines. Some of these animals have short spines. Others have long spines. The pictures show some well-known echinoderms.

A common echinoderm is the starfish. Most starfish have five arms that come out from the center part of the animal. On the underside of each arm are two rows of tiny tube feet. A **tube foot** is a hollow structure with a sucker at the end. Most echinoderms have tube feet. The picture below shows the tube feet on a starfish.

The starfish uses its tube feet to pull itself over the ocean floor. Tube feet also help the starfish

Sea cucumber

Sand dollars

Starfish and close-up of tube feet

39

get food. When a starfish finds a clam, it begins a kind of tug-of-war. The clam protects itself by tightly closing its two shells together. The starfish attaches its tube feet to both shells and begins pulling. It tries to pry the shells apart. Sometimes the tug-of-war goes on for a long time. But the starfish almost always wins.

Tube feet pulling open shellfish

Starfish attacking shellfish

Regenerating body parts

The starfish eats both oysters and clams. So people who gather this seafood do not like starfish. In the past, these people tried to get rid of starfish by cutting them into pieces. They threw the pieces back into the ocean. Instead of solving their problems, they made them worse. Some of the starfish pieces grew into whole new starfish. Why did this happen? The starfish is an animal with a very unusual ability. Like the planarian, it can regenerate, or regrow, body parts that are missing. When the pieces of starfish were thrown into the water, the number of starfish really got larger. Each piece grew into a whole new starfish.

Animals with a Soft Body

What are mollusks, and how do they look?

The clam and the octopus belong to a group of animals called the mollusks (mol'əsks). A **mollusk** is an invertebrate with a soft body. Some mollusks have two outer shells. Others live inside a one-piece shell or have no shell at all. Many mollusks live in the ocean. Others live in fresh water or on land.

The body of a mollusk is more complex than the body of an echinoderm. For example, the mollusk has the beginning of a true eye. The picture shows the eyes on the body of a scallop. Mollusks also have a more complex system for pumping blood. Blood is pumped through blood vessels into spaces in the animal's body.

Scallop with tiny blue eyes

Foot of scallop

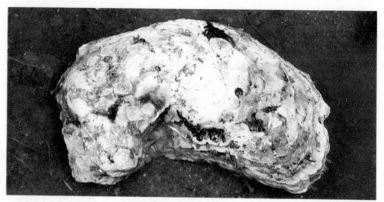

Oyster

Clams, oysters, and scallops are two-shelled mollusks. The shells are held together by muscles. The muscles open and close the shells like a hinge. The two-shelled mollusks have a part called a foot. This foot, made of a strong muscle, is used for digging. It is also used for pulling the animal along the ocean floor. Notice the foot of the scallop in the picture.

Snails and slugs are other common mollusks. Both have a large muscular foot. The foot gives off a layer of slime. Snails and slugs glide along on this layer of slime. The main difference between a slug and a snail is the shell. Usually slugs do not

Land snail on leaf

Slug

have a shell, while snails have a shell. The snail's shell protects it from enemies. When in danger, the snail can hide inside its shell. Some other mollusks in this group are limpets and periwinkles (per'ə wing kəlz). These two mollusks are shown in the pictures.

Periwinkles

Limpet

There are two other common mollusks that have no shell. These mollusks are the squid and the octopus. Both have long tentacles. The tentacles are lined with suckers. These suckers help them to catch other animals for food. The squid and the octopus have an unusual way to protect

Octopus and close-up of suckers

Squid

themselves. They give off a cloud of dark liquid when they are in danger. This dark liquid, called ink, keeps them from being seen while they escape from their enemies.

Mollusks such as clams, oysters, and scallops are a source of food for many people. In some countries certain land snails are gathered and cooked for food. The abalone (ab ə lō'nē) is an ocean snail that is gathered by divers. Its foot is so large that it is cut up and served as abalone steaks. Squid and octopus are also favorite foods of many people.

Do You Know?

Did you know that oysters can make pearls? Some oysters that live in tropical waters make pearls that are very valuable. A large, perfectly shaped pearl can be as valuable as a very expensive diamond. A pearl forms inside the shell of an oyster when a grain of sand or other particle enters the shell. Cells inside the oyster's shell produce a material called nacre (nā'kər). The particle becomes coated by many thin layers of nacre. After several years, the particle is completely covered. A shiny natural pearl has been formed.

Most of the pearls sold today are cultured pearls. People use their knowledge of oysters to produce pearls. The oyster can be "forced" to make a pearl. A small bead is inserted into each oyster. Oysters are then placed in oyster beds in the water. Several years later, the oysters are pulled out of the water and opened. Some of the oysters will contain a cultured pearl.

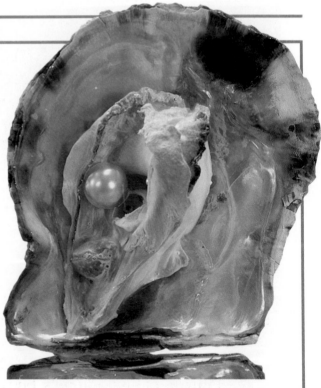

Animals with Jointed Legs

What are the four main groups of arthropods?

The arthropods (är'thrə podz) make up the largest group of animals. Some people think there may be as many as 10 million types. An **arthropod** is an invertebrate that has a segmented body and jointed legs. The body has two or three segments. The number of jointed legs is used to divide the arthropods into groups. Can you find the three body segments on the pictures of the ant?

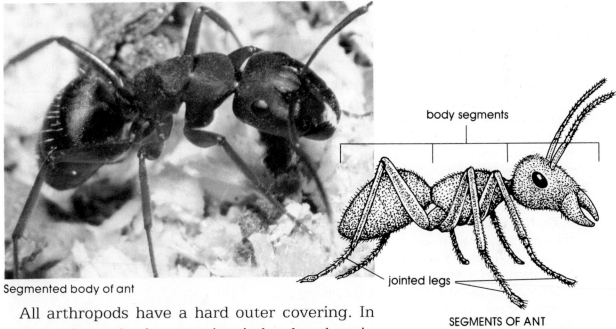

Segmented body of ant

SEGMENTS OF ANT

All arthropods have a hard outer covering. In some arthropods the covering is harder than in others. This hard outer covering is called the **exoskeleton** (ek sō skel'ə tən). It is like a skeleton on the outside of the animal's body. It protects the soft parts of the body. Arthropods also have well-developed sense organs and a head with special mouth parts.

Millipede

Centipede

There are four main groups of arthropods. The first group includes millipedes and centipedes. A millipede looks very much like a worm with many legs. The word *millipede* means "thousand legs." (*Milli-* means "thousand" and *-pede* means "foot.") Each segment of a millipede has two pairs of legs. The millipede is a harmless animal that eats plants. When in danger, it may curl up into a ball.

A centipede is also wormlike but has fewer legs than a millipede. The word *centipede* means "hundred legs." (*Centi-* means "hundred" and *-pede* means "foot.") Unlike a millipede the centipede eats other animals. It uses a pair of poison claws near its mouth to capture its food. With these claws the centipede can inject poison into another animal.

The second group of arthropods includes shrimps, lobsters, and crayfish. Animals in this

Lobster

Shrimp

group are also called **crustaceans** (krus tā′shənz). Almost all the arthropods in this group live in water. Shrimps and lobsters live in the ocean. Crayfish live in fresh water. Crustaceans have five pairs of legs. Their exoskeleton is divided into two main parts. These arthropods move by muscles attached to their exoskeleton.

Spider in web

The third group of arthropods includes animals such as spiders, ticks, and mites. These animals have four pairs of legs. They also have two main body parts. Most spiders are harmless. In fact, many are useful because they kill insects that are problems for people. You probably have seen spider webs. Why do you think spiders make webs?

Spider wrapping insect

47

A few spiders, such as the black widow, are poisonous. Ticks and mites are parasites that live by sucking blood from other animals. Ticks also are annoying to pets and carry disease to people.

Black widow

Tick on skin

The fourth and largest group of arthropods is made up of insects. There are more different kinds of insects than all other animals and plants. An insect is an arthropod that has three pairs of legs and a body that is divided into three parts. The three parts of the body are the head, the abdomen (ab'də mən), and the thorax (thôr'aks). The **abdomen** is the rear part of an insect's body. The **thorax** is the middle part of an insect's body. Wings and legs are joined to the thorax. The drawing shows the three main parts of an insect's body.

PARTS OF AN INSECT

head   thorax   abdomen

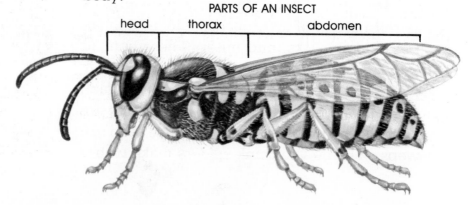

Compound eyes of insect

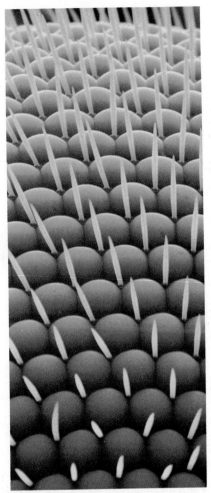

Close-up of compound eye

Insects have very unusual sense organs. Most adult insects have compound eyes. The compound eye has thousands of lenses, as you can see in the picture. It lets the insect see motion. For example, bees can see flowers moving in a slight breeze. But they cannot see the details of the flower.

An insect's head has two feelers, or antennae (an ten'ē). The **antennae** help the insect smell and feel. Sometimes the antennae are used for tasting and hearing.

Antennae

Activity

How can you make an imaginary invertebrate?

Materials   scrap art and craft materials / scissors / glue / felt-tip pens

Procedure

A. Use your imagination! Create a model of an invertebrate. Use any materials you wish. The animal does not have to look like any known invertebrate. But it must have body parts that help it to live and grow. Pick an environment for your invertebrate.

   1. Does your animal live on land or in the water?

B. Remember that your animal has to survive without help from you. The animal must be able to eat and to dispose of body wastes. Your animal must also have a way to escape from predators. The animal's body covering must protect it. (Remember that there are two main groups of invertebrates: those with soft bodies and those with hard outer coverings. Decide which kind you will make.)

   2. Does your animal have a soft body or a hard covering?

Results

1. Does your invertebrate look like any known invertebrate? If so, which one?
2. How does your invertebrate protect itself?
3. Describe any movements your animal can make.
4. Describe what each animal body part does.

Conclusion

1. How would your invertebrate animal's body parts help it to survive?
2. Look at the models your classmates have made. How is your model similar to other models? How is your model unusual?

Using science ideas

Draw a picture or prepare a diorama of the type of surroundings in which your animal could survive.

Insects have special mouth parts. These parts are formed for chewing, sucking, or piercing. The kind of mouth parts an insect has depends on the food it eats. For example, beetles and grasshoppers eat leaves. Their mouths have parts that cut and chew. Butterflies and moths have mouth parts that suck up juices from flowers. Mosquitoes have mouth parts for piercing the skin and sucking blood.

TYPES OF MOUTH PARTS

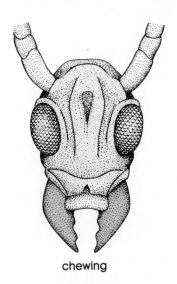
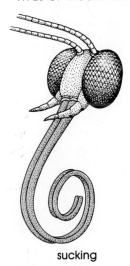
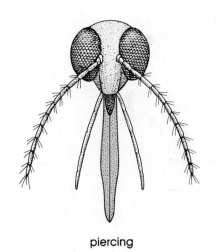

chewing   sucking   piercing

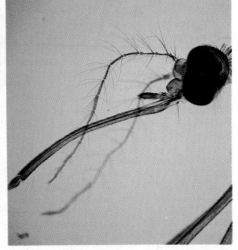

Chewing mouth parts   Sucking mouth parts   Piercing mouth parts

Dragonfly molting

An insect's body is covered with an exoskeleton. The exoskeleton does not grow as the insect grows. When the covering gets too small, the insect molts (mōlts). To **molt** means to "shed the outer covering." The insect's exoskeleton splits down the middle. The insect then works its way out. Once the old covering is shed, the insect gradually forms a new exoskeleton.

Insects are both harmful and helpful. Some insects feed on other insects that destroy crops. The ladybug is an example of this type of helpful insect. Many insects are also an important source of food for fish, birds, frogs, and other animals.

People consider some insects to be pests. An insect called the boll weevil (bōl wē′vəl) damages cotton crops. Termites, which live on wood, can destroy homes made mainly of wood. Some insects can carry diseases to animals and people. Mosquitoes can carry the serious disease called malaria.

Boll weevils

Ideas to Remember

▶ Scientists classify animals into groups by features that are alike.

▶ An animal with a backbone is called a vertebrate. An animal without a backbone is called an invertebrate.

▶ A sponge is a simple invertebrate with a body that contains many pores.

▶ Hydras, jellyfish, and sea anemones are invertebrates with stinging cells and tentacles.

▶ Scientists classify worms into three groups—flatworms, roundworms, and segmented worms.

▶ An echinoderm is a spiny-skinned invertebrate that lives in ocean waters.

▶ A mollusk is an invertebrate with a soft body. Some mollusks have two outer shells; some live inside a one-piece shell; others have no shell at all.

▶ An arthropod is an invertebrate that has a segmented body, jointed legs, and a hard outer covering.

Reviewing the Chapter

SCIENCE WORDS

A. Copy the sentences below. Use science terms from the chapter to complete each sentence.

1. Scientists _____ animals by their structure.
2. Shrimps, lobsters, and clams are examples of _____.
3. Another name for a spiny-skinned animal is a/an _____.
4. To shed the outer covering is to _____.
5. The animal or plant on which a parasite depends and which it often harms is called the _____.

B. Write the letter of the term that best matches the definition. Not all the terms will be used.

1. Animal with a segmented body and jointed legs
2. Segmented worm
3. Wormlike animal with many legs
4. Invertebrate with a body that contains many small holes
5. Animal or plant that depends on and harms another animal or plant
6. Middle part of an insect's body
7. Hard outer covering
8. Hollow structure with a sucker at the end
9. Insect's feelers
10. Flatworm that has two eyespots

a. stinging cell
b. planarian
c. tube foot
d. earthworm
e. exoskeleton
f. arthropod
g. sponge
h. tentacle
i. antennae
j. parasite
k. centipede
l. thorax

UNDERSTANDING IDEAS

A. Write the correct term for each number in the diagram.

antenna	jointed leg
abdomen	head
mouth part	thorax

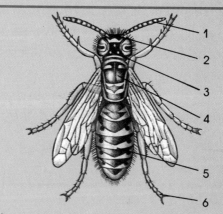

54

B. Make a chart like the one shown. Write the correct information under each heading. Then choose two of the groups. Explain how to tell animals in one group apart from animals in the other group.

Group	Special body part	Example
Sponges Animals with stinging cells Segmented worms Animals with spiny skin Animals with hard shells Animals with jointed legs		

USING IDEAS

Collect or draw pictures of invertebrates you have studied that are useful to people. Make a chart of the pictures to show how people use these animals.

THINKING LIKE A SCIENTIST

Answer the following questions. You may be able to answer some of the questions just by thinking about them. To answer other questions you may have to do some research.

1. Moles are animals that live in underground tunnels. Moles hunt for earthworms in the tunnels. When a mole finds more earthworms than it can eat, it takes the worms to a special storage area in a tunnel. The mole does not kill the worms, but it gives each one a bite in the back. What effect do you think the bite has on the earthworm?

2. How do you suppose sponges attach themselves to rocks on the ocean bottom?

Chapter 3

Animals With a Backbone

Can you imagine a baby that has a mass of over 7,000 kg and is over 7 m long? This is the mass and length of a baby blue whale when it is born. Its mother may have a mass of over 110,000 kg!

The blue whale belongs to a group of animals called the vertebrates. Vertebrates are animals with a backbone. There are five main groups of vertebrates. Fish, frogs, snakes, birds, and dogs are examples of animals from each main group. In this chapter you will learn about the animals from each of the groups. You will see how the animals are different and how they are alike.

Blue whale

Fish

What are the main characteristics of fish?

Fish are vertebrates that live in water. They are cold-blooded animals. A **cold-blooded animal** is an animal whose body temperature changes with the temperature of the water or air around it. When the air or water around such an animal is cold, the animal becomes cold. A cold-blooded animal becomes warm when the air or water around it is warm.

The skeleton (skel'ə tən) of a fish is simpler than that of other vertebrates. Most fish have skeletons made of bone. The shark and the sting-ray have skeletons made of cartilage (kär'tə lij). So some scientists believe that sharks and sting-rays are not true fish. **Cartilage** is a soft, bonelike material that bends. You can feel cartilage in the tip of your nose.

Most fish are covered with scales. A scale is a flat bony structure. Scales cover the body of a fish and protect it. Fish also have fins. A **fin** is a struc-

Trout

Shark

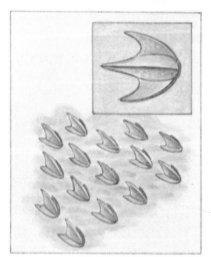

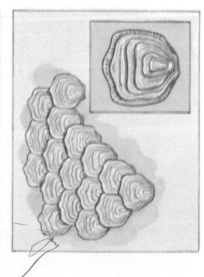

ture on a fish that helps it move through the water. The drawing shows the different fins on a fish. How many fins can you count on this fish?

All animals need oxygen. Animals that live on land get oxygen from the air. You may wonder how fish get oxygen under water. There is oxygen dissolved in the water. Fish take in the oxygen found in water through their gills. **Gills** are thin, feathery structures that are filled with blood. Fish use gills for breathing. To breathe, a fish takes water into its mouth. The water then

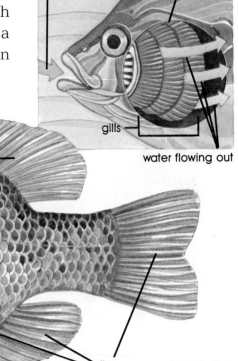

HOW GILLS WORK

gill cover cut away

water flowing in

gills

water flowing out

STRUCTURE OF FISH

fins

gill cover

scales

fins

flows over the gills. Oxygen from the water goes into the blood in the gills. Blood in the gills contains a waste material called carbon dioxide. Carbon dioxide passes through the gills and then out of the body into the water. At the same time, oxygen from the water goes into the blood in the gills. This is how the fish breathes under water.

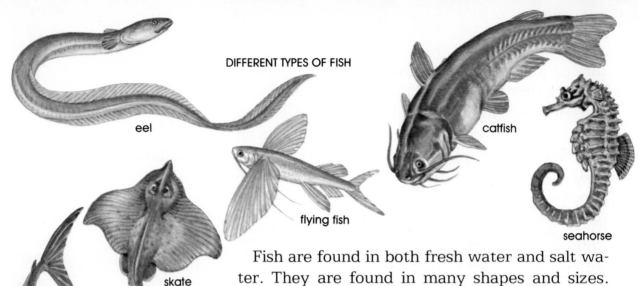

DIFFERENT TYPES OF FISH

eel

catfish

seahorse

flying fish

skate

swordfish

Fish are found in both fresh water and salt water. They are found in many shapes and sizes. Some fish look very different from most other fish. The seahorse looks like a tiny horse. The eel has a long slender body and small scales.

Fish are a major source of food for people. For thousands of years fish have been gathered from streams, rivers, lakes, and oceans. Each year about 66 billion kg of fish are caught. This is enough to feed each person on earth about 17 kg of fish a year.

Finding Out

How does water temperature affect a fish?

Observe a fish in a jar that contains water. Measure and record the temperature of the water. Count and record the number of times the fish opens and closes its mouth in one minute. Now add three or four ice cubes to the water. Carefully stir the water. Measure and record the water temperature after one minute and after several minutes. Count and record the fish's mouth movements for one minute. How does water temperature affect the speed of a fish's breathing?

Amphibians

What are the main characteristics of amphibians?

An **amphibian** (am fib'ē ən) is a cold-blooded vertebrate that lives part of its life in water and part on land. Frogs, toads, and salamanders are some common amphibians. The outside of an amphibian's body is usually moist and slimy. Amphibians do not have scales.

Bullfrog

Southern toad

Most adult amphibians live on land. They return to water to lay their eggs. A few amphibians spend almost their entire life in water. These include bullfrogs and some salamanders, such as mud puppies.

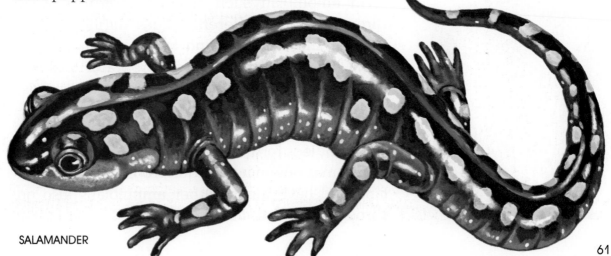
SALAMANDER

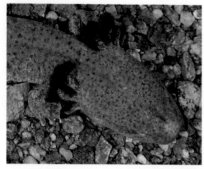

Mud puppy

Most adult amphibians breathe through lungs. **Lungs** are organs through which animals get oxygen from air. The mud puppy does not have lungs. It has gills outside its body through which it can breathe under water. Amphibians with lungs cannot live completely in water. They must come to the surface to breathe air. Amphibians can also get oxygen through the skin.

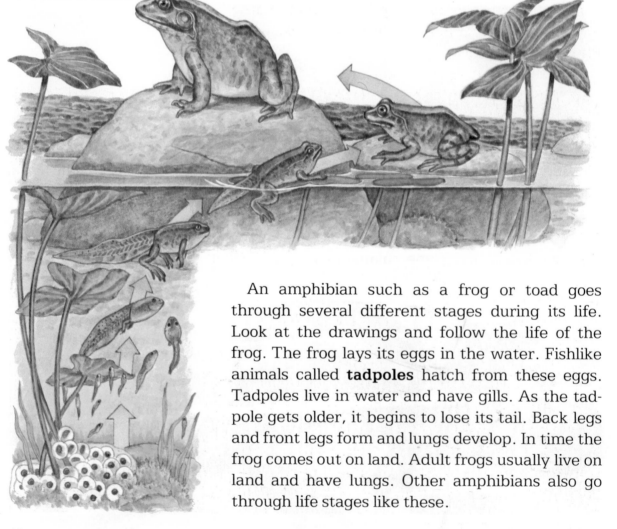

LIFE CYCLE OF A FROG

An amphibian such as a frog or toad goes through several different stages during its life. Look at the drawings and follow the life of the frog. The frog lays its eggs in the water. Fishlike animals called **tadpoles** hatch from these eggs. Tadpoles live in water and have gills. As the tadpole gets older, it begins to lose its tail. Back legs and front legs form and lungs develop. In time the frog comes out on land. Adult frogs usually live on land and have lungs. Other amphibians also go through life stages like these.

Reptiles

What are the main characteristics of reptiles?

A **reptile** (rep'tīl) is a cold-blooded vertebrate that has lungs and dry skin. Almost all reptiles have scales. Most reptiles live on land and lay eggs. Some give birth to live young. The eggs of reptiles are laid on land. These eggs have a tough covering that prevents the eggs from drying out on land.

There are four main groups of reptiles. These are the alligators and crocodiles, the snakes, the lizards, and the turtles.

Pine snakes hatching from eggs

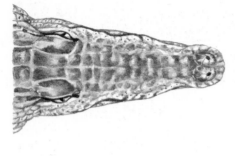

Alligators and crocodiles belong to the family of reptiles known as crocodilians. They are four-legged animals that breathe with lungs but spend much time in water. One way to tell alligators from crocodiles is by the shape of the head. An alligator has a wide head with a short, blunt snout. A crocodile has a triangular-shaped head with a long, narrow snout. The drawings show an alligator and a crocodile. Which is which?

Snakes make up the largest group of reptiles. They do not have legs, and their bodies are covered with thin scales. Snakes can be large or they can be small. The anaconda, from South America, can be more than 9 m long. The thread snake is only about 12 cm long.

Anaconda snake

Snake eating mouse and close-up of snake's curved teeth

Snakes have an unusual way of eating. They swallow their food whole. The picture shows a snake with a whole mouse in its mouth. Most of the things a snake eats are larger than its mouth. The snake's jaws allow its mouth to open very wide. Also, the lower jaw stretches sideways. This helps the snake swallow animals larger than its mouth. The snake's teeth are curved toward the back of the mouth. This makes it hard for an animal to escape from the snake's jaws.

Another group of reptiles is the lizards. There are many different kinds of lizards. Many live in deserts and other hot, dry areas. Lizards have claws on their toes, as shown in the picture. The body of a lizard is covered with scales.

Lizard and clawed foot

The chameleon (kə mē′lē ən) is one of the most interesting lizards. Chameleons live in trees and catch insects for food. They can change color. These lizards can change from brown to green to gray. The chameleon in the picture is changing color. These changes help these animals to blend in with their surroundings. How can this be helpful?

Turtles make up the last group of reptiles. The body of a turtle is protected by a shell. When in danger, some turtles pull their legs and head into the shell. How does this help the turtle survive? The turtles in the picture are box turtles. They can close their shells tightly. Some turtles live on land. Others spend most of their time in water.

Chameleon

Box turtles

Birds

What are the main characteristics of birds?

Birds are warm-blooded animals that are covered with feathers. A **warm-blooded animal** is an animal whose body temperature stays the same even when the temperature of the air or water around it changes. Birds are vertebrates with lungs. Like reptiles, birds lay eggs. Their eggs are in a hard shell. Wings and feathers make birds different from other vertebrates. Most birds use their wings to fly. Some birds, such as penguins, have feathers and wings but cannot fly. Birds can be found living on land, in trees, and on water. What birds can be found on water?

Penguins

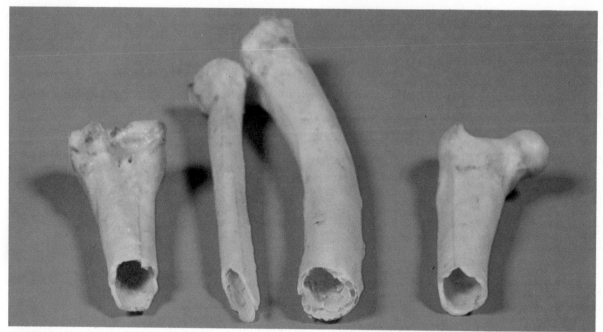
Bird bones

The bones and feathers of birds are made in a special way to help birds fly. The bones are hollow and light. The feathers have a hollow central shaft. This shaft makes feathers strong but light. Some large birds may have as many as 25,000 feathers. All birds lose and replace their feathers during a year. This regular loss of feathers is called molting.

The major use of feathers is to help birds to fly. Feathers are also needed to keep birds warm. Some birds fluff their feathers when they are cold. This fluffing forms more air spaces between the feathers and helps to keep the birds warm. Ducks and geese have small fluffy feathers called **down** near their skin. Down traps air and helps to keep the birds warm. Perhaps you have a jacket or blanket filled with down. These small feathers help to keep your body warm.

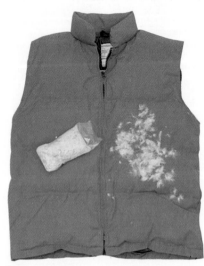
Down feathers

Oyster catcher

Snowy egret and young

Because birds are very active animals, they need a great deal of energy. So they eat a lot of food. Some birds spend most of their life hunting for food. The diet of birds is varied. Some birds eat nuts, while others eat seeds. Birds such as the one shown above eat oysters. Birds living near the water sometimes eat fish that they spear with their beaks. Still others, such as ducks and the flamingo below, eat tiny water plants and animals.

Flamingo

Nests of weaverbirds

Nest of plover

Birds show a great variety in nests and nest building. The nests of some birds are built by the male bird. Others are built by the female bird. Still others are built by both male and female. Nests are of all shapes and sizes. Some nests, such as those of the weaverbirds, are extremely large. As many as 600 birds may work together to build huge nests. Nests can be made of twigs, leaves, or feathers. They can also be made of mud or other substances that birds find. Nests can hang from tree branches or rest on the ground. Some nests are even built under piles of rotting leaves.

Some birds, such as pigeons, can harm people because they carry disease. But people enjoy many other kinds of birds because of their beautiful colors and their interesting calls and songs.

How do a bird's feathers and bones help it fly?

Materials   bird feather / scissors / hand lens / chicken bone / pliers / beef bone

Procedure

A. Look at the drawing of the bird feather on this page. Point out the central shaft and the side branches. Each side branch is called a barb.

B. Look at a bird feather. Find the central shaft. Use scissors to cut through the central shaft.
   1. Is the central shaft hollow or solid?

C. Find the barbs on the feather. Gently pull some of the barbs apart. Then put them together by pulling them through your fingers. The locked barbs trap air between them.

D. Look at the feather with a hand lens. Draw the feather as you see it through a hand lens.

E. Look at a chicken bone. Break it in half with pliers.
   2. Describe what you see inside the chicken bone.

F. Look at the inside of a beef bone. Compare the chicken bone with the beef bone.
   3. What are the differences between the two bones?

barb

shaft

Conclusion

1. When the barbs of a bird's feather lock together to trap air, how does this help the bird?

2. Describe a few important features of a feather and of a chicken bone. What features of a bird's feathers and bones help it to fly?

3. Why is a beef bone not suitable for flight?

Mammals

What are the main characteristics of mammals?

Mammals are the most complex group of vertebrates. All mammals are alike in four ways. First, they are warm-blooded. This means that a mammal's body temperature does not change when its environment gets warmer or colder. Second, mammals breathe with lungs.

Mammals share two other characteristics. All mammals have hair or fur on their bodies at some time in their lives. Not all mammals have the same amount of hair or fur. For example, a gorilla is a very hairy mammal. An elephant is a mammal

Springer spaniel and pups

with only a little hair. The fourth important characteristic of mammals is that the females have milk glands. The young feed on milk from these glands. The picture shows springer spaniel puppies feeding on milk from their mother.

Mammals differ from each other in many ways. Most mammals live on land. A few mammals, such as whales and dolphins, live in water. However, these mammals still breathe with lungs. From time to time they must come to the surface for air. Mammals also differ greatly in size. The blue whale is the largest mammal. It may grow to be as long as 32 m and have a mass of over 110,000 kg. The common shrew is one of the smallest mammals. It is only about 10 cm long and has a mass of less than 3 g.

Shrew

Do You Know?

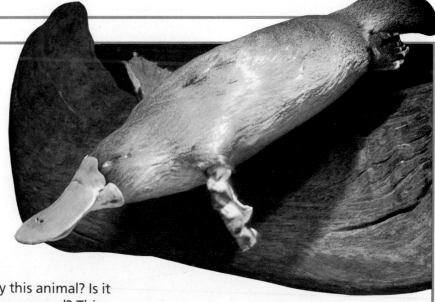

Suppose you found an animal like this: It has a bill and webbed feet, like a duck. It has fur on its body and a flat tail, like a beaver. The animal feeds its young with milk from its milk glands, like other mammals. But its young are hatched from eggs, like the young of reptiles.

How would you classify this animal? Is it a bird? Is it a reptile? Is it a mammal? This strange animal is an egg-laying mammal. It is called a duckbilled platypus (plat'ə pəs).

The home of the platypus is Australia and a nearby island named Tasmania. A platypus lives in a burrow it digs in the banks of streams. Its broad tail and webbed feet help it swim in the water. The platypus isn't a fancy eater. It lives on worms, snails, grubs, insects, and plants that live in the water and the mud.

Even though the platypus looks harmless, nature gave it some deadly weapons. On its hind legs the male platypus has spurs that are connected to poison sacs. The platypus can use these spurs to inject poison into animals. The poison can kill small animals or wound larger ones.

People used to hunt the platypus for its velvety fur. But laws have been passed to protect the platypus from hunters.

People are also mammals. Humans are warm-blooded and they breathe with lungs. They have hair on their bodies. Human mothers have milk glands with which to feed their babies. But people are different in some ways from all other mammals. People are the most intelligent mammals. They can reason, remember, communicate, and learn. This is because the human brain is the largest and most complex mammal brain. What is another way that people are different from other mammals?

The young of most mammals develop inside the mother's body. How does this help the baby to survive? Some mammals produce many young at

Elephant and baby

one time. For example, mice may give birth to as many as eight or ten babies at one time. But large mammals, such as elephants, usually have only one baby at a time. The time it takes for a baby animal to develop inside the mother is not the same for all mammals. Usually the time is related to the size of the animal. In small mammals, such as hamsters, the young develop in only 16 days. The young of a large mammal like a giraffe take about 442 days to develop. Puppies develop inside the mother for about 63 days. Baby whales develop in the mother for about 450 days.

Some mammal babies develop for a very short time inside the mother's body. When they are born, they are not fully formed. They are very small and helpless. They crawl into the mother's warm pouch and continue to develop there. The kangaroo and the opossum are mammals whose young develop in a pouch. The pictures show tiny opossum babies feeding inside their mother's pouch and a kangaroo with its young.

Certain mammals are important to people. Some mammals are used for food and other products. Cattle, pigs, and sheep are raised for meat. Foods such as cheese, butter, and ice cream are made from cows' milk. Mammal skins are used to make many leather products such as belts, shoes, and footballs. Mammals such as horses, donkeys, camels, oxen, and elephants are used to carry people and materials.

Some mammals, such as rats, are harmful to people. Rats spread disease and eat stored food, such as grain. Millions of dollars' worth of food are lost each year because of damage by rats.

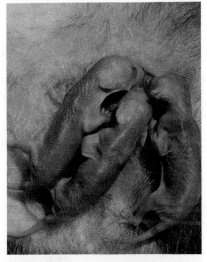
Baby opossums feeding

Kangaroo with young

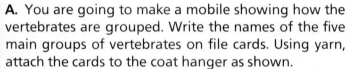

Activity

What are the characteristics of the five groups of vertebrates?

Materials 5 small file cards / coat hanger / yarn / construction paper / scissors / transparent tape / felt-tip pens or crayons / old magazines

Procedure

A. You are going to make a mobile showing how the vertebrates are grouped. Write the names of the five main groups of vertebrates on file cards. Using yarn, attach the cards to the coat hanger as shown.

   1. What are the five main groups of vertebrates?

B. Cut five strips of construction paper, all the same size. On these strips list the main characteristics of each group of vertebrates.

C. Using the yarn, attach the lists to the right cards as shown.

   2. Did you find any characteristics that appeared in more than one group?

   3. What are these characteristics? In which groups did these characteristics appear?

D. Below each list of characteristics, hang pictures of animals from that group. You may either draw the animals or cut out pictures of animals from magazines. Attach the pictures with yarn as shown.

Conclusion

What do all five groups of vertebrates have in common?

Using science ideas

You can use your mobile to play a science game called "The Vertebrate Detective." Think of one of the animals hanging on the mobile. On a file card list five characteristics of this animal. Read these characteristics, one at a time, to the class. Have members of the class guess the animal you are thinking of.

Ideas To Remember

▶ Vertebrates are animals with a backbone.

▶ The five major groups of vertebrates are fish, amphibians, reptiles, birds, and mammals.

▶ A fish is a cold-blooded vertebrate with fins. It uses gills to breathe under water. Most fish have scales.

▶ An amphibian is a cold-blooded vertebrate that lives part of its life in water and part on land.

▶ A reptile is a cold-blooded vertebrate that has lungs and dry skin. Most reptiles have scales and live on land.

▶ A bird is a warm-blooded vertebrate that has feathers and wings.

▶ A mammal is a warm-blooded vertebrate that is usually covered with fur or hair. It breathes through lungs and feeds milk to its young.

Reviewing the Chapter

SCIENCE WORDS

A. Write the letter of the term that best matches the definition. Not all the terms will be used.

1. Soft, bonelike material in a shark's skeleton
2. Thin, feathery structures filled with blood and used in breathing
3. Type of animal whose body temperature stays the same even when surrounding temperature changes
4. Cold-blooded vertebrate with lungs and dry skin
5. Small fluffy feathers near the skin
6. Structures that help fish move through water
7. Any animal with a backbone
8. Warm-blooded vertebrate with fur or hair on part or all of its body

a. warm-blooded
b. cartilage
c. down
d. cold-blooded
e. reptile
f. mammal
g. vertebrate
h. fins
i. gills

B. Identify each of the following.

1. It is a cold-blooded vertebrate. Its body is covered with scales. It can change color for protection. What is it?

2. It is a large mammal. It can have a mass of over 110,000 kg. It has lungs but it lives in the water. What is it?

UNDERSTANDING IDEAS

A. Each body part listed below belongs to one of the animals shown at the right. Match the body part to the animal.

1. Gills inside the body
2. Pouch for developing young
3. Scaly skin and feet with claws
4. Gills outside the body
5. Teeth that curve toward the back of the mouth
6. Skeleton made of cartilage

B. The pictures show the stages in the life cycle of a frog. Each picture has a number. Write the numbers in the correct order to show how the frog develops. Then describe what is happening in each stage.

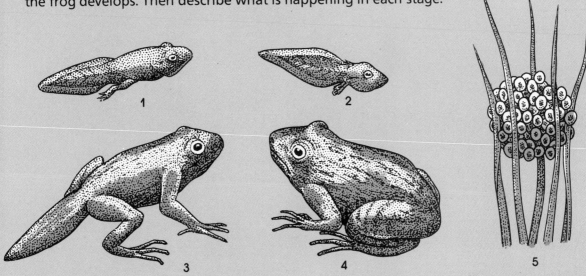

USING IDEAS

Keep a diary for a week. List all the vertebrates that you see during this time. You may include live animals as well as those you might see on television or in films.

THINKING LIKE A SCIENTIST

Answer the following questions. You may be able to answer some of the questions just by thinking about them. To answer other questions you may have to do some research.

1. An animal called the horned toad is often mistaken for an amphibian. But the horned toad is a reptile. What things that you might observe about the horned toad would tell you it is a reptile?

2. You have learned that fish use fins to move through the water. In your opinion, which fin is most important in help- ing a trout to swim forward? Can any fish swim backward? What fins would they use to do this? Use scientific reasoning and facts to support your opinion.

3. Most land-dwelling mammals have tails. Name a mammal that uses its tail in each of the following ways: as a warning device; to grasp tree limbs; for balance; for protection from insects; to keep warm.

Chapter 4

Living Communities

The picture shows a desert in Arizona. A desert is a hot, dry place. It does not seem like a place where plants and animals could live. Yet snakes, lizards, insects, birds, rats, and rabbits make their homes in the desert. What plants do you see in the desert shown?

In many ways the desert is like other parts of the earth. There are living and nonliving things in all parts of the earth. The living things affect each other and the nonliving things around them. And the living things are affected by the nonliving things. In this chapter you will learn about the ways in which the living and nonliving parts of the world can change.

The Living and Nonliving World

What is an ecosystem?

All living things exist in a world that contains other living, as well as nonliving, things. These living and nonliving things affect each other. Everything that surrounds and affects a living thing is called its **environment** (en vī'rən mənt). What are some living things in your home environment? What are some nonliving things? In what ways do these living and nonliving things affect each other? The study of how living and nonliving things affect each other is called **ecology** (ē kol'ə jē). Scientists who study this subject are called ecologists. For example, an ecologist might study how sunlight affects animals in a forest.

Look at the picture of the fish tank. What living and nonliving things do you see? The living and nonliving things in the tank affect, or interact with, each other. Both the fish and the plants need water to survive. The plants give off oxygen, which goes into the water. The fish, which

need oxygen to live, take the oxygen from the water. As they breathe, the fish give off carbon dioxide. The plants use the carbon dioxide to make food. Without the fish, the plants would die. And without the plants, the fish would die.

The fish tank is an example of an ecosystem (ē′kə sis təm). An **ecosystem** is a group of living things and their nonliving environment. An ecosystem includes all the ways the living things in a group interact with each other. It also includes the way living things interact with their nonliving environment.

An ecosystem can be as small as a single fish and a single plant in a fishbowl. Or an ecosystem can be as large as a forest, a desert, or an ocean. Look at the picture of the city park. The park is an ecosystem that may contain several smaller ecosystems. For example, under a rock you may find a small ecosystem that has many kinds of living things. A single tree in the park may be another ecosystem. The tree may be the home of squirrels, birds, and insects. Nongreen plants as well as green plants may also live on the tree.

Ecosystem under a rock

City park

Living Things in Ecosystems

What are communities and populations?

You have learned that an ecosystem is made up of living and nonliving things. The living things in an ecosystem are known as a community (kə-myü′nə tē). A **community** is all the plants and animals that live and interact with each other in a place.

Communities are often named for the kind of place in which they live. There are forest, marsh, and pond communities. What are some other kinds of communities?

Communities are made up of populations (pop-yə lā′shənz). A **population** is a group of the same kind of living thing in a community. In the picture at the left, all of the pine trees in the forest make up one population. It is a population of pine trees. What types of plant populations are shown in the picture below?

Members of the geese population can easily be seen in the picture of the marsh. What other animal populations live in a marsh? There are also many different plant populations in the marsh. The different populations in a community interact with each other. The geese feed on the marsh plants. When they feed on these plants, the geese make room for new plants to grow. The geese also release wastes into the soil. This enriches the soil and helps the new plants grow.

Activity

What populations are found in an ecosystem?

Materials meterstick or metric tape / 4 sticks / 4.5 m of string / hand lens / 2 large jars with lids / small shovel or trowel / white paper

Procedure

A. Choose a place outdoors to study. Measure a square area of ground 1 m on each side. Push four sticks into the ground to mark the four corners of your square. Tie string around the sticks to enclose the area.

B. Study the area closely for several minutes. Look for moving insects or other animals. Use a hand lens to help you see small plants and animals.

C. Collect a sample of each kind of plant and animal you find. Put these samples in one jar. Use a small shovel to collect a sample of the soil. Put this sample in the second jar.

D. Take your samples back to the classroom. Pour the soil sample onto a sheet of white paper. Examine the sample with a hand lens. Look for living things. Look at the samples in the other jar.

Results

1. How many kinds of animals did you find?
2. How many kinds of plants did you find?
3. Identify as many of the plants and animals as possible. List them on a sheet of paper.

Conclusion

1. What populations did you find in the ecosystem?
2. In what ways might these populations affect one another?
3. If all of the plants in your ecosystem suddenly died, what might happen to the animals?

Using science ideas

Suppose you studied this same ecosystem at another time of the year. How might this affect the number and kinds of populations you could find? Explain.

Every living thing in a community has a special place in which it is usually found. The special place in a community in which a plant or animal lives is called its **habitat** (hab'ə tat). You can think of an ecosystem as the neighborhood that a living thing is part of. The habitat can be thought of as its address in that neighborhood.

Some forest habitats

Within a community there are many habitats. In a forest the soil is the habitat of ants and earthworms. A rotten tree stump is the habitat of termites. Squirrels live in the trees. Mosses grow on the forest floor, in the shade of trees. Ants and earthworms, termites, squirrels, and mosses each have their own habitat. But these living things are all part of the same community.

The populations and habitats in a desert are different from those in a forest. Look at the picture at the right. The cactus plant is the habitat of the owl. The habitats of many other desert animals are burrows under the ground.

Owl in nest in saguaro cactus

Mouse in city building

Mouse in country field

The habitat of a plant or animal supplies it with many of the things that it needs to survive. Some living things are able to live in more than one habitat. Others can live in only one habitat. For example, flies can live in many habitats. They move to different places to get food. Mice can also live in more than one habitat. They are found in city buildings as well as in country fields.

Some animals are very limited in their habitat. Trout can only live in cool streams. The koala (kō-ä'lə) of Australia eats only one kind of plant. It eats the leaves of the eucalyptus (yü kə lip'təs) tree. So the koala can only live where this kind of tree grows. Food also limits the habitat of the panda. It only eats bamboo. How many different habitats could you live in?

Koala eating eucalyptus leaf

Science & Technology

▶ This bird is sitting in a tropical rain forest. But the rain forest is not in South America. It is inside a large wood and glass building at the Bronx Zoo in New York City. People at the zoo have created a habitat for many kinds of plants and animals.

▼ The temperature and humidity in the forest are kept high by machines. Other machines create clouds that rest in the treetops. Artists have created artificial rocks and riverbeds. Glass skylights let in the sun. Electric wires heat rocks to keep lizards warm. This special habitat provides a home for animals whose natural homes are being destroyed.

Many plants and animals share the same habitat. Earthworms share the soil with many plants. Termites share a rotten tree stump with ants and other insects. Birds share their tree habitat with squirrels. Although they share the same habitat, the way these animals live may be very different from each other. The role that each living thing plays in a habitat is called its **niche** (nich).

Female cardinal

Red squirrel

Some squirrels and birds share the same habitat. Yet these animals each have a different niche. Squirrels gather nuts and stay close to their habitat. Some birds are insect eaters. They travel great distances from their habitat to get food. Both animals share the same habitat. But they do not have a great effect on each other.

Sometimes the niche of one population does affect other populations. A creek is the habitat of a population of beavers. The beavers build dams across the creek. The dams they build create ponds. The ponds become the habitat of fish and plants. The beavers also cut down many trees. How does this affect the tree population?

Beaver cutting down tree and building dam

Changes in Populations

What factors affect the size of a population?

Ecologists study communities of living things. They try to find out what living things are present. They also want to know the size of each population. They try to learn whether the populations are changing in size. Ecologists want to know if populations are getting larger, getting smaller, or staying the same.

Ecologist studying a bird population

When an animal population changes in size, it often means there is a change in the birth rate or the death rate. The birth rate is the number of animals that are born in a period of time. What is the death rate? Many factors can cause a change in the birth rate or the death rate.

Young male white-tailed deer eating

Why might the birth rate of a population go up? Suppose a deer population has a large supply of food and water. Deer eat plants. If the deer are healthy, many will live long enough to produce young deer. So the birth rate will go up.

As the birth rate goes up, the deer population will get larger. After a while, the kinds of plants that deer eat will be scarce. Some deer may move away in search of food. What will this do to the size of the deer population? The deer that stay will still have little food. Some deer will get sick and die. Other deer may become very weak. They may be unable to run from other animals that hunt them for food.

Buck and does, members of a white-tailed deer population

The size of a population may also change because of a sudden change in the amount of food that can be found. Suppose a fire or a disease destroys the deer's food source. Then the death rate of the deer population would go up. As the death rate goes up, population size goes down.

Lynx and snowshoe rabbit

The size of a population may also be affected by the presence of a predator (pred'ə tər). A **predator** is an animal that hunts other animals for food. The animal that is hunted is the **prey** (prā). The picture shows a predator with its prey. The predator is a lynx (lingks). A lynx is a small catlike animal. The prey is a snowshoe rabbit. Both animals live in the United States and Canada.

Suppose the number of snowshoe rabbits goes up. Then the number of lynx goes up, too. This is because the lynx now have a larger food supply. But an increase in the lynx population means more rabbits will be eaten. After a while, there will be very few rabbits left. With less food, many of the lynx will starve to death. This decreases the number of lynx. What will then happen to the size of the rabbit population?

Activity

What factors affect the size of a population?

Materials metric ruler / pencil / paper / buttons

Procedure

A. Draw a grid like the one shown. Each box should be 2 cm on a side. There should be six squares across and six squares down. The grid represents a forest.

B. Suppose each box represents the amount of space, food, and water needed by one deer. Use buttons to represent deer. Begin with two deer. Put each deer into a different box on the grid.

C. Imagine that a year has passed. The deer population has doubled in size. Add the correct number of buttons to the grid.

   1. How many deer are there now?

D. Another year passes and the deer population has doubled again. Add the correct number of buttons to the grid.

   2. How many deer are there now?

E. The next year three deer die of disease. Remove three buttons. Then the remaining deer population doubles once again. Add the correct number of buttons to the grid.

   3. How many deer are there now?

F. Suppose that from now on, the deer population doubles each year and no more deer die.

   4. In how many more years will there be too many deer for the amount of space, food, and water in the forest?

Conclusion

1. What is the greatest number of deer that could live in the forest?

2. What are some reasons for a decrease in the size of a population?

Changes in Communities

What is succession and what causes it?

You learned that a sudden major change, such as a fire, can affect the size of populations. Sudden changes can also affect whole communities.

On May 18, 1980, a volcano in Washington erupted. The volcano, Mount St. Helens, exploded with great force. The force was equal to almost 10 million metric tons of dynamite. One picture shows how the area looked before the blast. The other shows the same area 4 months

Mount St. Helens before the eruption

Mount St. Helens 4 months after the eruption

Trees blown down by eruption

after the blast. Millions of trees were blown down. Many plants were burned or covered with layers of ash as much as 180 m deep. Scientists believe that thousands of bear, deer, and other animals lost their lives. Few living things in the area survived.

A fire destroyed many square kilometers of the forest below. Trees, shrubs, grasses, and other plants were burned in the fire. Many animals were also killed. Among these were snakes, lizards, rabbits, and baby birds. Some animals were able to escape the fire, and so they lived. But many of the animals that lived lost their food supply and their habitat.

Colorado forest destroyed by fire

People also cause changes in communities. The picture shows a major change in a redwood forest. People are cutting down the trees to use the wood. What changes might result from clearing the trees in this forest? In what ways are these changes like the changes from a forest fire? What are some living things that will lose their habitat?

People clearing a redwood forest

How has your environment changed?

Interview some adults who have lived in your neighborhood for a long time. Or do some research at the library about your neighborhood. Try to find out what the area was like many years ago. What changes have there been? Find out whether each change was brought about by people or by nature. Try to find out about the kinds of plants and animals that have lived in the neighborhood. Learn how these living things were affected by each change. Find out about the effect that the changes might have had on people.

What happens after a sudden major change destroys a community? The same community does not come back right away. It may take 100 or more years for it to return. During this time there are many changes in the kinds of living things in an ecosystem. The series of changes in the communities of an ecosystem is called **succession** (sək sesh′ən).

These drawings show succession in a forest after a fire.

1. Before the fire a forest of beech and maple trees is the habitat of many living things.
2. A fire burns the trees and other plants.
3. Several years after the fire the area has become a field. There are grasses and other low plants. Insects, birds, groundhogs, and other animals live in the field.
4. In a few years shrubs and young trees grow.
5. The beech and maple trees reappear after 100 years. What animals live in the forest?

Ecologists have found different stages in the succession of any ecosystem. The first stage of succession is called the **pioneer** (pī ə nir′) **stage.** What is the number of the drawing that shows the pioneer stage in the succession of the forest? The picture on the right shows the beginning of the pioneer stage after the Mount St. Helens blast. New plants are growing out of the ash.

The last stage in the process of succession is called the **climax** (klī′maks) **stage.** Which drawing shows the climax stage? The climax stage in a community is usually stable. This means that it rarely changes. What might cause it to change?

Pioneer stage, Mount St. Helens

Many times succession does not result from a sudden change. Succession is more often a natural process in an ecosystem. These drawings show succession in a pond community.

1. Many kinds of plants and animals live in and around the pond. Each year some animals and many plants die and sink to the bottom.
2. After many years the remains of once-living things form soil and the pond fills in.
3. As the pond fills in, a marsh develops. The marsh plants grow and die.
4. In time the marsh dries up and a field develops. Grasses and shrubs grow in the field. A few years later trees appear.
5. Finally a forest community develops. What is this last stage of succession called?

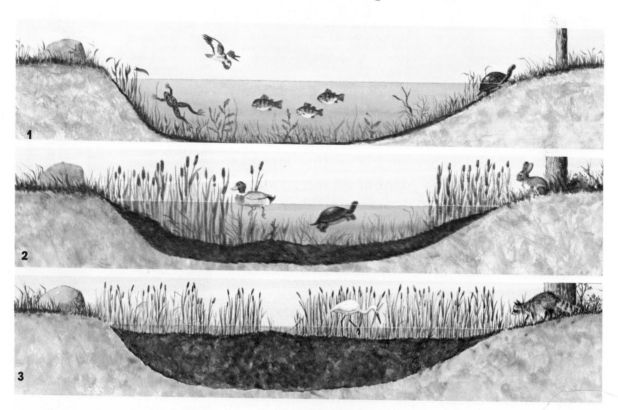

Ideas to Remember

▶ The environment is everything that surrounds and affects a living thing.

▶ An ecosystem is a group of living things, their nonliving environment, and the interactions among them.

▶ A community is all the plants and animals that live and interact with each other in a place.

▶ A population is a group of the same kind of living thing in a community.

▶ A habitat is the special place in a community in which a plant or animal lives.

▶ The role that each living thing plays in its habitat is called its niche.

▶ Many factors affect the size of populations.

▶ Succession is the series of changes that take place in the communities of an ecosystem.

Reviewing the Chapter

SCIENCE WORDS

A. Copy the sentences below. Use science terms from the chapter to complete each sentence.

1. A group of living things and their environment is a/an _____.
2. The series of changes in the communities of an ecosystem is called _____.
3. All the plants and animals that live and interact with each other in a place is called a/an _____.
4. The special place in a community in which a plant or animal lives is called its _____.
5. The study of how living and nonliving things affect each other is called _____.
6. Everything that surrounds and affects a living thing is called its _____.
7. The last stage of succession is called the _____ stage.
8. A group of the same kind of living thing in a community is called a/an _____.
9. The role that each living thing plays in a habitat is called its _____.
10. The first stage of succession is called the _____ stage.

B. Identify each of the following.

1. It is an animal that hunts other animals for food. What is it?

2. It is an animal. It is hunted by other animals for food. What is it?

UNDERSTANDING IDEAS

A. A *cause* makes things happen. An *effect* is what happens. For each pair of sentences, write which is the cause and which is the effect.

1. a. A population of predators increases in size.
   b. A population of prey increases in size.
2. a. A marsh develops.
   b. Many plants and animals die and sink to the bottom of a shallow pond.

3. a. A population of predators increases in size.
   b. A population of prey decreases in size.
4. a. Many members of a deer population starve to death.
   b. A fire burns all the plants in a forest.

B. Renumber the drawings below to show the correct order. Then describe what is happening at each stage.

1

2

3

USING IDEAS

Collect old magazines and cut out pictures that show different communities. List as many plant and animal populations as you can see in each.

THINKING LIKE A SCIENTIST

Answer the following questions. You may be able to answer some of the questions just by thinking about them. To answer other questions you may have to do some research.

1. Many scientists must become experts in more than one area of science. Why would an ecologist become an expert in chemistry?
2. What problems would plants and animals living in a cave ecosystem have? What features might these living things have that would help them overcome the problems?

3. Most states have hunting laws that limit which animals can be hunted as well as when and where they can be hunted. Why do most hunters support this practice?
4. In some places in the world, there are islands that are battered by hurricanes every two or three years. What would succession be like on such an island?

Science in Careers

Many people who have pets know that working with animals can be both rewarding and fun. Some people who like animals choose careers in which they take care of animals.

A **veterinarian** (vet ər ə nãr′ē ən) is an animal doctor. Veterinarians treat animals that are ill or injured. They also give checkups to animals.

Animal keepers take care of animals in places such as zoos and circuses. Animal keepers see that the animals are properly fed and sheltered. They also check that the animal cages are kept clean and in good repair.

If you have an interest in plants, you may want to prepare for a career as a **botanist** (bot′ə nist). Botanists are scientists who study plants. Many botanists are teachers or researchers.

Flowers are used to add beauty indoors and outdoors. They can help people express feelings. A **floral designer** is someone who arranges flowers into designs for other people. Classes in flower arranging are offered in many adult education programs. Some people are trained on the job.

Botanist

Veterinarian

People in Science

LIBBIE HYMAN
(1888–1969)

Few people have done more for the study of invertebrates than the zoologist (zō ol'ə-jist) Libbie Hyman. Between 1940 and 1967, Hyman published six books about the biology of invertebrates. These books earned her the respect of the scientific world. Her books gave detailed information about invertebrates. They also showed the importance of studying and then describing living things. Before her books were written, scientists made guesses about the body structure of many invertebrates.

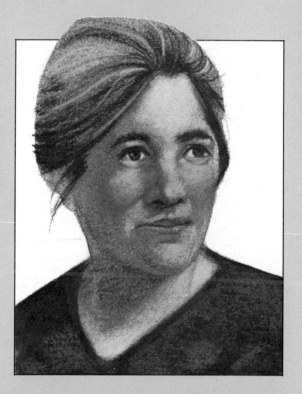

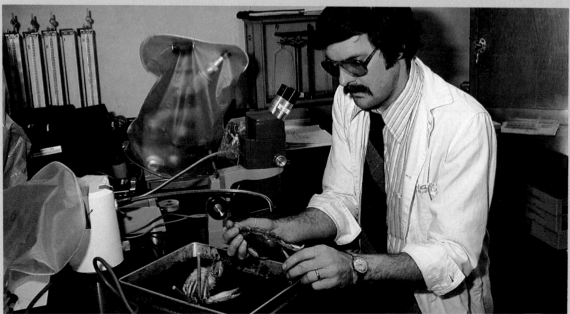

Zoologist studying a blue crab

Developing Skills

WORD SKILLS

At the back of this book is a section called the Glossary and another section called the Index. A glossary lists the important terms in a book and their definitions. An index lists the main topics covered in a book and the pages on which they can be found. Subtopics and their page numbers are listed under some of the main topics.

Use the Glossary and Index of this book to answer these questions.

1. In what order are the terms listed in the Glossary and Index?
2. Besides definitions, what other information is in the Glossary?
3. On what page can you find information about cumulus clouds?
4. What is the meaning of the term *hinge joint*?
5. Use the Glossary to find the term *turbine*. How is it pronounced?
6. What are two meanings of the term *cartilage*?
7. Find the term *vein* in the Glossary and write the definitions. Now find this term in a dictionary and write the definitions. How does a glossary differ from a dictionary?
8. In the Index, what subtopics are listed under the main topic *Energy*?
9. Which topics and subtopics would help you locate information on electricity? Write the topics, the subtopics, and their page numbers.

READING A LINE GRAPH

Look at the line graph on the next page. A line graph can show how things change. This line graph shows the population of the world in the past. The graph also shows how the population might change in the future. Use the graph to answer the following questions.

1. What was the population of the world in 6000 B.C.?

2. What was the population of the world in 2000 B.C.?

3. What was the population of the world in A.D. 1985?

4. How much did the world's population increase from A.D. 1 to A.D. 1985?

5. What might the population of the world be in A.D. 2000?

6. Make your own line graph. Find the temperature outside your home or school at the same time every day for one week. Use this data to make a graph. On what day was the temperature the highest? On what day was it the lowest? Use your graph to describe what happened to the temperature during the week.

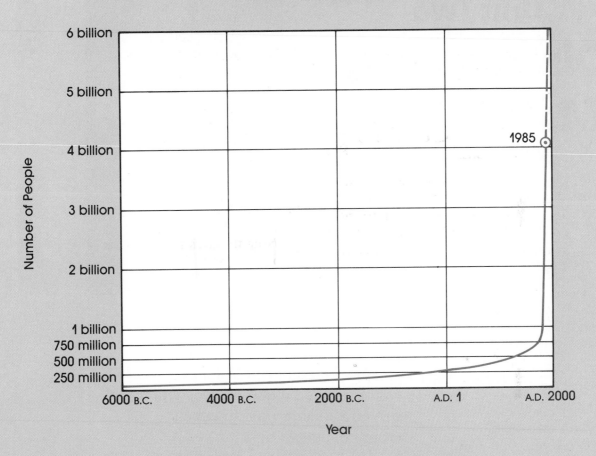

POPULATION OF THE WORLD

USING THINKING SKILLS

As the world's population increases, many things are affected. One of these things is the supply of food on the earth. Think about this as you answer the following items.

1. Besides food, what other things are affected by an increase in the world's population?

2. Should the world's population be controlled? Explain your answer.

3. Find out about ways that China controls its population.

Unit Two
Discovering Matter and Energy

Chapter 6–Physical Changes in Matter You can see many colors of paint in the picture. What changes happen when different colors of paint are mixed together? You will learn about some ways in which matter changes.

Chapter 5–Building Blocks of Matter Pennies are made of two basic kinds of matter—copper and zinc. In this chapter you will discover how scientists study what matter is made of and how it changes.

Chapter 8–Sources of Energy This solar furnace uses the sun to heat water. The heated water produces steam and runs an engine. You will learn in this chapter how many sources of energy are used.

Chapter 7– Understanding Electricity In the picture, electrons are moving between two points to produce heat and light. This chapter explains how electricity works and how it is used.

Chapter 5

Building Blocks of Matter

Have you ever tried to put together a picture puzzle? Some puzzles are very hard to put together. To complete the puzzle, you need to look at the sizes, shapes, and colors of the small pieces. Then you try to find ways that they fit together. The small pieces give you clues that help you form the completed picture.

Scientists also use clues to help explain the world around them. Like a jigsaw puzzle, matter is made up of many small parts. The small parts give clues about what matter is like. In this chapter you will learn about the small parts that make up matter.

Studying Matter

How do scientists study the world around them?

Look around you. Almost everything you see is matter. You are matter and so is the air around you. Your pencil, your chair, and the walls of your classroom are all made of matter. **Matter** is anything that has mass and takes up space. You know that **mass** is a measure of the amount of matter in an object.

How do scientists study matter? Scientists begin by asking questions. Suppose a scientist asks the question, "How is food made in a leaf?" The scientist then gathers information to answer the question. Scientists first try to observe matter

Collecting water samples

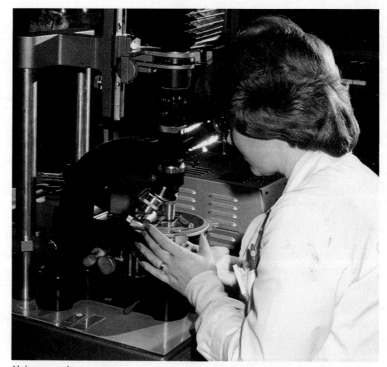

Using a microscope

Using a telescope

directly. To do this they use their senses of sight, smell, hearing, taste, and touch.

Sometimes scientists use special devices to observe very small things or things that are far away. They use microscopes to see very small objects such as cells. They use telescopes to study the stars and other bodies in space. All the scientists in the pictures on both pages are gathering information about matter.

Information that scientists collect while observing matter directly is called direct evidence. For example, a scientist can observe a leaf's structure under a microscope. This evidence can help answer questions about how the plant makes food in the leaf.

When scientists cannot observe matter directly, they study matter in an indirect way. They use indirect evidence. **Indirect evidence** (in də rekt' ev'ə dəns) is a set of clues that scientists use to make logical guesses about things they cannot see or test directly. When you see a footprint in the sand, you know a person has walked there. You have found indirect evidence of a person.

Scientists study many kinds of indirect evidence. Look at the fossil shown below. Fossils give scientists information about plants or animals. A fossil also can give clues about the land and area where it was found. This fossil gives you some indirect evidence. What can you learn from it?

In the example above you made a guess about a fossil. But it was not a wild guess. It was a logical guess, based on evidence. In the same way, scientists have used direct and indirect evidence to make logical guesses about the nature of matter. Such a logical guess is called a **hypothesis** (hī-poth'ə sis).

Scientists have made hypotheses about what matter is made of. In the next lesson you will learn more about the structure of matter.

What can you learn from indirect evidence?

Materials sealed box with unknown object / metric ruler / balance and masses /magnet

Procedure

A. Lift and shake the box.

   1. Are you collecting direct or indirect evidence?

   2. What did you find out about the object in the box by shaking it?

B. Gather all the information you can. Use the balance to measure the object's mass. Move the magnet along the outside of the box. Measure the box.

C. Make a chart like the one below. List each thing you did and what you learned.

Result of shaking	Effect of magnet	Mass	Size of box

D. Study your chart.

   3. From your evidence, what do you guess is in the box?

E. Open the box and look inside. Compare your guess with what actually is in the box.

   4. In what ways was your guess correct?

   5. In what ways was it wrong?

Conclusion

You have just collected indirect evidence. How did indirect evidence help you guess what the object was?

Using science ideas

List some other ways you could learn about the contents of a sealed box.

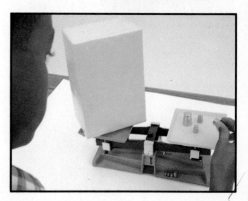

115

The Atom

What is matter made of?

Matter is made of particles too small to be seen, even with a powerful microscope. So scientists have used indirect evidence to learn about these particles. Each tiny particle is called an **atom** (at'əm). An atom is the basic unit of all matter.

Scientists have made logical guesses about what atoms are like. But how can scientists describe what an atom is really like if they can't see it? One way is to make a model of the atom.

Model airplane

A model is a way to describe how something looks or acts. A model can be made of wood or clay. Or it can be a picture or diagram. A model can also be words that describe an idea. The picture shows a model airplane. This model is much smaller than the real thing.

Models of atoms are much larger than the real thing. Atoms are very small. Suppose a million of the smallest atoms were stacked one on top of another. The stack would not be as thick as one page in this book.

For many years scientists have been making models of the atom. What do the models show? Scientists think the atom has a central part called a **nucleus** (nü′klē əs). The nucleus of an atom contains two kinds of particles, **protons** (prō′tonz) and **neutrons** (nü′tronz). Protons and neutrons are tightly packed together in the nucleus. Tiny particles called **electrons** (i lek′tronz) travel around the nucleus. The drawing shows a model of a helium atom.

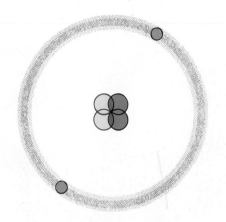

An atom is almost all empty space. Suppose you were to make a model of a helium atom. The nucleus of the atom would be the size of a tennis ball. The electrons would be in the space outside the tennis ball. Your model of the atom would be about 22 football fields across!

The electrons in your model would be very small. They would each be smaller than the head of a pin. The electrons would be moving quickly all around the tennis ball. This shows that in a real atom there is mostly empty space between the nucleus and the electrons.

Elements

What are elements and their symbols?

You have learned that matter is made of tiny particles called atoms. But all atoms are not alike. A silver atom is different from a helium atom. Suppose a silver bar is broken down into the smallest particle that is still silver. The smallest particle of the silver bar would be a silver atom. A silver atom cannot be broken down into a simpler kind of matter and still be silver.

Silver bar

Silver is an element (el'ə mənt). An **element** is matter that is made up of only one kind of atom. It is a basic kind of matter. The smallest particle of an element is an atom.

Scientists have discovered 92 different elements. These 92 elements occur naturally on the earth. Additional elements have been made by scientists using special machines. The total number of elements is about 109.

The atoms of these elements are different from one another. One way in which they differ is in the number of protons. Different kinds of atoms have different numbers of protons. For example, an atom of silver has 47 protons. An atom of gold has 79 protons. The picture on the right shows objects made mainly of only one element. Can you name the elements that make up the objects in the picture?

Made mainly of one element

Each element has its own symbol. A **symbol** is a short way to write the name of an element. Symbols are sometimes called a chemist's shorthand. Symbols are important for two reasons. They are a short, easy way to write the names of elements. Scientists all over the world use these symbols.

Do You Know?

Some of the elements were named in an interesting way. For example, the name of the element helium comes from the Greek word *helios,* which means "sun." Evidence of helium was first found in the sun's light.

The element tungsten was discovered in Sweden and in Spain at the same time. In Sweden it was found in a heavy yellow rock. The element was named tungsten.

The name comes from two Swedish words. *Tung* means "heavy" and *sten* means "stone." The Spanish scientists called the same element wolfram. It was found in a mineral called wolframite.

Today, in most parts of the world, the element is called wolfram. In the United States it is called tungsten. But it is known by the symbol *W.* The picture shows a bulb with a tungsten filament.

How can you group the elements?

One way scientists group the elements is to put all metals in one group and all nonmetals into a second group. Most metals are good conductors of electricity and are shiny. Most nonmetals are poor conductors of electricity and are not shiny. Many nonmetals are gases. Which of the objects shown here is made mainly of a metal? Which is made mainly of a non-metal? Which of the elements in the following list are metals? Which are nonmetals?

aluminum   carbon   helium   lead   nickel   oxygen

Helium-filled balloons

The table on page 121 lists some elements and their symbols. It describes how the elements look. Look at the list of symbols. You will see that sometimes the symbol for an element is the first letter of its name. For example, the symbol for carbon is *C.* Sometimes the symbol is two letters. For example, the symbol for calcium is *Ca.* A two-letter symbol is sometimes used because the names of some elements begin with the same letter. So the symbol *Ca* stands for calcium and the symbol *Co* stands for cobalt.

Look at the symbol for iron. It is *Fe.* The word for iron in Latin is *ferrum* (fer'əm). So the symbol for iron comes from that word. Find the symbol for silver. It is *Ag.* The word for silver in Latin is *argentum* (är jen'təm). The symbol for silver comes from that word. The symbols for some other elements also come from their names in Latin and other languages. Find mercury in the table. It is an unusual metal. Is mercury a solid, a liquid, or a gas at room temperature?

Diamond—a form of carbon

SOME COMMON ELEMENTS		
Element	Symbol	Description
Calcium	Ca	Silver-white metal
Carbon	C	Black solid or colorless crystal
Chlorine	Cl	Greenish-yellow poisonous gas
Cobalt	Co	Silver-white metal
Gold	Au	Heavy yellow metal
Helium	He	Light gas with no color, taste, or odor
Hydrogen	H	Gas with no color, taste, or odor
Iron	Fe	Gray-white metal
Mercury	Hg	Heavy silver-colored metal; liquid at room temperature
Nitrogen	N	Gas with no color, taste, or odor
Oxygen	O	Gas with no color, taste, or odor
Silver	Ag	Shiny white metal
Sodium	Na	Soft silvery metal
Sulfur	S	Powdery yellow solid

Mercury used
in thermometer

Molecules and Compounds

What happens when atoms combine?

You have learned that the smallest particle of matter is the atom. Atoms do not usually exist alone on earth. They combine, sometimes in pairs, sometimes in threes. Sometimes hundreds of atoms combine. New substances form when atoms of different elements combine. These new substances are called **compounds** (kom'poundz). The simplest particle of many compounds is a **molecule** (mol'ə kyül). Molecules are made of two or more atoms.

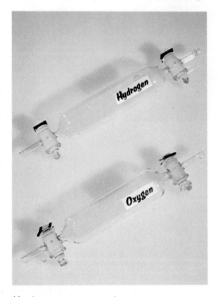

Hydrogen gas and oxygen gas

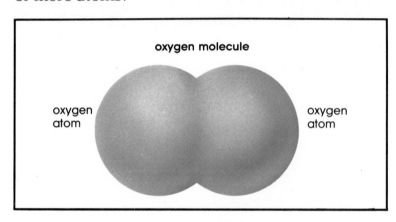

Sometimes two atoms of the *same* element combine to form a molecule. Think about these examples. Two atoms of the element oxygen join to form a molecule of oxygen. In the same way, two atoms of the element hydrogen join to form a molecule of hydrogen. Look at the drawing above. It shows a molecule of oxygen. You can see that two oxygen atoms have joined to form this molecule. The oxygen and hydrogen molecules are not compounds. Compounds are formed only when atoms of *different* elements join.

How does steel wool form a compound?

Materials 2 test tubes / steel wool pad / magnet / metric ruler / water / 2 test-tube clamps / ring stand / 600-mL beaker / wax crayon or pencil /hand lens

Procedure
A. Steel wool is made of fine strands of steel. Steel is a form of iron. Test a steel wool pad with a magnet.
  1. What happens when you hold a magnet near the steel wool?

B. Wet the steel wool with water. Fill the lower 2 cm of a test tube with a piece of the steel wool. Use a pencil to push the steel wool into the tube.

C. Half fill a beaker with water. Set up the two test tubes with the beaker and a ring stand. One test tube will be empty. Use a wax crayon or pencil to make a mark 2 cm from the open end of each test tube, as shown. Make sure the marks are even with the surface of the water.
  2. Predict what will happen in each test tube.

D. Observe the test tubes for 5 days. Note any changes that occur inside the test tubes each day.
  3. How has the steel wool changed?
  4. How has the water level changed?

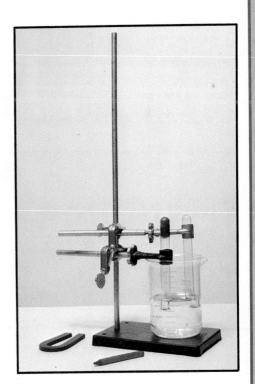

E. After 5 days, carefully remove the steel wool. You may need to use your pencil. Look at the steel wool with a hand lens. Test it with a magnet.

Results
  1. Describe how the steel wool looks.
  2. Is the steel wool attracted to the magnet?

Conclusion
A new compound has been formed. It is called iron oxide. Iron oxide is made from iron and oxygen. Another name for iron oxide is rust.
  1. Where did the iron come from?
  2. Where do you think the oxygen came from?
  3. Why do you think the water level changed?

Salt and salt crystals

You have learned that the atoms in a compound are from different elements. Table salt, for example, is made of the elements sodium and chlorine. Sugar is another compound. It is made of atoms of the elements carbon, hydrogen, and oxygen. A compound may be very different from the atoms it is made of. Sugar is a white crystal that tastes sweet. It is formed of the elements carbon, hydrogen, and oxygen. Are these three elements very different from sugar?

Sugar and sugar crystals

Look at the table of the compounds on page 125. The table lists four common compounds. It shows the elements they are made of and describes these elements. Find the description of the elements that make up sugar. You will find that the elements making up sugar are different from the compound sugar.

Find the elements that make up table salt. Do the elements sodium and chlorine look like table salt? No. Sodium is a silvery metal. Chlorine is a greenish-yellow poisonous gas. Table salt is a white crystal used to season food. Notice that the compound salt is different from the elements that make it up.

FOUR COMMON COMPOUNDS

Compound	Description of compound	Elements in compound; symbol for elements	Description of elements
Table salt	Salty-tasting white crystal used to season food	Sodium (Na)	Soft silvery metal
		Chlorine (Cl)	Greenish-yellow poisonous gas
Water	Liquid found over three fourths of the earth's surface	Hydrogen (H)	Gas with no color, taste, or odor
		Oxygen (O)	Gas with no color, taste, or odor
Sugar	Sweet-tasting white crystal used to sweeten food	Carbon (C)	Black solid found in coal, charcoal, and diamonds
		Hydrogen (H)	Gas with no color, taste, or odor
		Oxygen (O)	Gas with no color, taste, or odor
Ammonia	Strong-smelling gas that dissolves in water	Nitrogen (N)	Gas with no color, taste, or odor
		Hydrogen (H)	Gas with no color, taste, or odor

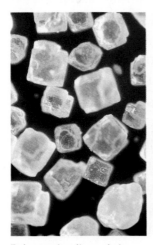
Enlarged salt crystals

Water droplets

Enlarged sugar crystals

Ammonia in water

Water for recreation

Here is another example. Water is a compound formed from elements that are different from water. On the earth water can be found as a liquid, as a solid, and as a gas. We drink it and we bathe in it. It makes up about two thirds of our body.

Water is made up of the elements hydrogen and oxygen. Hydrogen is a gas that has no color, taste, or odor. Oxygen is also a gas. It, too, has no color, taste, or odor. It makes up about one fifth of the air. The elements that make up water are very different from the compound water.

Remember that scientists use symbols for the names of elements. It is easier to write the symbol for an element than to spell out its name. Scientists also use these symbols to write the names of compounds. Water is written H_2O. H_2O stands for one molecule of water. The symbol for hydrogen (H) is joined with the symbol for oxygen (O).

The small number 2 after the H means there are two atoms of hydrogen in a molecule of water. Notice that there is no number after the O. This means there is only one atom of oxygen in a molecule of water.

Science & Technology

▶ Many robots are at work in the United States. Robots are moving computers. They do everything from putting together cars to packing candies in boxes. This robot even moves across the floor. A robot does a task by following directions stored in its computer. This robot's "hands" open and close. What tasks do you think it can do?

One of the most important uses for robots is in a laboratory. Robots can work with substances that are dangerous to people. Some elements and compounds give off radiation. Others are poisonous if touched or smelled. Robots can take the place of people in handling these dangerous things.

▶ At the right you can see one kind of robot used in a laboratory. It can use its hands to pick up objects. The robot's hands are very gentle and make exact movements. They can hold glass test tubes. They can also pour and mix chemicals.

Of course, the robot doesn't work alone. A person behind a shield wall works controls that move the robot. Some robots have cameras. The camera gives the person at the controls a close-up view of the robot.

Suppose you could design a robot. Name a task that you would like the robot to perform. What would your robot look like?

H_2O is the formula (fôr′myə lə) for water. A **formula** is a group of symbols and numbers that stands for a compound. The symbols in a formula

oxygen atom

hydrogen atom

hydrogen atom

water molecule

show the kinds of atoms in a compound. The numbers in a formula show the number of atoms in the smallest particle of a compound.

Every compound can be written with a formula. The formula for one type of sugar is $C_{12}H_{22}O_{11}$. What does this formula show you? It shows you that one molecule of sugar contains atoms of carbon, hydrogen, and oxygen. It also shows you there are 12 atoms of carbon, 22 atoms of hydrogen, and 11 atoms of oxygen. You can see that a formula shows the structure of a compound.

Ideas to Remember

▶ Matter is anything that has mass and takes up space.

▶ Indirect evidence gives clues that scientists use to make guesses about things they cannot see or test directly.

▶ An atom is the basic unit of all matter. An atom is the smallest particle of an element.

▶ The central part of an atom is the nucleus, which contains protons and neutrons. Electrons travel around the nucleus.

▶ An element is matter that is made up of only one kind of atom.

▶ A symbol is a short way to write the name of an element.

▶ A molecule is the simplest particle of many compounds.

▶ A compound is matter formed when two or more atoms of different elements are combined. Scientists use formulas to write the names of compounds.

Reviewing the Chapter

SCIENCE WORDS

A. Copy the sentences below. Use science terms from the chapter to complete the sentences.

1. Scientists call a group of symbols and numbers that stands for a compound a/an _____.
2. The central part of the atom is called the _____.
3. Matter made of only one kind of atom is a/an _____.
4. A logical guess based on direct and indirect evidence is a/an _____.
5. A substance formed when atoms of different elements combine is a/an _____.
6. A tiny particle that travels around the nucleus of an atom is a/an _____.
7. Anything that has mass and takes up space is _____.
8. A set of clues that scientists use to make logical guesses about things they cannot see or test directly is _____.
9. A measure of the amount of matter in an object is its _____.

B. Identify each of the following.

1. It is a very tiny particle. It is part of an atom. It travels around the nucleus. What is it?
2. It is made of numbers. It is made of symbols. It stands for a compound. What is it?

C. Unscramble each group of letters to find a science term from the chapter. Write a sentence using each term.

ulelomec   notrop

tunnero   myblos

UNDERSTANDING IDEAS

A. The drawing shows a water molecule. For each numbered atom, write the name of the element. What is the formula for this compound?

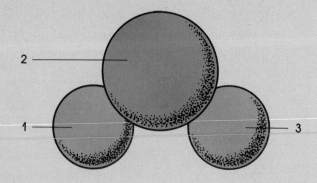

B. Make a chart like the one shown below. Write the correct information in the empty boxes.

Element	Symbol
Hydrogen	
Carbon	
	Fe
	Ag
Mercury	
Sodium	
	Au
	O

USING IDEAS

You can use indirect evidence to play a game. You will need at least four players. Collect objects from around your home or school. Put each object into a paper bag. Each player is given a bag and looks at the object. He or she gives clues to the other players about what is in the bag. The winner is the person whose object is guessed with the fewest clues.

THINKING LIKE A SCIENTIST

Answer the following questions. You may be able to answer some of the questions just by thinking about them. To answer other questions you may have to do some research.

1. In what ways is a model of an atom like a model of the solar system? How are they different?
2. Soda water is made by adding carbon dioxide to water. Is soda water a compound? Explain your answer.
3. Why would a scientist studying dinosaurs depend on indirect evidence more than would a scientist studying bird migration? Write three science questions that cannot be answered without using indirect evidence.
4. As a scientist, answer the questions below. State the reasons for your opinions.
   A. Is it possible that scientists will discover more elements that occur naturally on the earth?
   B. Is it likely that more elements will be made by scientists?

Chapter 6

Physical Changes in Matter

What kinds of matter do you see here? Besides the trees, you can see water. Some of the water is liquid. Because the air temperature is cold, some of the liquid water has changed to solid ice. In addition, some water in the clouds has changed to snow. Then the snow has fallen to the ground. But snow, liquid water, and ice are all still water.

Matter changes in many different ways. In this chapter you will learn about how matter changes in size and shape. You will find out about other kinds of changes in matter. You will also learn how matter can be identified.

Physical Properties

What are physical properties of matter?

The children in the picture are playing a game. The girl is blindfolded and then asked to smell two different kinds of food. She must identify which is a piece of onion and which is a piece of orange. The girl is using odor as a way of identifying matter.

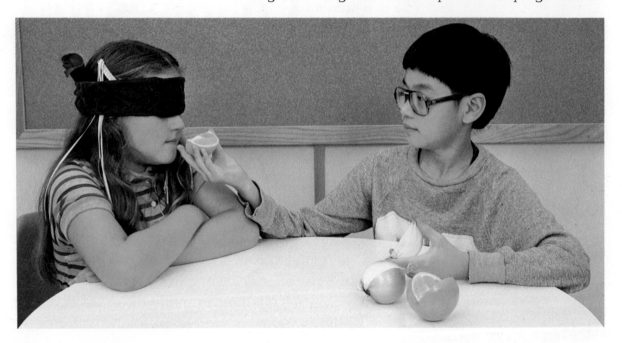

These pictures show two elements—gold and carbon. How can you tell the piece of gold from the piece of carbon? One way to tell is by observing how each one looks. The color of gold is different from the color of carbon. Based on color, which piece is gold and which is carbon?

Odor and color are physical properties of matter. A **physical property** is one that can be used to identify matter. Two other physical properties are shape and hardness.

Density is also a physical property of matter. It is the mass of a certain volume of a substance. Volume is a measure of the amount of space that matter takes up. Density compares mass with volume. For example, suppose you have two identical pails like those shown in the picture. Suppose you fill one pail with clay and one pail with cotton balls. The volume, or the space that is filled, is the same in both pails. Then you use a balance to find the mass of each pail. The mass of the pailful of clay will be greater than the mass of the pailful of cotton balls. This means that clay is more dense than cotton balls.

You can use the property of density to help you identify matter. In the picture below, the two glasses labeled *A* and *B* each contain a colorless liquid. One liquid is water and the other is alcohol. Water has a greater density than alcohol. An ice cube has been put into each glass. Ice floats in the denser liquid and sinks in the less dense liquid. Which glass contains alcohol, *A* or *B*? How do you know this?

Physical Changes

What kinds of physical changes occur in matter?

Matter can change in different ways. The pictures show a log before and after it was chopped. Chopping the wood changes its size and shape. This kind of change is a physical change. A **physical change** is a change in the size, shape, or state of matter. New materials are not formed when there is a physical change. The same kind of matter is present both before and after a physical change. The pieces of chopped wood no longer are the same shape or size as the log. But you can see that the pieces are still wood.

Changes in size and shape are common physical changes. Suppose you make a mistake on a paper you are writing. You erase the mistake with a rubber eraser. Bits of the eraser are rubbed off onto the paper. But the tiny particles that make

up the eraser have not changed. They have just been spread around on the paper.

When wood is chopped or an eraser crumbles, a physical change happens. But the atoms and molecules in the matter do not change. The same kind of matter is present before and after each physical change.

Matter can exist in three forms, or states. The three states of matter are solid, liquid, and gas. Many kinds of matter can change from one state to another. A change in state is another kind of physical change.

Water is one of the few kinds of matter that commonly exists in all three states. Rain is liquid water. Ice cubes and icebergs are solid water. Water as a gas is invisible. It is called water vapor. Although you cannot see it, there is always water vapor in the air. How many states of water can you see in the picture? How many do you think there are?

How do the three states of matter differ? Remember that all matter is made of tiny particles. Different states of matter differ in how far apart these particles are. There is an attraction between the particles in matter. The strength of this attraction varies with the amount of space between particles. Also, the way in which particles in each state of matter move is different. The drawing below shows how particles in a solid, a liquid, and a gas might look.

Particles in solid matter are packed very close together. This causes the attraction between these particles to be strong. The particles move rapidly back and forth in a very small space. Because the particles have a strong attraction for each other, they do not move around very much. For this reason, solids have a definite shape and a definite volume. A cube of sugar and a brick are solids. What are some other solids?

Particles in liquid matter are not as close together as those in a solid. So the attraction between particles in a liquid is weaker than in a

solid   **liquid**   **gas**

The three states of matter

solid. In a liquid, this weak attraction allows particles to move and slide over each other. Because of the way the particles move, a liquid has no definite shape. A liquid takes the shape of the container it is in. For example, a liter of milk can be contained in a milk carton or in a pitcher or in several glasses. Even if the shape of the container changes, the volume of one liter of the milk remains the same.

The picture shows containers of different sizes and shapes. The same volume of water is in each one. What property of liquids does this show?

Particles in a gas are spread farther apart than particles in a liquid. The attraction between the particles is very weak. So particles of a gas move about freely. Because the attraction is so weak and the spaces so great, gases have no definite shape or volume. Particles of gases spread out to fill any container they are in.

Solids, liquids, and gases are different states of matter. But matter can change state. Solids can

Melting ice

become liquids; liquids can become gases. Energy, usually in the form of heat, can cause matter to change from one state to another. Heat energy causes the particles in solids and liquids to move faster. This increases the spaces between the particles and weakens the attraction. So a solid changes to a liquid and a liquid to a gas.

If a glass of ice cubes is left out on a hot summer day, the ice will melt. Melting is the change of state from a solid to a liquid. When heat is added to a solid, what happens to the particles in the solid? How does this explain why the solid melts? A solid changes to a liquid at a certain temperature called the **melting point.**

Cooking food often involves boiling liquids. When something boils, it changes from a liquid to a gas. As heat energy is added, some particles in the liquid have enough energy to escape from the liquid. The escaped particles are now particles in a gas. A liquid changes to a gas at a certain temperature called the **boiling point.**

Boiling water

Finding Out

How fast and how far can particles in a gas move?

Get a bottle of perfume and some cotton. Have several of your classmates stand together about 5 m away. Open the bottle of perfume and pour a small amount of it onto the cotton. Note the time. Recap the bottle. Ask your classmates to raise their hands when they smell the perfume. Note the time again. How long did it take for them to smell the perfume? What conditions in the room might have affected how quickly the perfume moved through the air?

Most substances have a definite melting point and boiling point. Melting point and boiling point are physical properties of matter. The melting point of water is 0°C. Its boiling point is 100°C.

Sometimes a gas changes to a liquid and a liquid changes to a solid. How do these changes of state happen? In both cases, energy must be removed, or taken away. The energy that is removed is usually heat energy. When heat energy is removed, the particles of matter slow down. They move closer to one another. What happens to the attraction between particles? How does this cause a liquid to change to a solid? How is the liquid orange juice changed to a solid?

Melting, boiling, and other changes in state may not seem like physical changes, but they are. Suppose aluminum is melted. Then it is poured into a mold where it hardens. The material is still aluminum. Physical changes do not change the particles that make up matter. They only change the size, shape, or state of matter.

Liquid orange juice

Solid orange juice

Liquid aluminum

Solid aluminum

Mixtures

What are the properties of a mixture?

The children in the picture below are making a salad. They are mixing some lettuce, carrots, green peppers, and other vegetables. A salad is a mixture (miks'chər) of different vegetables. A **mixture** is a material formed by the physical combining of two or more different materials. Mixed nuts are another example of a mixture.

The materials in a mixture are not combined as they are in a compound. In a compound, substances have combined to form a new substance. But the materials that are in a mixture do not change to something else. Lettuce remains lettuce when it is mixed with carrots. The materials in a mixture can be physically separated. How could you separate the pieces of vegetable in the salad mixture?

A mixture of nuts

How can you separate the parts of a mixture?

Materials spoon / table salt / sand / dark-colored paper / hand lens / 2 jars / filter paper / funnel / paper towel / glass or plastic dish

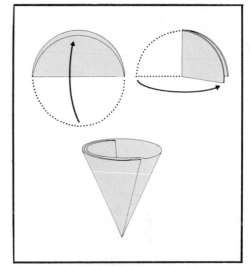

Procedure

A. Put a spoonful of table salt and a spoonful of sand on a sheet of dark paper. Use a hand lens to look at the sand and the salt. Draw some particles of each.

  1. How are the particles of salt different from the particles of sand?

B. Mix the sand and the salt together. Half fill a jar with water. Add the salt-sand mixture to the water in the jar. Stir the mixture.

  2. What happens?

C. Fold a piece of filter paper as shown. Put the filter paper into a clean funnel. Put the funnel into another jar so it rests on the mouth of the jar.

D. Slowly pour all the salt-sand-water mixture into the funnel. Take the filter paper out, open it, and place it on a paper towel. Allow the material to dry.

E. Pour a small amount of liquid from the jar into a dish. Allow the liquid in the dish to evaporate.

  3. What material do you predict will be left in the dish after the water evaporates?

Results

Use the hand lens to look at the dried materials on the filter paper and in the dish.

  1. What material is left on the filter paper?
  2. What material is left in the dish?

Conclusion

1. When you made the salt-sand-water mixture, what kind of change in matter occurred?

2. Describe how the materials in the mixture were separated.

The pieces or particles in a mixture can be of different sizes. The pieces of vegetable in the salad are large. Suppose you mix sand and salt together. The particles are small, but they can be seen. They can also be separated from each other by physical means.

Mixtures are found everywhere. Almost all foods are mixtures. Nearly all the water on the earth is a mixture. If you have ever tasted ocean water, you know it is salty. Ocean water is a mixture of water and different kinds of salts. What mixtures are shown at the left?

Science & TECHNOLOGY

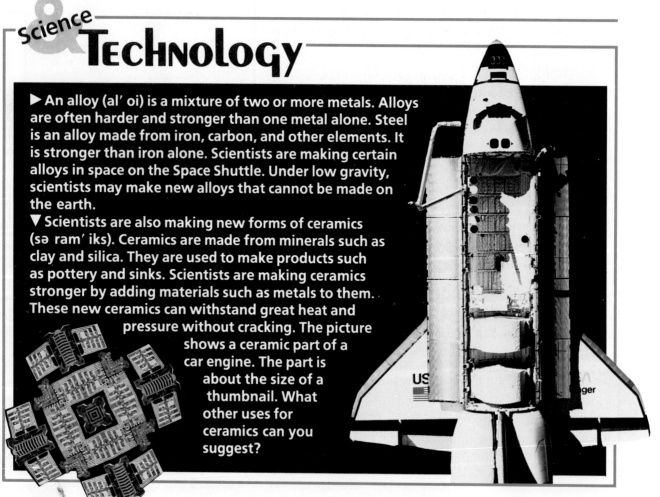

► An alloy (al′ oi) is a mixture of two or more metals. Alloys are often harder and stronger than one metal alone. Steel is an alloy made from iron, carbon, and other elements. It is stronger than iron alone. Scientists are making certain alloys in space on the Space Shuttle. Under low gravity, scientists may make new alloys that cannot be made on the earth.

▼ Scientists are also making new forms of ceramics (sə ram′ iks). Ceramics are made from minerals such as clay and silica. They are used to make products such as pottery and sinks. Scientists are making ceramics stronger by adding materials such as metals to them. These new ceramics can withstand great heat and pressure without cracking. The picture shows a ceramic part of a car engine. The part is about the size of a thumbnail. What other uses for ceramics can you suggest?

Two Kinds of Mixtures

How are a solution and a suspension different?

Sometimes the particles that make up a mixture are large. For example, you can see large particles in a mixed nut mixture. Suppose you mix sand and water together. You can still see the separate particles of sand in the water.

But sometimes you cannot see the particles that make up a mixture. What happens when you stir sugar into a glass of water? The mixture of sugar and water forms a solution. A **solution** (sə-lü′shən) is a mixture that forms when one substance dissolves in another. In a solution the particles are evenly mixed together. Many solutions are solids dissolved in liquids. Such solutions are always clear, even if they are colored.

In a sugar-and-water solution, the sugar particles seem to disappear, but they do not. How do you know? The solution has the sweet taste of sugar. The sugar has dissolved in the water. This

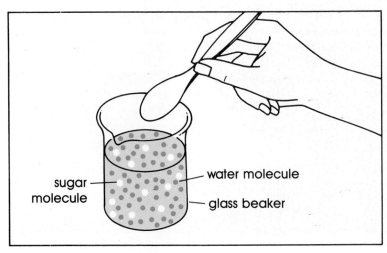

sugar molecule — water molecule — glass beaker

A solution of sugar and water

means that the sugar molecules are evenly mixed with the water molecules. The particles that make up the sugar-and-water solution are molecules that you cannot see. What will happen if the water in the solution evaporates?

A solution has two parts. The **solute** (sol'yüt) is the substance in a solution that dissolves. In a sugar-and-water solution, sugar is the solute. Water is the solvent. The **solvent** (sol'vənt) is the substance in a solution that does the dissolving.

Not all solutes dissolve in the same amount of time. Stirring makes a solute dissolve faster. Temperature also affects how fast a solute dissolves. Most solutes dissolve faster in a warm solvent than in a cold one. The picture shows powdered tea in hot water and in cold water. The same amount of tea was put into each glass at the same time. Why is there a difference in the amount of tea dissolved in each glass?

The size of the solute particles also affects how fast the solute dissolves. Small solute particles dissolve faster than large solute particles. For example, small grains of sugar will dissolve faster than a whole sugar cube.

What conditions affect how fast a solute dissolves?

Materials   4 sugar cubes / paper / two plastic bags / twist ties / 4 jars, all the same size / labels / 4 plastic spoons

Procedure

A. Wrap two sugar cubes in separate pieces of paper. Place each one in a separate plastic bag and close the bags with twist ties. Crush the cubes into a powder by stepping on the plastic bags. Be careful not to tear the bags.

B. Label two jars *Hot* and two jars *Cold.* Half fill the two *Hot* jars with hot water. Half fill the two *Cold* jars with cold water.

C. Carefully take the wrapped, crushed sugar out of one bag. Do not spill any of it. Pour the sugar into one of the jars of hot water. Quickly drop a whole sugar cube into the other jar of hot water. Use the same procedure for the two jars of cold water.

   1. In which of the four jars do you predict that the sugar will dissolve first?

   2. In which of the four jars do you predict that the sugar will dissolve last?

Results

Make a table like the one shown. Watch the jars to see in which one the sugar dissolves first. Record in the table the water temperature and form of sugar in that jar. Follow the same procedure for the other three jars.

Dissolving Order	Water Temperature (Hot or Cold)	Particles (Cubes or Crushed)
1st		
2nd		
3rd		
4th		

Conclusion

1. How does the size of the solute particles affect how fast a solute dissolves?

2. How does the temperature of the solvent affect how fast a solute dissolves?

The picture on the left shows what happens when crushed chalk is mixed with water. You can see that the water becomes very cloudy. But the chalk and water do not form a solution. The particles of chalk do not dissolve in the water. The chalk particles float in the water. The mixture of chalk and water is called a suspension (sə-spen'shən). A **suspension** is a mixture in which particles of a substance do not dissolve in another substance. Suspensions are cloudy mixtures.

In the chalk-and-water mixture, the chalk particles are suspended in the water. If they are not disturbed, the particles that are in a suspension will separate from the liquid. They will settle to the bottom. The picture on the right shows the chalk-and-water mixture after 2 days. The chalk particles have settled to the bottom.

You may have seen bottles labeled *Shake well before using.* Many such bottles contain some kind of suspension. A vinegar-and-oil salad dressing is a suspension. Orange juice and some liquid medicines are also suspensions.

A suspension of chalk and water

Settled chalk particles

148

Another Kind of Change

What is a chemical change?

You have learned about many different physical changes in matter. But matter can change in another way. When a piece of wood burns, it changes into new substances. Burning wood is an example of a chemical change. A **chemical change** is a change in matter in which one or more different kinds of matter form.

iron

The physical properties of matter change when there is a chemical change. You can see that iron is a dark-gray metal. Iron is attracted by a magnet. Sulfur is a yellow powder that is not attracted by a magnet. When iron and sulfur are mixed together, they can easily be separated. Neither substance has changed. But when iron and sulfur are heated together, a chemical change takes place. A new substance is formed. This substance is iron sulfide. It is brown-black in color. And it is not attracted to a magnet.

sulfur

iron sulfide

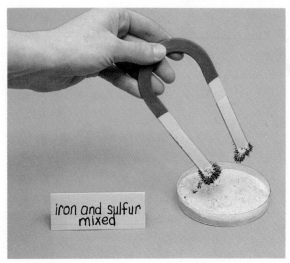

iron and sulfur mixed

Some chemical changes take place slowly. The rust on the body of this car formed from a slow chemical change. Oxygen from the air joined with iron and moisture to form the compound iron oxide. Iron oxide is commonly called rust. How does paint help stop rust from forming?

Rusting—a slow chemical change

Other chemical changes take place more quickly. When vinegar is poured on baking soda, a rapid chemical change takes place. There are new substances formed. One new substance is carbon dioxide gas.

A rapid chemical change

Ideas to Remember

▶ A physical property is one that can be used to identify matter. Color, odor, shape, hardness, and density are physical properties.

▶ A physical change is a change in the size, shape, or state of matter.

▶ The three states of matter—solid, liquid, and gas—differ in how particles move, in how far apart particles are, and in the strength of attraction between particles.

▶ Melting point and boiling point are physical properties.

▶ A mixture is a material formed by the physical combining of two or more different materials.

▶ A solution is a mixture that forms when one substance dissolves in another. A suspension is a mixture in which particles of a substance do not dissolve in another substance.

▶ A chemical change is a change in matter in which one or more different kinds of matter form.

Reviewing the Chapter

SCIENCE WORDS

A. Copy the sentences below. Use science terms from the chapter to complete the sentences.

1. The temperature at which a solid changes to a liquid is the _____.
2. The same kind of matter is present both before and after a/an _____ in matter.
3. Density is a/an _____ that can be used to identify matter.
4. A substance changes from a liquid to a gas when that substance reaches its _____.
5. When iron and sulfur are mixed together and then heated, a new substance is formed. A/An _____ has taken place.

B. Write the letter of the term that best matches the definition. Not all the terms will be used.

1. Mixture in which particles of a substance do not dissolve in another substance
2. Substance in a solution that dissolves
3. Mixture that forms when one substance dissolves in another
4. Substance in a solution that does the dissolving
5. Material formed by the physical combining of two or more different materials

   a. solute
   b. particle
   c. mixture
   d. solution
   e. liquid
   f. suspension
   g. solvent

UNDERSTANDING IDEAS

A. Identify each of the following as matter that is solid, liquid, or gas.

1. It is the state of matter in which particles move and slide over and around one another. Matter in this state has no definite shape, but it does have a definite volume.
2. It is the state of matter in which particles move freely and are spread far apart. Matter in this state has no definite shape or volume.
3. It is the state of matter in which particles move rapidly back and forth in a very small space. Matter in this state has a definite shape and a definite volume.

B. Write whether each drawing shows a physical change or a chemical change.

1

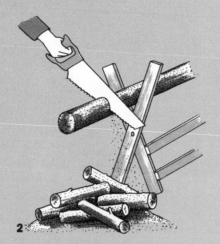

2

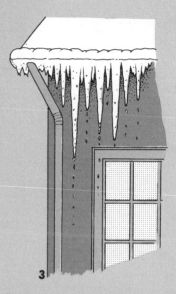

3

USING IDEAS

Gallium is a silver-white metal that can be liquid or solid. It is a solid at room temperature, or about 21° C. But gallium becomes a liquid when it is held in the hand. Body temperature is 37° C. What do these facts tell you about the melting point of gallium?

THINKING LIKE A SCIENTIST

Answer the following questions. You may be able to answer some of the questions just by thinking about them. To answer other questions you may have to do some research.

1. Why do helium balloons float?
2. Air contains the gases oxygen, nitrogen, argon, and carbon dioxide. Scientists describe air as being a mixture. What does this tell you about the gases in air?
3. Why, do you think, is it so difficult to mix oil and water? What kinds of liquids mix together easily?

4. How are liquids like honey, tree sap, tar, and glue different from liquids like water, milk, and orange juice? Explain the difference in terms of the movement of particles.
5. What physical and chemical changes in matter can be caused by water?

Chapter 7

Understanding Electricity

You live in a world that depends on electricity. Look around. You may have many things in your home that run on electricity. A television, a stereo, and a radio use electricity. The lights in your home, the clock on the wall, and the toaster in the kitchen all need electricity. You may have toys and games that run on electricty. Your home may be heated by electricity. Your food may be cooked in an electric oven.

The boy in the picture is looking at the many electrical devices on display. Can you imagine your life without electricity?

In this chapter you will learn what electricity is. You will learn how it is produced, used, and measured. You will also learn about some of the dangers of electricity and how it can be used safely.

Electricity

What is electricity?

You depend a great deal on electricity. But what *is* electricity? You cannot see it. You can only see what it does. For a long time scientists have been interested in what electricity is and what it does.

What is known about electricity? Scientists know that everything is either matter or energy. Matter has mass and takes up space. Since electricity does not have mass or take up space, it must be energy.

Train running on electricity

You know that electricity can do work. What kind of work is being done in the picture?

To understand electrical energy, you must understand matter. Remember that all matter is made of atoms. Knowing the structure of the atom will help solve the mystery of electricity.

You have learned that the atom has a central part called a nucleus. There are particles in the nucleus. Some of these particles have a positive charge. They are called protons. Moving around the nucleus are other particles, called electrons. The electrons in an atom have a negative charge. If the number of protons and the number of electrons in an atom are the same, their charges balance one another. When this happens, the atom has no charge. An atom with no charge is neutral (nü′trəl). Under normal conditions the atoms in most matter are neutral. As the drawing shows, the number of electrons and protons is balanced.

NEUTRAL ATOM

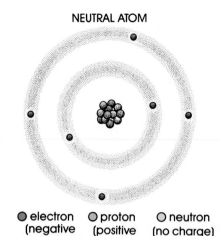

● electron (negative charge) ● proton (positive charge) ○ neutron (no charge)

Look at the drawing of the children playing tug-of-war. You can see that the teams are not balanced. One team has six children and the other has four. To balance the teams, some children will have to move. They can move in only one direction. Some children will have to move from the side with the larger number to the side with the smaller number. How many children will have to move to balance the teams?

In some ways electricity is like this game of tug-of-war. Suppose the number of protons and the number of electrons in an atom are not the same. This happens when an atom gains or loses electrons. If an atom has more electrons than protons, the atom has a negative charge. An atom with more protons than electrons has a positive charge.

Look at the drawings of the atoms. As you can see, atoms can gain or lose electrons. Atom **A** is losing an electron. Atom **B** is gaining an electron. This movement of electrons produces electricity. Which atom has a positive charge? Which atom has a negative charge?

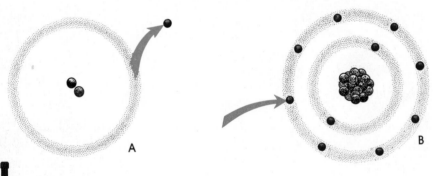

- ● electron
- ● proton
- ● neutron

A

B

Finding Out

Does clear tape have an electric charge?

Objects that have like electric charges, repel, or push away from, one another. Objects that have opposite electric charges attract one another. Remove two strips of tape, each about 8 cm long, from a roll of clear tape. Touch only one end of each strip. Slowly move the sticky sides toward each other. What happens? Now slowly move the two smooth sides toward each other. Watch what happens. Do the pieces of tape have an electric charge? How can you tell?

Kinds of Electricity

What are two kinds of electricity?

It was a cold, dry day. This boy walked across a carpet, touched a doorknob, and felt a shock. What happened? As he walked, his shoes rubbed electrons off the carpet. When two objects are rubbed together, electrons move from one object to the other. The electrons collected on his body and stayed there. The extra electrons gave his body a negative charge. Such a buildup of electrons on an object is called **static electricity.**

collection of electrons

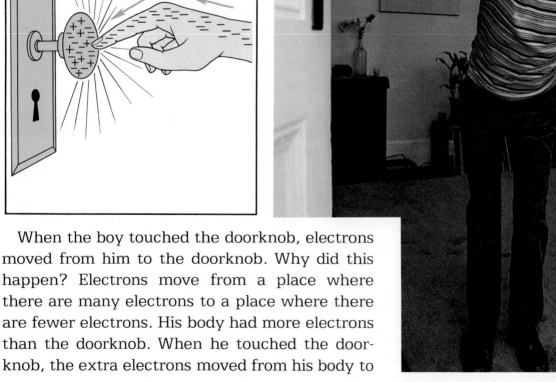

When the boy touched the doorknob, electrons moved from him to the doorknob. Why did this happen? Electrons move from a place where there are many electrons to a place where there are fewer electrons. His body had more electrons than the doorknob. When he touched the doorknob, the extra electrons moved from his body to

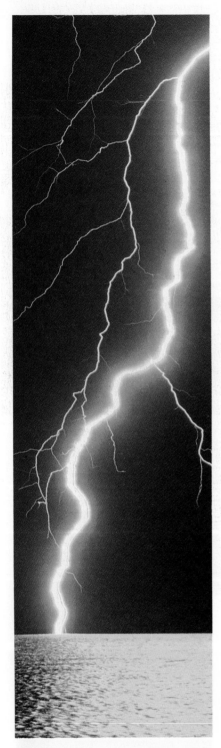

Electric discharge

the doorknob. This movement of the extra electrons is called an **electric discharge** (dis'chärj). After the electric discharge, the boy became neutral again.

Lightning is another example of a discharge of static electricity. Lightning is often caused by a buildup of electrons on a cloud. In the drawing below, the cloud has more electrons than the ground. When the difference between the charge on the cloud and the charge on the ground is great enough, an electric discharge occurs. You see this discharge as lightning.

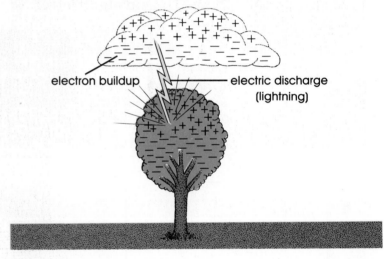

electron buildup — electric discharge (lightning)

Electrons move when they jump from a finger to a doorknob. They also move when lightning strikes the earth. In both cases the buildup of electrons is static electricity. But when the electrons move, there is current electricity. **Current electricity** is the movement of electrons from one place to another.

When an electric shock occurs or lightning strikes, electrons move through air. But electrons

Electricity powers computers of all kinds. Computers are helping athletes to train. In labs, athletes are wired with sensors. Then they are filmed as they work out. Their movements show up on computer screens. The athletes can spot what they are doing wrong and correct problems.

Runners are getting help from computer shoes. First the runner counts his or her various running strides. Then he or she enters these numbers into the computer. The runner wears the computer shoe during the run. After the run is finished, the runner connects the shoe to the computer. The computer tells the runner the length of the run, how long it took, and how many calories were used. The computer also keeps records in table and graph forms. How do you think this information helps the runner?

also move through other forms of matter, such as metal. Matter through which electrons move easily is called a **conductor** (kən duk'tər). Most metals are good conductors. Some metals are better conductors than others. Gold, silver, and copper are all good conductors. Copper is low priced and easy to obtain. So it is often used as a conductor.

Not all kinds of matter are good conductors. Electrons do not move easily through wood, rubber, and glass. Matter that is not a good conductor is called an **insulator** (in'sə lā tər). Rubber is used as an insulator around copper wire. The rubber helps to keep electrons from moving out of the wire and to prevent electric shock.

Activity

Which materials are conductors of electricity?

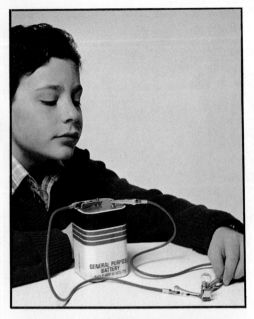

Materials 6-volt battery / light bulb and socket / 3 test leads / copper penny / cardboard strip / toothpick / aluminum foil / paper clip / rubber band

Procedure

A. You are going to test different materials to see if they are conductors or insulators. If the bulb in your setup lights when a material is tested, the material is a good conductor. If the bulb does not light, the material is a good insulator.

B. Connect the battery, test leads, and light bulb, as shown in the first picture.

C. Remove one of the test leads from the bulb. Clip it to a copper penny. Use another test lead to connect the penny to the bulb, as shown in the second picture.
  1. What happens to the bulb?
  2. Is the penny a conductor or an insulator?

D. Repeat step **C** for each of the other materials. Make a chart for your results like the one below.

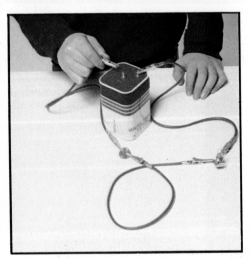

Results

Material tested	Conductor	Insulator
copper penny		
toothpick		
cardboard strip		
aluminum foil		
paper clip		
rubber band		

Conclusion

1. Which materials are conductors of electricity? How do you know?
2. Which materials are insulators? How do you know?
3. How are all of the conductors alike?

Electric Circuits

What are two kinds of electric circuits?

As you know, current electricity is the movement of electrons along a conductor. The path on which the electrons move is called a **circuit** (ser'kit). You can see a circuit in the drawing at the right. Trace the path of electrons in this circuit. Begin at the dry cell that produces energy that moves the electrons. From the dry cell the electrons move along the conductor, or wires, to the bulb. The bulb lights. Then the electrons follow the path back to the dry cell.

Note that the dry cell, wires, and bulb are connected in a complete, unbroken path. An electric circuit must be complete for electrons to move through it. A circuit that is complete is called a closed circuit.

If the circuit is broken, electrons will not move. There will be no current electricity. A circuit that is broken, or incomplete, is called an open circuit. A switch can be used to open or close a circuit. If the switch is open, electrons stop moving and the circuit is broken. What happens when the switch is closed?

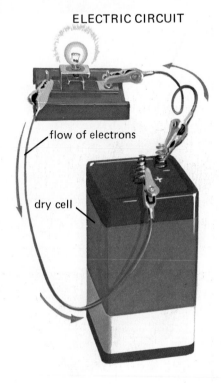

ELECTRIC CIRCUIT

flow of electrons

dry cell

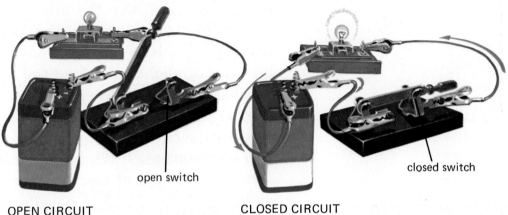

open switch

OPEN CIRCUIT

closed switch

CLOSED CIRCUIT

163

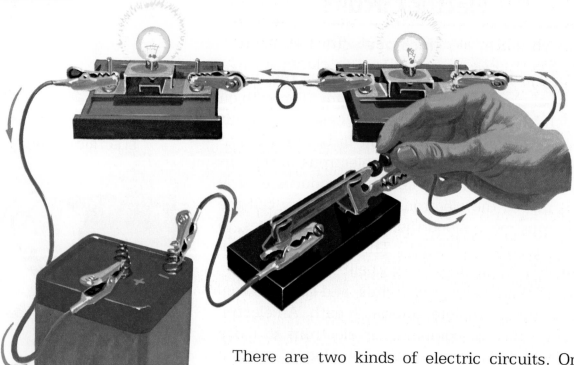

There are two kinds of electric circuits. One kind is a series (sir'ēz) circuit. A **series circuit** is one in which the electrons can follow only one path. An open switch or a broken wire stops the movement of electrons in a series circuit.

The drawing shows a simple series circuit. Is this a complete circuit? How can you tell? Trace the path of electrons in this series circuit. Start with the dry cell. Use the arrows to follow the path of electrons through the wires and the switch. From the switch, electrons move through wires to each light bulb. Find the path the electrons follow back to the dry cell.

If one of the bulbs in a series circuit burns out, it breaks the circuit. If this happened, would the other bulb still light?   Why or why not?

The second kind of electric circuit is called a parallel (par'ə lel) circuit. A **parallel circuit** is one in which electrons can follow more than one path. Look at the drawing of this circuit. Trace the paths on which electrons move. Start at the dry cell. Electrons move through the closed switch and over wires. But notice that there are two different paths that electrons can follow to the bulbs. Some electrons follow a path to the green bulb. Other electrons follow a path to the red bulb. Eventually all electrons return to the dry cell.

Most circuits used in homes are parallel circuits. If you turn off one light in your home, the others stay on. The parallel circuit provides another path for the electrons to follow. It is like taking a detour on a road. Traffic still flows from one point to another, but sometimes it may go along a different route. What would happen if the lights in your home were wired in series circuits instead of parallel circuits?

PARALLEL CIRCUIT

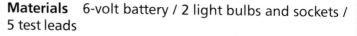
Are bulbs brighter in a series circuit or a parallel circuit?

Materials 6-volt battery / 2 light bulbs and sockets / 5 test leads

Procedure

A. Connect two test leads to the terminals of a battery. Connect the opposite ends of the leads to each side of a small light bulb. The first picture shows this circuit.

   1. Do you have a complete circuit?
   2. What kind of circuit is this?
   3. Observe the brightness of the bulb. Is it bright or dim?
   4. Predict what would happen if you added one more bulb to the circuit.

B. Add one more bulb to the circuit. Use another test lead to connect two bulbs in series, as shown in the second picture.

   5. Are the two bulbs each as bright as the one bulb was? Was your prediction correct?

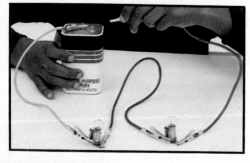

C. Now connect the two bulbs, test leads, and battery to form a parallel circuit. The third picture shows this circuit.

   6. Are the two bulbs brighter or dimmer than the two bulbs were in step **B**?
   7. Are the two bulbs as bright as the one bulb was in step **A**?

Conclusion

1. Which circuit had the brightest bulbs?
2. Explain in your own words the difference between a series circuit and a parallel circuit.

Using science ideas

1. Draw a series circuit that has 5 bulbs. What would happen if one bulb burned out?
2. Draw a parallel circuit that has 5 bulbs. What would happen if one bulb burned out?

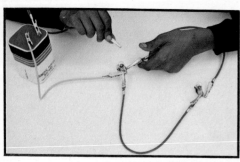
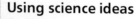

Producing Electricity

How can a magnet be used to produce electricity?

Have you ever used a magnet to pick up pins or paper clips? Did you know that a magnet can also be used to produce electricity? This property of magnets was known in 1831. A scientist named Michael Faraday found that a magnet can be used to produce electricity.

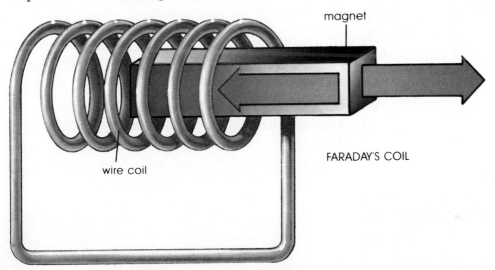

magnet

wire coil

FARADAY'S COIL

The drawing shows, in a simple way, what Faraday did. He moved a strong magnet back and forth through a coil of wire. Electrons moved along the wire! How did this happen? Electrons were not moving along the wire before the magnet was passed through the coil.

You may know that a magnet has lines of force around it. These lines of force cause some metal objects to move toward the magnet. They can also make electrons move inside a wire. Moving electrons produce an electric current.

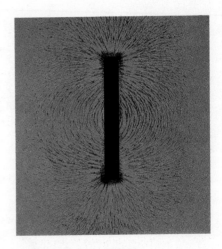

Magnetic lines of force

Faraday's discovery was used to make a machine that is still in use today. This machine is a **generator** (jen'ə rā tər). A generator changes energy of motion into electrical energy. When coils of wire cut through a strong magnetic field, electrons move through the wire. To keep the electrons moving, either the wire or the magnet must be kept moving.

To produce electricity, a generator needs energy from an outside source. Most of this energy comes from the burning of fuels, such as coal, oil, and gas. Another source of this energy is moving water.

The pictures show how a generator produces electrical energy through water power. Look at the pictures as you follow each step.

1. This power plant uses moving water to produce mechanical energy. The first picture shows a dam on a river. It also shows the water flowing out of the power plant.

1

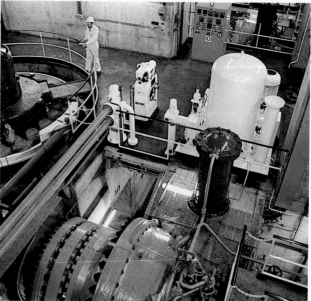

2

2. The moving water turns the blades of a **turbine** (ter'bin). A turbine is a device that is made of a wheel and blades. You can see a turbine in the second picture.

3. The turbine is attached to a generator. The generator, shown in the third picture, is a magnet inside a coil of wire. As the turbine moves, it turns the magnet. This produces an electric current inside the coil of wire.

4. The electric current produced by the generator is carried by wires to a power station, shown in the fourth picture. Eventually, the current is carried by wires to many locations.

Generators are not the only way to produce electricity. You may own flashlights or toys that need a supply of energy. They do not have generators. Instead they use a device commonly called a battery. A battery is two or more electric cells joined together. An **electric cell** is a device that changes chemical energy to electrical energy.

3

4

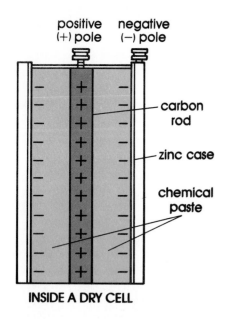

positive (+) pole   negative (−) pole

carbon rod

zinc case

chemical paste

INSIDE A DRY CELL

One type of electric cell is called a dry cell. A **dry cell** uses a chemical paste, carbon rod, and zinc case to produce a flow of electrons. Chemical reactions occur inside the dry cell. One reaction causes the walls of the zinc case to become negatively charged. Another reaction causes the carbon rod to become positively charged. The zinc case is called the negative pole. The carbon rod is called the positive pole. If the dry cell is connected to a circuit, electrons flow from the negative pole to the positive. This movement of electrons forms an electric current.

A true battery is made of two or more cells. Most car batteries are made of six cells. A car battery does not use a chemical paste to make electricity. Instead it uses acid and water, which react with metal plates. The chemical reaction of the metal and acid produces a flow of electrons. Such a battery is called a **wet cell battery.** The car battery, below, is a wet cell battery.

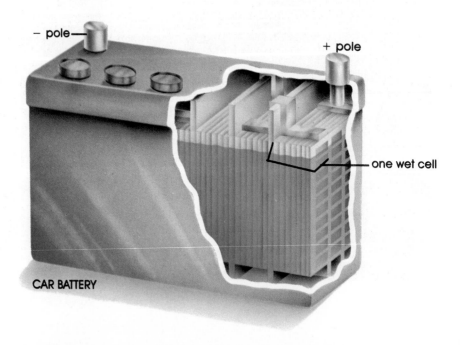

− pole

+ pole

one wet cell

CAR BATTERY

Using Electricity

How is electricity used?

Every day you use electricity in many ways. You may wake up to the sound of an electric alarm clock. You may eat breakfast cooked on an electric stove. You use electricity at home and in school. It is also used in stores and factories. Look at the drawing of the house. How many uses of electricity can you find?

To be useful, electricity must be changed to other kinds of energy. Think back to what you know about magnets. The electromagnet is a magnet that forms when a current passes through a wire coiled around a metal core. A giant electromagnet can be used to lift heavy metal objects in a scrapyard. This is an example of how electricity can be changed to another kind of energy.

Electrical energy can also be changed to mechanical (mə kan'ə kəl) energy. **Mechanical energy** is energy of moving machine parts. You can see this change in an electric motor. An **electric motor** is a machine that changes electrical energy to mechanical energy. When you plug a motor into a wall outlet, the electricity turns the motor. Mixers, fans, and power tools all have motors. Look again at the drawing of the house on page 171. Where are motors used?

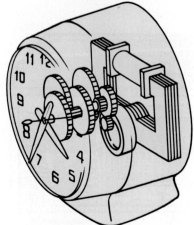

Motors in electric appliances

Electricity is also an important source of light and heat. For example, in a light bulb or a toaster, electricity is changed to light or heat energy.

Let's see how a light bulb produces light. The light bulb has a glass cover, a base, and a filament. The **filament** (fil'ə mənt) is a thin coil of wire. When a current moves through the filament it becomes hot. The hot filament glows and gives off light. The glass cover prevents air from reaching the filament. What would happen if air reached the glowing filament?

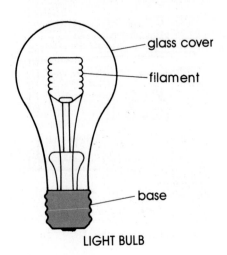

glass cover

filament

base

LIGHT BULB

Measuring Electricity

How is the flow of electricity measured?

Each day great amounts of electrical energy are used in homes, schools, and offices. How is electricity used in the picture of the office building? You use a certain amount of electricity when you watch television for an hour. You use a different amount when you read for 2 hours by the light of a lamp. Have you ever had someone tell you to turn off a light? Energy use costs money. Someone must pay for all the energy you use. But before you can pay for it, it has to be measured. The person in the picture is reading a meter that measures the amount of electricity used.

Reading an electric meter

Electricity is used to do work. The more work a device does, the more electricity it uses. Also, the faster a device works, the more electricity it uses. The amount of work that is done in a certain period of time is called **power.** Small amounts of electric power are measured in units called **watts** (wots). Large amounts of power are measured in kilowatts. A **kilowatt** (kil'ə wot) is 1,000 watts.

The World Trade Center, New York City

173

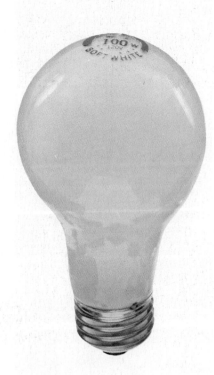

Most electric devices have the number of watts they use printed on them. One motor may have *50 watts* printed on it. Another motor may have *100 watts* printed on it. The 100-watt motor uses twice as much energy as the 50-watt motor in the same amount of time. Look at the light bulbs in the picture. How many watts does each bulb use? Which one uses the most power?

Electric companies measure how much electricity a customer uses in kilowatt-hours. A **kilowatt-hour** is equal to 1,000 watts of electricity used for 1 hour. A 100-watt motor can run for 10 hours before it uses a kilowatt-hour of electricity. How long can a 50-watt light bulb burn before it uses a kilowatt-hour of electricity?

Meters measure the amount of electricity used in a building. Do you know where the meter is at your house? The meter shows how many kilowatt-hours of electricity were used in your home. Each kilowatt-hour costs a certain amount of money. Look at the picture of an electric bill. How many kilowatt-hours of electricity were used during the month? How much did the electricity cost?

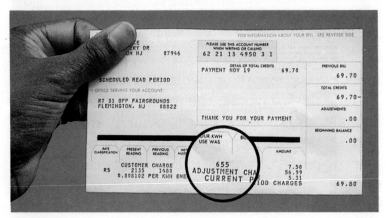

Electric bill

Using Electricity Safely

How can a building be made electrically safe?

Every building has safety devices to help keep electricity safe. **Fuses** (fyüz'ez) and **circuit breakers** protect buildings against fire. How do they do this? Each circuit is made to handle a certain amount of electric current. If too many appliances are plugged into a circuit, the wires may become too hot. When this happens, fuses and circuit breakers help to keep fires from starting.

Fuse box

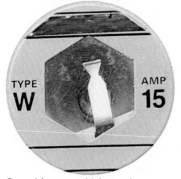 

Good fuse and blown fuse

These two safety devices are made to break the circuit if the wires become too hot. A metal strip inside a fuse melts and the fuse blows. This breaks the circuit. A special switch in a circuit breaker turns off to break the circuit.

Electricity should not be allowed to flow again until the cause of the problem is found. The number of appliances on the circuit should be checked. There may be too many. There may also be something wrong with one of the appliances.

When the circuit has been checked, the current can be turned on again. The blown fuse can be replaced with a new fuse. The switch on the circuit breaker can be turned on again.

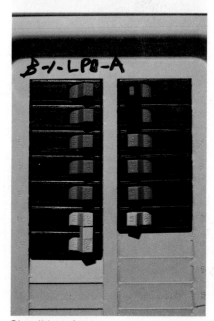

Circuit breakers

You too can help prevent electrical accidents. The following simple rules will help protect you from harm:

DON'T put anything except an electrical plug into an electrical outlet.

DON'T touch any electric appliance while you are wet.

DON'T use an electric appliance that has a frayed cord.

DON'T run an electrical cord under a carpet.

DON'T plug too many electric devices into one outlet.

DON'T touch a fallen power line.

DON'T fly a kite near power lines.

DON'T swim, play in an open field, or stand under a tree during a lightning storm.

Ideas to Remember

► There are two kinds of electricity—static electricity and current electricity.
► Static electricity is the buildup of electrons on an object.
► Current electricity is the movement of electrons from one place to another.
► A series circuit is one in which electrons can follow only one path.
► A parallel circuit is one in which electrons can follow more than one path.
► A generator is a machine that changes mechanical energy into electrical energy.
► An electric cell is a device that changes chemical energy to electrical energy.
► An electric motor is a machine that changes electrical energy to mechanical energy.
► The amount of electricity used is measured in kilowatt-hours.
► Fuses and circuit breakers are safety devices in electric circuits.

Reviewing the Chapter

SCIENCE WORDS

A. Identify each of the following.

1. It protects your home from fire. It is made of glass and metal. You can hold it in your hand. What is it?
2. It is coiled and it glows. Electric current passes through it. It is inside a glass case. What is it?
3. It contains a chemical paste. A carbon rod passes through the middle of it. Moving electrons produce electric current inside it. What is it?

B. Write the letter of the term that best matches the definition. Not all the terms will be used.

1. Unit for measuring small amounts of electric power
2. Circuit in which electrons can follow only one path
3. Matter through which electrons move easily
4. Device that changes chemical energy to electrical energy
5. Atom that has no charge
6. Path through which electrons move
7. Circuit in which electrons can follow more than one path
8. Machine that changes energy of motion into electrical energy

   a. circuit
   b. generator
   c. parallel circuit
   d. static electricity
   e. neutral
   f. watt
   g. current electricity
   h. series circuit
   i. electric cell
   j. conductor
   k. turbine
   l. insulator

UNDERSTANDING IDEAS

A. Look at the drawing of the house on page 171. List all the electrical appliances shown.

B. Explain how electrical energy is produced by a generator. Describe how you could make a model of a generator.

C. Name five safety rules that should be followed when using electricity. Explain the reason for each rule.

D. Describe a closed electric circuit. Explain how a series circuit differs from a parallel circuit.

E. Write the correct term for each number in the drawings.

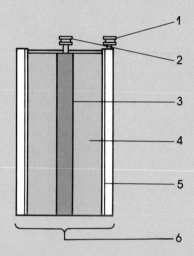

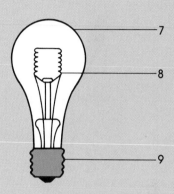

USING IDEAS

1. Do a survey of electrical safety in your home. Look for things that do not follow the safety rules found on page 176. Discuss with your family how the hazards can be corrected.

2. Look at the next electric bill you get at your home. How many kilowatt-hours did you use? How much do you have to pay for each kilowatt-hour?

THINKING LIKE A SCIENTIST

Answer the following questions. You may be able to answer some of the questions just by thinking about them. To answer other questions you may have to do some research.

1. Suppose you attend a magic show. The magician takes a page of a newspaper and waves a wand over it. Then he walks over to a clean blank wall, places the paper on the wall, and rubs the paper with a wool cloth. Presto! The paper stays on the wall! Explain this so-called magic act in scientific terms.

2. Why are extension cords for large appliances and outdoor tools much thicker than other extension cords?

3. Benjamin Franklin observed the effects of static electricity on objects. He proposed a theory that there must be an "electric fluid" in the objects. Was he right? Explain your answer.

4. Many people are trying to produce an electric car that will run as well as a gasoline-powered car. What problems do you think an electric car would have? What advantages would it have?

179

Chapter 8

Sources of Energy

Think about how you used energy today. You used energy to get dressed. This energy came from the food you ate. Perhaps you rode to school in a bus or a car. Where do buses and cars get energy to move?

The "solar power tower" in the picture is a modern device that uses the sun as a source of energy. The many mirrors focus sunlight onto the tower. The sunlight is used to produce electricity.

The sun is one source of energy that people use. The earth has other energy sources. Some of these sources are plentiful but hard to collect. Others are scarce. In this chapter you will learn about these energy sources and some of the problems involved in using them.

Energy from Fossil Fuels

What are three fossil fuels and their uses?

All machines need energy to do work. Some machines get their energy from muscle power. A bicycle is a machine that runs on muscle power. But most machines that are used today do not run on muscle power. They use another source of energy. This major energy source is fossil fuels. A **fossil fuel** is a fuel that forms from the remains of dead plants and animals. Coal, oil, and natural gas are fossil fuels.

Millions of years ago the earth was warm and wet. Much of the earth's surface was swampy. The drawing below shows what these swamps may have looked like. Many green plants grew and died in these swamps. Each plant had energy stored in it. Year after year, more plants died and piled up. The land sank beneath the weight of the

Swamp plants from which coal formed

plants. Seas began to form. Streams emptying into the seas carried sand and other material. The weight of all this matter pushed down hard on the dead plants. Over the years, heat and pressure caused the dead plants to change into coal.

In other places, the earth of the past was covered with shallow seas. Tiny living things in these seas died and fell to the bottom. After many years, they became covered with sand, mud, and other material. Heat and pressure changed the remains of these living things to oil and natural gas.

Coal, oil, and gas are taken from the earth. Coal and gas do not have to be changed for use as fuels. Oil that is taken from the earth is called **crude oil**. Before crude oil can be used, it must be changed. Crude oil is changed to useful products in a **refinery** (ri fī'nər ē). These products include fuels such as gasoline, diesel (dē'zəl) fuel, and home heating oil.

Oil well

gasoline

diesel fuel

home heating oil

Oil refinery

Fossil fuels have many uses. The most important use is as a source of energy. But before their energy can be used, fossil fuels must be burned. This process is called combustion (kəm bus′chən). In **combustion**, oxygen from the air combines with a fuel, producing heat and light.

Most of our electricity comes from the heat of burning fossil fuels. Look at the drawing. It shows coal being burned to heat water. When the water boils, it changes to steam. The steam is forced against a fan-shaped turbine. The force of the steam turns the blades of the turbine. The turbine is attached to a generator. The turbine turns the generator, which produces electricity. Power lines carry the electricity to other places.

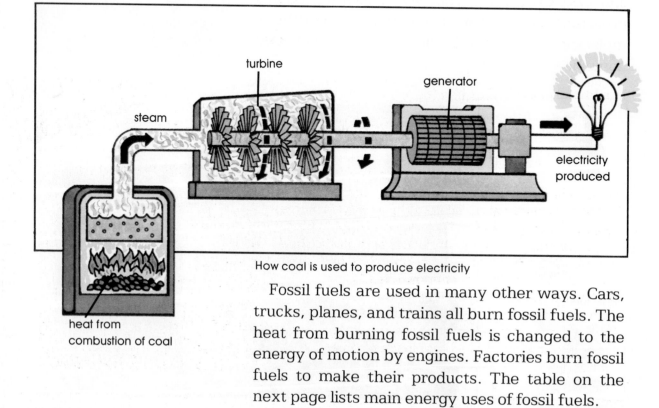

How coal is used to produce electricity

Fossil fuels are used in many other ways. Cars, trucks, planes, and trains all burn fossil fuels. The heat from burning fossil fuels is changed to the energy of motion by engines. Factories burn fossil fuels to make their products. The table on the next page lists main energy uses of fossil fuels.

ENERGY USES OF FOSSIL FUELS	
Fossil fuel	**Main energy uses**
Coal	Electricity production Manufacturing, such as making steel Home heating
Crude oil	Gasoline for automobiles Diesel fuel for cars, trucks, and trains Jet fuel Kerosene for home heating Oil for home heating
Natural gas	Home heating Cooking Bottled gas for campers and outdoor grills

Supplies of fossil fuels are limited. Once they are used, they are gone forever. They cannot be replaced. The world will someday run out of this major energy source. So people must make wise use of fossil fuels.

Finding Out

What are some materials used to conserve energy?

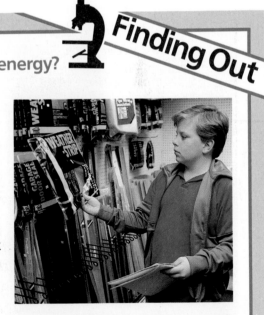

With permission from your parents or other adults, visit a hardware or building supply store. Look for a display of materials used to save energy in homes. Such materials might include caulking material, weatherstripping, foam insulation, and plastic sheets to put on windows. You might also find plastic "bubbles" for basement window wells.

Find as many materials as you can. Describe them carefully. Record the prices of the materials. Think about how each material can save energy. Which ones might you be able to use in your home?

Energy from Atoms

How is energy obtained from an atom?

The second major source of energy being used in the world is nuclear (nü′klē ər) energy. What is nuclear energy? You have learned that the atom is a small particle from which all matter is made. You have also learned that there is a nucleus in the center of every atom. The energy stored in the nucleus of an atom is called **nuclear energy**. This energy has to be released before it can be used.

There are two ways to release the energy that is stored in an atom. The most common process used is called fission (fish′ən). In **nuclear fission** the nucleus of an atom is split, releasing energy. The atom that is most often used in fission is the uranium (yủ rā′nē əm) atom.

Nuclear power plant

The other process used to release the energy that is stored in the atom is called fusion (fyü′zhən). Fusion is the opposite of fission. In **nuclear fusion** the nuclei (nü′klē ī) of atoms are combined, releasing energy. (The word *nuclei* means "more than one nucleus.") In both fission and fusion large amounts of energy are released.

The most important use of nuclear energy today is to produce electricity. Fission is the process used to produce energy for electricity. Fission takes place in a special structure called a **nuclear reactor**. The large amounts of heat energy that result from fission are controlled in the reactor. In nuclear power plants the heat from fission is used to change water to steam. Look at the drawing below. Just as in coal-burning power plants, the steam is used to turn a turbine. The turbine is attached to a generator that produces electricity.

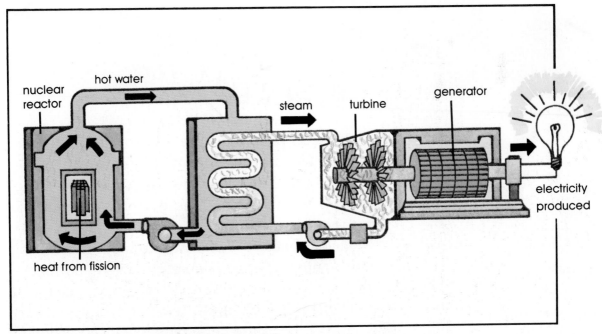

How nuclear energy is used to produce electricity

Fusion is not used today to produce useful energy. This is because scientists have not yet learned to control the great amount of energy released from fusion. Scientists are using the nuclear test reactor shown to help them learn to control fusion.

Nuclear test reactor

Although people cannot control fusion at present, almost all the energy on the earth comes from fusion. This is because the sun is the source of most of the earth's energy. And the sun produces energy from fusion.

Nuclear energy is one way to meet the world's energy needs. Some people think its benefits outweigh its problems. People who favor using nuclear energy say it helps save fossil fuels. It takes much less uranium than coal or oil to produce a

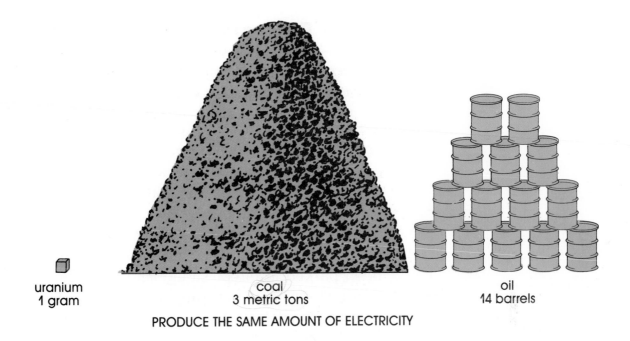

uranium	coal	oil
1 gram	3 metric tons	14 barrels

PRODUCE THE SAME AMOUNT OF ELECTRICITY

certain amount of electricity. In fact, just 1 gram of uranium produces as much energy as 3 metric tons of coal or 14 barrels of oil.

Supporters of nuclear energy also say that it is clean energy. It does not release harmful smoke into the air, as happens when coal is burned. Why do nuclear power plants not give off smoke?

But other people point to the problems in using nuclear energy. The fuel used inside these power plants gives off radiation (rā dē ā′shən). Radiation is the release of energy and particles from atoms. It can harm living things. Some people fear that radiation inside power plants might leak to the outside.

Another problem is where to put the wastes from nuclear reactors. Some of these wastes give off harmful radiation for hundreds of years. So storing them until they are safe is important. Scientists are looking for ways to do this.

Energy from the Sun

How is solar energy used, and what are some problems with its use?

The sun is the source of most of the earth's energy. Energy from the sun is called **solar** (sō'lər) **energy.** People use solar energy to produce heat. Some office buildings and homes are heated with solar energy.

One way to use solar energy is to "trap" it. Have you ever gotten into a closed car that had been parked in direct sunlight? If so, you know that a lot of heat was trapped in the car. The air in the car may have been much warmer than the air outside.

How does the air in the car become warmed? Solar energy passes through the glass windows. When it strikes the material inside the car, the solar energy changes to heat. This warms the air inside the car. Because the car is sealed, very little heat escapes to the outside. So the air in the car becomes warmer and warmer. This buildup of heat is called the **greenhouse effect**.

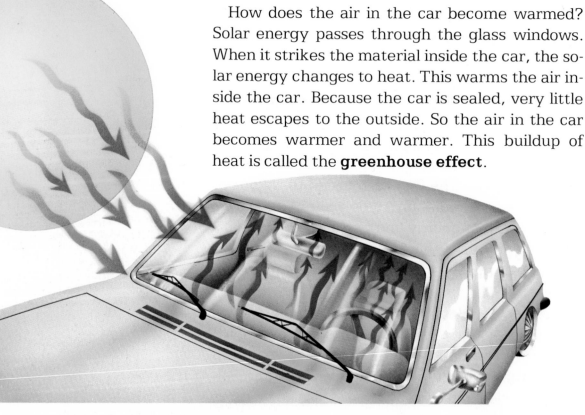

Look at the picture of the greenhouse. Why are the walls and roof made of glass? The greenhouse effect is used to heat some houses and other buildings. This kind of heating is called passive solar heating.

Another kind of heating system uses large solar collectors. A **solar collector** is a device that collects sunlight and changes it to another form of energy. You can see solar collectors on the apartment building in the picture at the right.

Inside the solar collectors are rows of black tubes carrying water or air. Sunlight strikes the tubes and heats the water or air inside them. The tubes carry the heated water or air to pipes that run throughout the building. The heated water or air is pumped through the pipes. If the heat is not needed, the heated material goes to a storage tank. On a cloudy day or at night, the stored heat can be used. This kind of system, with pumps or other moving parts, is called active solar heating.

Solar collectors on roof

191

In addition to producing heat, solar energy can also be used to produce electricity. This can be done in two ways. One way is an indirect method. Solar energy is first used to produce heat. The heat changes liquid water to steam. The steam turns a turbine that is attached to a generator.

The type of solar collector shown below uses an indirect method to produce electricity. It has mirrors that gather sunlight. Another picture of this type of collector is on pages 180–181 of this

Solar collector that uses mirrors

chapter. The sunlight is reflected onto a small area on the tower. Inside the tower is a boiler that holds water. How can solar collectors such as this be used to produce electricity?

Another way to use solar energy to produce electricity is a direct method. A device called a **solar cell** changes solar energy into electrical energy. Solar cells are an energy source for many spacecraft and some buildings. There are solar cells covering the four arms of this spacecraft. Why would solar cells be useful in spacecraft?

Solar cells on *Viking* spacecraft

Solar energy seems to be a perfect energy source. It is clean, plentiful, and free! But there are problems in using solar energy. One problem is that not all places receive enough sunlight to make solar energy useful. Also solar energy is not constant. If there are several cloudy days in a row, the stored heat or electrical energy may be used up.

Science & Technology

▲ Solar power is running everything from watches to spacecraft. On this satellite, solar cells collect light from the sun. The cells change the light energy into electricity. The electricity is changed into microwaves that are sent to the earth. On the earth the microwaves are changed back into electricity that is used by the electric companies.

◀ An airplane called the *Solar Challenger* uses 16,128 solar cells for power. The solar cells power two small motors that turn the plane's propeller. On July 5, 1981, the *Solar Challenger* flew from France to England, more than 267 km. The plane reached an air speed of over 75 km/h. The only fuel it used was energy from the sun!

◀ You may have seen solar cells on small radios, watches, and calculators. Solar cells are also used in places that are hard to reach with electric lines. For example, some buoys at sea use solar cells. In mountain jungles of New Guinea, solar cells power the phone system. What other uses for solar cells can you name?

Does the north or south side of a building receive more solar energy?

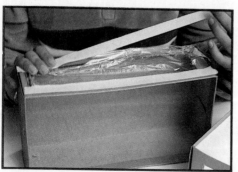

Materials 2 cardboard shoe boxes with lids / scissors / clear plastic wrap / transparent tape / 2 thermometers / compass

Procedure

A. Use scissors to cut out a rectangular hole in one side of each of two shoe boxes. Cover the hole in each box with a piece of clear plastic wrap. Use transparent tape to attach the plastic wrap.

B. Place a thermometer inside each box and put the lids on. Then make a chart like the one shown.

C. Take the boxes outdoors on a sunny day. They represent buildings that receive solar energy. Use a compass to find north and south. Place one box so that its "window" faces south. Place the other box so that its "window" faces north.

D. Open the boxes and check the temperature in each box. Record these numbers as the starting temperatures in your chart. Now close the boxes.
1. Predict how the temperatures in the two boxes will change during the next 40 minutes.

E. Every 10 minutes, for the next 40 minutes, record in your chart the temperature inside each box.

Results

1. In which box was the final temperature greater?
2. Make a graph showing how the temperature in each box changed.

Conclusion

1. What was the difference between the starting and final temperatures in each box?
2. Which lets in more solar energy, a north-facing window or a south-facing window?
3. In which direction should the windows face in a house that uses passive solar energy? Why?

Time	Temperature	
	North	South
0 min		
10 min		
20 min		
30 min		
40 min		

Energy from Water

What are two ways that moving water is used for energy?

Moving water is an important source of energy used to produce electricity. In a **hydroelectric** (hī drō i lek'trik) **power plant,** moving water turns turbines attached to generators that produce electricity. Hydroelectric power plants, such as the one shown below and the one on pages 168–169, are built as part of dams on rivers. Falling water flows through pipes inside the dam. The water flows over turbine blades at the bottom of the dam. The moving blades turn generators.

Hydroelectric power plant

The number of places where hydroelectric power plants can be built are limited. Also when dams are built on rivers, large land areas may be flooded. This can destroy places where many plants and animals live.

There is another way of using the energy of flowing water. Have you ever spent a day at an ocean beach? If so, you have probably seen that

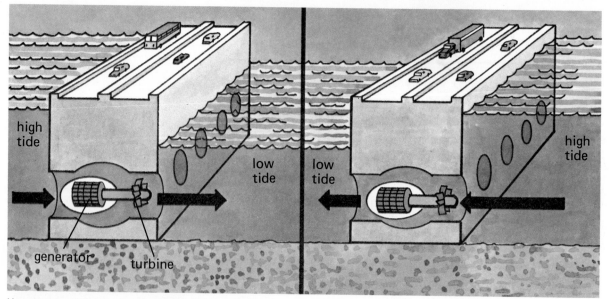

tide

low
tide

low
tide

high
tide

generator   turbine

How tidal energy is used to produce electricity

Tidal power plant

the water level along the shore rises and falls. In most areas the water level rises and falls twice a day. These daily movements of the water level along the shore are called **tides.**

Tidal (tī′dəl) energy is another energy source. **Tidal energy** is the energy of rising and falling tides. It can be used to produce electricity. To see how this is done, look at the drawing. A dam is built across a narrow opening to the ocean. During high and low tides, water moves in and out of the openings in the dam. As it moves through the openings, the water flows over turbine blades inside the dam. The turbines turn generators.

Very few tidal power plants are in use today. The picture shows one that was built on a river in France. Tidal energy will probably never be a major energy source. For tidal energy to be used, there must be a large difference in the height of the water between low and high tides. But there are only a few places in the world where tides are high and low enough to produce much energy.

196

Energy from Heat in the Earth

How is geothermal energy used?

You have learned that almost all energy on the earth comes from solar energy. But there is also an energy source that is deep inside the earth. This kind of energy is called **geothermal** (jē ə-thėr'məl) **energy.** It is energy from natural heat trapped beneath the earth's surface. This heat melts rock inside the earth. Melted rock inside the earth is called **magma** (mag'mə). In some places the magma comes close to the earth's surface. The magma collects in areas beneath the surface called hot spots. These **hot spots** are areas of geothermal energy.

How can geothermal energy be used to produce electricity? When water in the ground comes in contact with hot spots, the water turns to steam. By drilling wells into the earth in hot spots, this

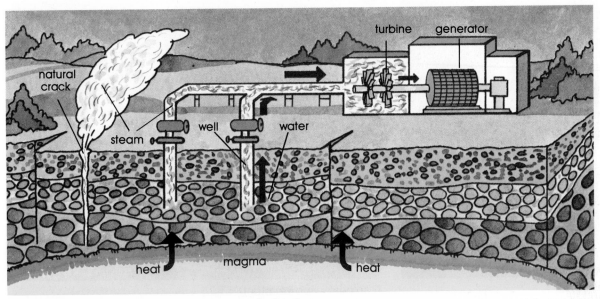

How geothermal energy is used to produce electricity

steam can be released. The released steam can be used to turn turbines that run generators.

In some places steam and hot water come to the surface without drilling. There are deep cracks in rock inside the earth through which the steam and hot water can move. When they reach the surface, the steam and hot water may gush out of the ground. This is called a geyser (gī′zər). You can see one geyser, Old Faithful, in the picture on the left.

The geothermal power plant in the picture is the largest in the world. This plant, called The Geysers, is located in California. It supplies enough electricity to run a large city. There are plans to expand The Geysers.

There are problems with geothermal energy. Many areas of geothermal energy are far from any large towns or cities. Electricity produced in these places would have to be carried great distances. This can be very costly.

A geyser

Geothermal power plant

Energy from the Wind

How is energy from the wind used?

The wind has been used as a source of energy for more than a thousand years. Wind energy is the energy of moving air. Long ago people used windmills to grind wheat into flour. Today windmills are being used to make electricity.

Old windmill used for grinding wheat

Modern windmills look different from the windmills of long ago. However, they work in much the same way. The wind turns blades at the top of the windmill. The blades are connected to a generator that produces electricity. This device is often called a wind turbine.

The high cost of other sources of energy has made windmills popular in some places. But there are problems with wind energy. One problem is that there are not many places where the wind blows strong and steady. Another problem is the high cost of building and fixing windmills. So energy from the wind is not likely to do much to help the world's future energy needs.

Modern wind turbine

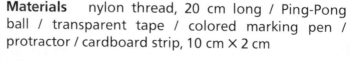
Can the wind make electricity where you live?

Materials   nylon thread, 20 cm long / Ping-Pong ball / transparent tape / colored marking pen / protractor / cardboard strip, 10 cm × 2 cm

Procedure

A. Tape one end of a piece of nylon thread to a Ping-Pong ball. Use a marking pen to color the thread so that it will be easier to see. Tape the free end of the thread to the center of a protractor, as shown. Then tape a cardboard strip to one end of the protractor. This will serve as a handle. You have now made a device to measure wind speed.

B. Take your device outdoors. Hold the protractor so that the flat edge is level with the ground, as in the bottom picture. When the wind blows the ball, the thread will line up with marks on the protractor. Record the number of the highest mark that the thread reaches. Use the table below to find out what this number equals in wind speed.

   1. What is the wind speed?

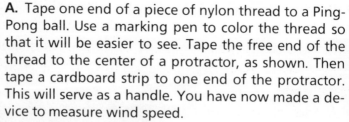

Number of mark	90	85	80	75	70	65	60	55	50	45	40	35	30	25	20
Wind speed (km/h)	0	9	13	16	19	21	24	26	29	31	34	37	41	46	52

C. Take wind speed readings several times a day for 4 to 5 days. Record your findings.

   2. What is the highest speed you recorded?

D. For a wind turbine to produce electricity, wind speed must be 13 km/h or over.

   3. What was the average speed of the wind that you measured?

Conclusion

1. Can the wind make electricity where you live?
2. How would the steadiness of wind speed affect the ability of a wind turbine to produce electricity?

Energy from Living Things

How is energy from living things used?

You have learned that millions of years must pass before the remains of living things become fossil fuels. Today scientists are looking for ways to produce energy directly from plant and animal matter. Plant and animal matter is called **biomass** (bī′ō mas). Biomass can be used to produce energy. The process of changing biomass into usable energy is called **bioconversion** (bī ō kən-vėr′zhən).

A campfire is an example of bioconversion. Wood is the biomass that is changed to produce energy. In recent years many people in the United States have bought wood-burning stoves. They use them to heat their homes. People save money by using wood as a fuel, since oil and natural gas are so costly. What could happen if a great many people use wood-burning stoves?

Wood-burning stove used to heat home

Bioconversion power plant

There is biomass in the trash that people throw away. In the United States, the average person produces more than 1 kg of trash each day. Much of it can be burned to make heat. This heat can be used to change water to steam. The steam can run generators. Bioconversion of trash helps in two ways. It produces useful energy from low-cost fuel. And it gets rid of unwanted materials. The picture on the left shows trash that will be burned to produce electricity.

Trash containing dead plant and animal matter can be used to make energy in yet another way. By using tiny living things called bacteria (bak-tir'ē ə), trash can be changed to fuel. The bacteria use the biomass in trash as a source of food. In the process, they produce a fuel called methane (meth'ān) gas. Methane gas can be burned for heat energy.

There is another way plants can be used for energy. The girl in the picture is filling the car's

Gasohol—a gasoline-and-alcohol mixture

tank with a gasoline-and-alcohol mixture. Alcohol is added to gasoline to help stretch the supply of this fuel. The alcohol comes from a process in which corn and yeast (yēst) are mixed. Yeasts are tiny nongreen plants. They use sugar as food. As the yeasts use the sugar that is stored in corn, they produce alcohol. You can see that there are many ways in which living things and the remains of living things help supply energy.

Ideas to Remember

► A fossil fuel is a fuel that forms from the remains of dead plants and animals.
► Fission and fusion are processes used to release the nuclear energy of atoms.
► Solar energy can be used to heat buildings and produce electricity.
► Moving water can be used to produce electrical energy in hydroelectric and tidal power plants.
► Geothermal energy is energy heat trapped beneath the earth's surface.
► Modern windmills use the energy of the wind to produce electricity.
► Plant and animal matter can be changed into useful forms of energy through bioconversion.

Reviewing the Chapter

SCIENCE WORDS

A. Use all the terms below to complete the sentences.

nuclear fusion   fossil fuel   refinery   nuclear reactor
crude oil   nuclear energy   combustion   nuclear fission

Oil is one kind of __1__. Oil that is taken from the earth is called __2__. It is changed to useful products in a/an __3__. During __4__, oxygen from the air combines with a fuel, producing heat and light.

The energy stored in the nucleus of an atom is called __5__. Scientists are trying to learn to control the energy released when the nuclei of atoms are combined in the process of __6__. The nucleus of an atom is split in the process of __7__. The splitting of atoms takes place in a structure called a/an __8__.

B. Write the letter of the term that best matches the definition. Not all the terms will be used.

1. Device that collects sunlight and changes it to another form of energy
2. Melted rock inside the earth
3. Plant and animal matter
4. Areas of geothermal energy
5. Device that changes solar energy to electricity
6. Daily movements of the water level along the shore
7. Energy from the sun

    a. biomass
    b. hot spots
    c. solar energy
    d. tides
    e. wind turbine
    f. solar collector
    g. hydroelectric power plant
    h. magma
    i. solar cell

UNDERSTANDING IDEAS

A. Write the term that best matches each picture on the top of page 205.

tidal energy   bioconversion
greenhouse effect   energy from a fossil fuel
geothermal energy   hydroelectric power

B. Describe three ways to use energy from the sun.

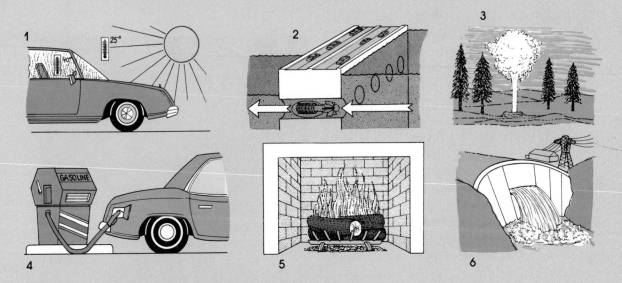

C. List one problem in using each energy source shown above.

USING IDEAS

Suppose you had to design a house for you and your family to live in. Which energy source or sources would you use to provide heat and electricity? Tell where you would have the house built. Explain how its location relates to the energy source or sources you choose. Also list the benefits and problems for each energy source.

THINKING LIKE A SCIENTIST

Answer the following questions. You may be able to answer some of the questions just by thinking about them. To answer other questions you may have to do some research.

1. Why did Americans 200 years ago use much less fossil fuel than Americans today use?

2. A plant can be used to produce energy. How do you think this plant clock works? What other objects could be used instead of plants?

Science in Careers

A person who studies the properties of matter is called a **chemist.** There are many different kinds of chemists. Food chemists test foods for quality and also make chemicals that help keep foods from spoiling. Other chemists invent new materials. Much of the clothing sold today is made from new materials developed by chemists.

The electrical energy needed to run telephones is carried by large cables. **Telephone cable workers** put these cables in place. When the cables break, as can happen during a storm, the cable worker repairs them. Cable workers must understand how electricity works.

Today many people see the value of using solar energy. **Architects** (är′kə tekts) who specialize in designing buildings that use solar energy are much in demand. These architects plan additions to older buildings so that solar energy can be used. They also plan new homes and factories that make use of devices such as solar collectors.

Telephone cable worker

Architect

People in Science

PERCY JULIAN
(1899–1975)

Dr. Julian spent his life studying uses for chemicals taken from the soybean plant. In 1935 he discovered a chemical that cures a disease which causes blindness. Another discovery made by Julian greatly lowered the cost of a drug used to help people suffering from arthritis. In all, Dr. Julian owned more than 1,000 patents. These patents included one for a fire-fighting chemical that saved many lives during World War II.

Dr. Julian in his chemistry laboratory

Developing Skills

WORD SKILLS

Prefixes and suffixes are word parts that change the meanings of the base words to which they are added. A prefix is added to the beginning of a base word. A suffix is added to the end of a base word. The tables show how prefixes and suffixes are used to change the meanings of words.

Use the tables to help you write a definition for each of the following words. If you do not know the meaning of the base word, look it up in a dictionary.

1. mechanical
2. semiconductor
3. generator
4. fissionable
5. diatromic
6. insoluble
7. electrify
8. antifreeze

Prefix	Meaning	Example
anti-	against	antisocial
di-	two	dioxide
in-	not	indirect
semi-	half, partly	semicircle

Suffix	Meaning	Example
-able	that can be	obtainable
-al	of, like	musical
-fy	make, cause to be	horrify
-or	person or thing performing an act	conveyor

READING A PICTOGRAPH

A pictograph is a way to show information, using pictures as symbols. Look at the pictograph on the next page. It shows the amount of oil that could be saved in 1 year using different methods. Use the pictograph to answer the following questions.

1. How much oil could be saved in 1 year if all clothes were washed in cold water?

2. Which energy-saving idea saves the most oil? How much is saved?

3. Which two of the energy-saving ideas save the same amount of oil? How much is saved?

4. Which of the energy-saving ideas saves 570,000 barrels of oil?

5. If all cars carried one more person and all cars averaged 8.9 km/L of gasoline, how much oil would be saved in 1 year?

6. How much oil would be saved in 1 year if all houses had 15 cm of insulation and all thermostats were set at 16°C?

7. Make a pictograph of the number of students in different classes in your school. Your teacher will help you find the data you need for your pictograph. Which class has the most students? Which class has the fewest students?

AMOUNT OF OIL SAVINGS IN ONE YEAR

If all houses had 15 cm of insulation	
If all thermostats were set at 16°C	
If all appliances were 20% more efficient	
If all cars carried 1 more person	
If all cars averaged 8.9 km/L of gasoline	
If all clothes were washed in cold water	

Each equals 100,000 barrels of oil per year

USING THINKING SKILLS

There is a limited supply of oil left in the world. This will cause problems because people depend on oil for many things. For example, gasoline made from oil powers cars and buses. Gasoline also powers trucks that bring food from farms to people. Oil is also used to heat homes and to produce electricity. Think about this as you answer the following questions.

1. Some people think that there should be laws that require people to conserve oil. What do you think?

2. Some people think that we should keep looking for new sources of energy that can replace oil. What do you think?

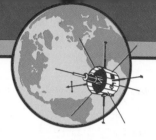

Unit Three
Discovering the Earth and Universe

Chapter 10–Cleaning Up the Earth The smoke from these stacks makes the air dirty and unsafe for health. People can protect the air, water, and soil from wastes.

Chapter 9–Changes in the Earth Waves crash against these rocks along the shore. The water wears away the rock and creates caves. In this chapter you will find out about many ways in which the earth is changed.

Chapter 11–Changes in the Weather   The clouds in the picture have been swept into a spiral shape by hurricane winds. These winds cause great changes in the weather.

Chapter 12–Beyond the Solar System   Scientists at this observatory study the stars beyond the sun. This chapter will explain some of the things scientists have discovered about stars.

Chapter 9

Changes in the Earth

Have you ever seen a place that looked like this? What caused the rocks to be shaped in these ways? This place is Bryce Canyon in Utah. The rocks in Bryce Canyon were shaped by the movement of water over millions of years.

The shape of the earth has changed many times during its history. The forces of moving water, ice, and air have caused these changes. In this chapter you will learn how the earth is worn away in some places. You will also learn how it is built up in other places. You will see how water, ice, and wind move materials from place to place.

Weathering Changes the Land

How does physical weathering occur?

If you view the earth while flying in a plane, you can see many features of its surface. You may see hills, flat land, valleys, and cliffs. The surface of the earth is always changing. It is changed by natural processes. Over a period of time, flat land may become mountains. Hills and mountains may slowly be worn down. The land is worn down by weathering. **Weathering** is all the processes that break rock into smaller pieces. There are two different types of weathering—physical weathering and chemical weathering.

Physical weathering is all the processes that break apart rock without changing its chemical makeup. This weathering causes rock to change its size and shape. The rock is broken into smaller pieces. But the small pieces have the same makeup as the rock they came from. The only change that the rocks have gone through is a physical one.

The effect that the freezing and melting of water has on rock is a type of physical weathering. In some mountain regions the daytime temperatures are above the freezing point of water. Water seeps into cracks in rock. At night, temperatures drop below the freezing point. So the water turns to ice.

When water freezes, it expands. As the water in a crack expands, it pushes with great force against both sides of the crack. This causes the crack to become larger. Each time water freezes and melts in the crack, the crack becomes larger. At some point the rock breaks apart into smaller pieces. This kind of physical weathering is called **frost action.**

Ice on rock

Cliffs weathered by frost action

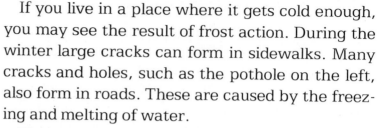

If you live in a place where it gets cold enough, you may see the result of frost action. During the winter large cracks can form in sidewalks. Many cracks and holes, such as the pothole on the left, also form in roads. These are caused by the freezing and melting of water.

Plants can also cause rocks to crack and break apart. Small plants and trees can grow in soil found in the cracks of rocks. As they grow, the plants push against the sides of the cracks. They cause the cracks to get larger. In time they split the rocks. The tree trunk on the left has split the large rock.

If you look carefully in your neighborhood, you may see places where plants have split some rocks and sidewalks. There may also be places, such as the one shown in the picture below, where tree roots have lifted up parts of the sidewalk.

How can growing plants weather rocks?

You will need 6 lima bean seeds, a clean tin can, ¼ cup of sand, a cup of plaster of Paris, water, and a plastic spoon. Soak the seeds in water for two days. Then put the plaster and sand into the can. Stir and add water until the mixture looks like thick soup. Use the spoon to smooth the top of the plaster. Now "plant" the seeds in the plaster about 1 cm below the surface. Smooth the plaster to cover the holes. Leave the can in a warm place. In a few days, observe the top of the plaster. What does it show about how growing plants weather rocks?

Physical weathering can also be seen along an ocean shore. Large waves pound rocks at the shore. When waves crash against rocky cliffs, such as those on the right, cracks can form. After a while, rocks may break away and fall into the ocean. The rocks may be lifted and dropped many times by the waves. As they are moved, the rocks strike other rocks. In time the rocks may be ground into small stones and pebbles. Waves may throw the stones and pebbles back against the cliffs. This helps to weather the rocks and cliffs even more.

Have you ever picked up smooth stones from a beach? This is another example of physical weathering by ocean waves. Many of the rocks weathered by waves are smooth and round.

Wind can also weather rocks. Wind can blow small pieces of sand against rocks. This can polish and smooth the rocks. But the wind alone does not weather rocks very much.

Another Kind of Weathering

How does chemical weathering occur?

Rock is also broken apart by chemical weathering. **Chemical weathering** is all the processes that break apart rock by changing its chemical makeup. Some places on earth contain large amounts of limestone and water in the ground. Chemical weathering is common in places like this. As rain falls, it mixes with carbon dioxide gas in the air. Some carbon dioxide dissolves in the water. This forms carbonic (kär bon'ik) acid. Water that contains this weak acid drains into cracks in the earth, as shown in the top drawing.

After many years, the acid reaches cracks in the limestone, as shown in the second drawing. The carbonic acid begins to dissolve the limestone. This makes the cracks become larger. After thousands of years, more and more limestone dissolves. A system of tunnels and caves may form, as shown in the third drawing. The picture below shows one of the largest caves formed in this way.

How limestone caves form

Limestone cave

Chemical weathering also breaks up rocks that contain iron. Rainwater contains oxygen from the air. The oxygen is dissolved in the water. Iron in rocks joins with the oxygen in rainwater. Iron oxide, or rust, is the new substance that forms. Iron oxide is soft and easily breaks off rock. When it breaks off, even more of the rock's surface can be changed by falling rain. The red-orange color in the rock on the right is caused by iron oxide.

Mosses and lichens (lī'kənz) also weather rock by chemical action. Lichens and mosses grow on rock and send out rootlike parts. The rootlike parts grow into tiny openings in the rock. They produce acids that dissolve some of the rock.

Rock containing iron oxide

Lichens on rock

Mosses on rock

Both physical and chemical weathering cause rock to break down. Chemical weathering happens at a fast rate in places that are wet and fairly warm. Physical weathering is greatest in wet places that are cooler. Dry places show little weathering effects, except for those caused by wind. Both kinds of weathering result in the forming of soil. Pieces of weathered rock mix with remains of living things. This forms soil.

Water Changes the Land

How does water change the land?

Most weathered materials are carried to other places. The movement of weathered rock and soil from one place to another is called **erosion** (i rō′zhən). Water, ice, and wind are called the **agents of erosion.** This is because moving water, moving ice, and moving air carry away weathered materials.

The most important agent of erosion is water. The force behind water erosion is gravity. Gravity causes water to run downhill. The steeper the hill, the faster the water will flow down it. The faster the water flows, the greater the rate of erosion. The amount of water also affects the rate of erosion. The more water there is, the more erosion there will be.

Erosion may begin when raindrops hit the soil. The falling drops break up large lumps of soil. Some of the water from rain and melting snow flows over the earth's surface. This water is called **runoff.** As runoff moves downhill, it may form small streams. Small streams may come together to form a larger stream. Several larger streams may join to form a river. Rivers flow into lakes or oceans.

rain

runoff

streams

river

ocean

As water moves over the surface, it may erode soil and rocks. The amount of material that is moved depends partly on the amount of water. The speed of the water is an even more important factor. Fast-moving water erodes far more material than slower-moving water. If there are no plants growing in soil, moving water may erode a lot of soil.

The erosion of soil by runoff can be a problem for farmers. The top layers of soil are rich in materials that plants need. So it is important for farmers to prevent erosion of this soil. The picture below shows one way this is done. There is a lot of erosion in hilly places. So farmers plant rows of crops around the sides of hills. The rows follow the curve of the land. When it rains, the rows hold the water and soil in place.

Erosion of soil by runoff

Crops following curve of land to prevent erosion

Terraces built to prevent erosion

Another way to prevent soil erosion on hills is to build terraces. Terraces, such as those on the left, are flat areas cut into a hillside. They, too, keep water and soil from washing down the hillside. Soil erosion can also be reduced by not clearing the land of all plants. How does this help?

Soil erosion is not the only effect of moving water. As water flows in a river, it wears away the riverbed. The riverbed is the rock under the river. The moving water carries materials that act like sandpaper. They grind rock and wear it away. The weathered materials are then carried by the moving water in the river.

The downward cutting of a riverbed can create a deep valley with steep sides. Such a valley is called a **canyon**. The Colorado River has been cutting the rocks of its riverbed for millions of years. This has formed the Grand Canyon, which is over 1.5 km deep.

Two views of the Grand Canyon and Colorado River

Ocean waves can erode sand from beaches along the shore. In some places the shoreline may lose as much as 380 cubic meters of sand each day. The pictures show a lighthouse at the tip of Long Island, New York. The picture on the top was taken almost 90 years ago. Compare it with the recent picture. Notice how much land has been eroded by ocean waves.

You have learned that erosion is greatest in fast-moving water. As a river flows downstream, the water starts to slow down. This slowing down causes the river to drop some sediments (sed′ə-mənts). **Sediments** are the materials that are dropped by the agents of erosion. Sediments include sand, soil, and rocks. The dropping of sediments by the agents of erosion is called **deposition** (dep ə zish′ən).

Erosion and deposition are related. Weathered materials are picked up and carried from one place. They are dropped, or deposited, as sediment in another place. In this way the land is constantly changing. In some places it is worn down by erosion. At the same time it is built up in other places by deposition.

In the spring, snow on the ground melts and there is often a lot of rain. So spring floods are common in some places. Flooding can erode valuable soil and destroy property. But flooding of rivers can be helpful because of deposition.

Spring flood

The floodwaters that overflow the banks of a river carry a lot of material. When these floodwaters soak into the ground, sediments are depos-

Rich farmland deposited by floodwaters

ited on the land along the river. These sediments enrich the soil. So land near rivers is often good farmland.

Most rivers empty into the ocean. The place where a river empties into the ocean is called the mouth of the river. The water at the mouth of a river moves very slowly. Much of the material carried by the river is deposited at the mouth of the river. The sediments form a fan-shaped landmass called a **delta.** Deltas are made up of sediments of weathered rock.

Mississippi River delta

The delta shown on the right is at the mouth of the Mississippi River. It is the largest delta in the United States. The picture was taken from an airplane, using special film. Other large rivers also have deltas.

The few remaining sediments that are not deposited on the delta are carried out to sea by ocean currents. Waves may carry some of these sediments and deposit them back on the shore. This forms sand beaches. Sediments may also be deposited as sandbars near the shore.

Sandbar

225

What factors affect the rate of erosion by water?

Materials   sand-and-gravel mixture / rectangular metal baking pan / metric ruler / 2 books / plastic squeeze bottle / clock or watch with second hand

Procedure

A. Put some sand-and-gravel mixture into one half of a pan. The mixture should be about 2 cm deep.

B. Use a book to raise the same end of the pan that contains the mixture. This represents material on a hillside.

C. Fill a plastic squeeze bottle with water. Begin to drop water onto the mixture at the rate of one drop each second.
   1. What do you observe?

D. Increase the water flow to a steady stream.
   2. Compare the amount of erosion with that in step **C**.

E. Put another book under the same end of the tray.
   3. What does this do to the angle of the tray? Does it make the hill steeper or less steep?

F. Squeeze water in a steady stream onto the mixture. Compare your results with those in step **D**.

Results

1. What did the water do to the sand-and-gravel mixture?

2. Did increasing the water flow affect the amount of material moved? Explain.

3. Did increasing the angle of the tray affect the amount of material moved? Explain.

Conclusion

When water flows down a hillside, what factors affect the rate of erosion?

Ice sheet

In some places glaciers exist today. Ice sheets, much like the glaciers of the ice ages, are found in Greenland and the South Pole region. Smaller mountain glaciers are found in high mountains, such as the Alps and the Rocky Mountains. Mountain glaciers are sometimes called rivers of ice. Why is this a good name?

Mountain glaciers scoop out material from valleys. This widens the valleys and gives them a U shape. The drawing shows a cutaway view of a U-shaped valley formed by a mountain glacier.

Glaciers of past ice ages have had a great effect on changing the shape of the land. The amount of erosion done by today's glaciers is limited. But some scientists believe that ice sheets will return someday and spread across the earth. If this happens, glaciers will reshape the land once again.

Mountain glacier

glacier

U-shaped valley formed by glacier

How does a glacier change the land?

Materials sand-and-gravel mixture / small paper cup / metric ruler / freezer / metal baking pan / modeling clay

Procedure

A. Measure and place a mark about 2 cm from the bottom of a paper cup. Add enough sand-and-gravel mixture to reach the mark.

B. Fill the cup with water and stir the mixture. Place the cup in a freezer. Allow the mixture to freeze overnight.

C. Line the bottom of a baking pan with a layer of modeling clay about 1 cm thick. Put a layer of sand-and-gravel mixture over the clay. This layer should also be about 1 cm thick.

D. The next day remove the paper cup from the freezer. Peel the paper cup away from the ice. Examine the ice mixture. This represents a glacier.

E. Place the ice mixture in the pan. Press down as you slowly move the ice mixture across the tray.

Results
1. What happens to the sand-and-gravel mixture?
2. What happens to the clay?

Conclusion
1. What do the particles frozen in the ice represent?
2. As glaciers move, how do they affect rock and soil?
3. How do glaciers affect layers of smooth, soft rock? Which material in the pan showed this effect?

Using science ideas
What must happen to cause a glacier to deposit the material it carries?

Wind Changes the Land

How does wind change the land?

Like water and ice, wind carries materials from one place to another. When the wind blows, it lifts and carries small dry particles. Most of the particles carried by wind are sand, soil, and dust. When these particles are blown against rock, they can cause physical weathering of the rock.

As wind blows sand from one place to another, the speed of the wind may be slowed by rocks or plants. When the wind slows, it deposits the sand it carries. This causes the sand to pile up. The deposition of wind-carried sand causes piles of sand, called **sand dunes,** to form. Some sand dunes may be as much as 50 m high. Sand dunes have many shapes. The forming of sand dunes is another way the earth is changed by building up.

Sand dunes

Desert pavement

In some places in the desert, wind blows away all loose sand. Only coarse pebbles and other small rocks are left behind. Such areas are known as desert pavement. The picture on the right shows desert pavement. Once desert pavement forms, almost no wind erosion will occur. Why?

Science & Technology

Did you know that sand dunes can move nearly 30 m in a year? Sand blown by wind can cause problems for people. Moving sand dunes have buried farms, towns, and forests. So new ways to control the movement of dunes are being tried.

In some areas, moving dunes are being stopped by dune grass. When the Pilgrims landed at Cape Cod, the dunes were covered with grasses, bushes, and trees. These plants helped to keep the dunes in place. When people removed the plants, the dune sand was left open to the blowing wind. This man is planting dune grass on Cape Cod. The grass will help to hold the dunes in place once more.

Dust storm during 1930s

Sometimes wind erosion can affect a large region. During the 1930s there were several years of drought (drout) in the Great Plains of the United States. A drought is a long period without rain. Many kinds of plants died, and the land became bare. Strong winds eroded the loose dry topsoil. The land affected by this drought and erosion became known as the Dust Bowl. It was named this because of the many dust storms that occurred. Some dust storms were so bad that they blocked out all the sunlight during the day.

There are ways for farmers to help prevent wind erosion. One way is to plant rows of trees or bushes. These plants act like fences or walls.

Windbreak

They block the force of the wind. Something that blocks the force of the wind is called a **wind-break.** Where fields are not being used, farmers can plant ground cover. Ground cover consists of low plants that hold soil in place and prevent erosion.

Ideas to Remember

► Weathering is all the processes that break rock into smaller pieces.

► Physical weathering is all the processes that break apart rock without changing its chemical makeup.

► Chemical weathering is all the processes that break apart rock by changing its chemical makeup.

► Erosion is the movement of weathered rock and soil from one place to another.

► The agents of erosion are moving water, moving ice, and wind.

► Deposition is the dropping of sediments by the agents of erosion.

Reviewing the Chapter

SCIENCE WORDS

A. Identify each of the following.

1. It is formed when moving water cuts downward into a riverbed. It is a valley. It has steep sides. What is it?
2. It is made of sediment deposited by the waters of a river. It forms at the mouth of a river. It is a fan-shaped landmass. What is it?

B. Write the letter of the term that best matches the definition. Not all the terms will be used.

1. Movement of weathered rock and soil from one place to another
2. Dropping of sediments by moving water, moving ice, and wind
3. Processes that break apart rock by changing its chemical makeup
4. Freezing and melting of water that causes large rocks to break apart
5. Moving water, moving ice, and wind
6. Slow-moving mass of ice on land
7. Materials dropped by moving water, moving ice, and wind
8. Pile of sand deposited by wind
9. Row of trees or bushes that block the force of the wind
10. Water from rain and melting snow which flows over the earth's surface

a. frost action
b. physical weathering
c. sand dune
d. canyon
e. agents of erosion
f. runoff
g. chemical weathering
h. deposition
i. delta
j. windbreak
k. sediments
l. erosion
m. glacier

UNDERSTANDING IDEAS

A. Identify whether each of the following resulted from erosion or deposition. Then write whether moving water, moving ice, or wind was involved.

1. Sand dune
2. Canyon
3. U-shaped valley
4. Delta
5. Hilly ridge of rocky material
6. Dust storm

B. Make a chart like the one shown. Write each example of weathering under the correct heading in the chart.

Physical weathering	Chemical weathering

1. Plants growing in the crack of a rock split the rock
2. Mosses and lichens produce acids that dissolve rock
3. Ocean waves pound rock cliffs and crack them
4. Carbonic acid dissolves limestone, forming caves
5. Iron oxide forms and breaks off rock
6. Frost action

USING IDEAS

1. Look in your neighborhood for examples of physical weathering, chemical weathering, erosion, and deposition. List all the examples you find and identify which process each one is. Draw pictures of the examples or, whenever possible, bring in samples.

2. Design an experiment to show one way that erosion of soil by wind or water can be prevented.

THINKING LIKE A SCIENTIST

Answer the following questions. You may be able to answer some of the questions just by thinking about them. To answer other questions you may have to do some research.

1. Why doesn't metal rust in Antarctica?
2. Does weathering occur underground? What kind of weathering do you think takes place in underground caves?
3. Why must engineers who design bridges be experts in frost action?
4. In 1848, gold was discovered in a stream at Sutter's Mill in California. Within a year, 80,000 people rushed to California to look for gold. Many of these people simply dipped a pan into a stream and sifted out gold. Where did this gold come from?
5. Suppose a space probe sent back pictures of a cold, lifeless planet that has no atmosphere. What would you look for in the pictures to tell whether the planet once had an atmosphere?

Chapter 10

Cleaning Up the Earth

All forms of life on Earth need water. People need clean, pure water for drinking, bathing, and swimming. When wastes produced by people are dumped into water, the water becomes dirty. The wastes in the water can harm people's health.

In the picture you can see one part of a waste-treatment plant. At this plant, water that contains waste is treated. The first stage of treatment takes place in the tank shown. The heaviest solid material and some germs are removed. Later stages of treatment remove other solids and germs from the water.

Each year, huge amounts of wastes pour into the air, water, and soil. In this chapter you will learn about the sources of these wastes. You will learn about how the wastes affect the air, water, and land. You will also learn about what is being done to control these wastes.

Natural Resources

Why is there a shortage of some resources?

Look around at the things you use. You use paper, pencils, and books. You walk on the land, drink the water, and breathe the air. All these things are natural resources or come from natural resources. A **natural resource** is a useful material found in or on the earth. The paper, pencils, and books you use come from trees. Trees are natural resources found on the earth. So are all other plants. Air, water, and land are also valuable natural resources. Can you name some other natural resources?

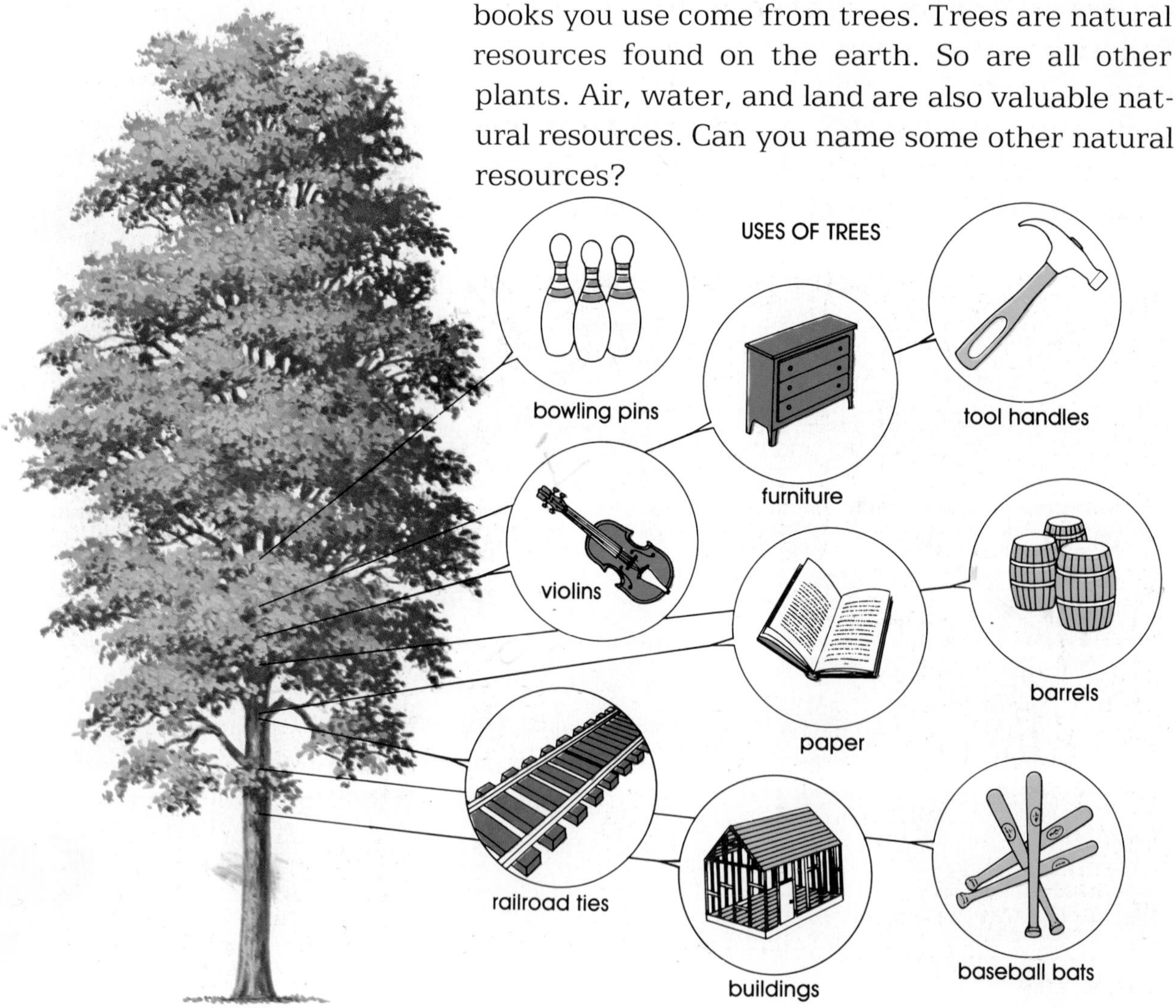

USES OF TREES

bowling pins

furniture

tool handles

violins

paper

barrels

railroad ties

buildings

baseball bats

Some resources can be replaced after they are used. For example, as trees are cut down for wood, new trees can be planted. A tree is a renewable (ri nü′ə bəl) resource. A **renewable resource** is one that can be replaced. Air, water, and soil are some other examples of renewable resources.

Since some resources can be renewed, there should be no shortages. There should be a large enough supply for everyone. But the supply has become smaller because of pollution (pə lü′shən). **Pollution** is the presence of waste or other unwanted materials in a resource. The substances that cause pollution are called **pollutants** (pə-lü′tənts). Pollution of air, water, and land has reduced the useful supply of these resources.

Littered forest

Planting tree seedlings

Air Pollution

What causes air pollution?

Pure air is made up of nitrogen, oxygen, and other harmless gases. The graph below shows the gases in air. The air you breathe often contains unwanted substances. When these substances are added to pure air, air pollution results. Most pollutants in air come from cars, trucks, homes, factories, and power plants. Some come from burning leaves and garbage. Some pollutants in nature are fumes and smoke from forest fires and volcanoes.

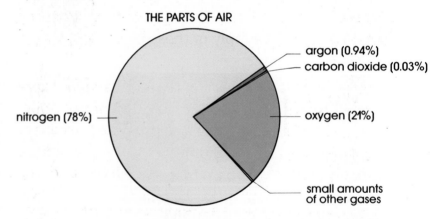

THE PARTS OF AIR

argon (0.94%)
carbon dioxide (0.03%)
nitrogen (78%)
oxygen (21%)
small amounts of other gases

Cars, trucks, homes, and factories burn fossil fuels for energy. Fossil fuels include coal, oil, and gas. Over the past 100 years, the use of fossil fuels has increased. Millions of cars and trucks are now on the roads. There are also many more factories than in the past. As a result, more fossil fuels are burned and more waste products are given off into the air.

Carbon dioxide and carbon monoxide (kär'bən mon ok'sīd) are examples of waste products given

Traffic on bridge

off by burning fuels. Smoke from burning fuels carries soot, ash, and dust into the air. These light particles may float in the air for a long time. Winds can carry them far from the source of pollution.

Coal-burning power plant

In parts of the United States and Canada, there is much concern over a special kind of pollution. The major cause of this pollution is the burning of fossil fuels. Volcanoes and forest fires also add to this kind of pollution. When fuels burn and volcanoes erupt, chemical wastes enter the air. Water vapor in the air combines with these chemicals to form weak acids in the air. These weak acids fall to the ground in snow or rain. They are called **acid rain.**

Acid rain falls on the land and into lakes and streams. When it reaches lakes and streams, it increases the amount of acid in the water. This change kills fish and other living things. Acid rain also breaks down minerals in the soil. The breakdown of minerals robs plants of important materials for growth. So some plants cannot live where there is acid rain.

Statue damaged by acid rain

Acid rain even damages buildings, water systems, and statues. Scientists know the causes of acid rain. People must use this knowledge to stop acid rain from forming.

Another kind of pollution occurs in towns and cities that have many factories, cars, and trucks. This pollution is called smog. Some **smog** is a mixture of smoke and fog. Smog occurs when calm, moist air near the ground is trapped and does not move away. The air remains in the area for several days. The longer the air stays in one place, the worse the pollution becomes. In the pictures below, you can see the effects of smog. Smog can be harmful. It can even cause death. In certain cities, smog is not as common as it once was. These cities have tried to control air pollution.

Today, people are aware that air pollution is a big problem. There are many ways that pollution can be controlled. Cars cause much of the pollu-

New York City in smog

New York City on a clear day

tion. Instead of driving cars, people can walk, ride bicycles, or take trains and buses. Or they can join car pools to get to school or work. Fewer cars on the roads will help reduce pollution.

Using trains and buses

Today new cars must have devices that trap or burn up harmful gases in car exhaust. Most new cars are built so that they burn only unleaded gasoline. Burning gasoline that has lead in it causes harmful substances to be released. The picture shows the testing of car exhaust.

Factories are required to use special devices in their smokestacks. These devices use an electrical charge to attract particles from smoke. They also remove harmful waste gases.

An important law, the Clean Air Act, was passed in 1970. This law limits the amount of pollution allowed in the air. When the amount gets too high, factories are ordered to stop burning certain fuels. When pollution is reduced to a safe level, the factories can begin burning these fuels again. The picture shows a machine that tests for air pollutants.

Checking car exhaust

Checking air pollutants in air

243

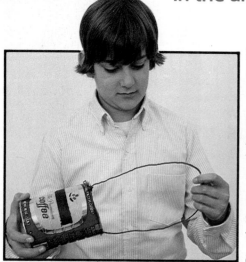

Are there solid particles in the air you breathe?

Materials large empty coffee can / 1 m of wire / scissors / white paper / glue / petroleum jelly / hand lens

Procedure

A. Wrap one end of a piece of wire once around the top edge of an empty coffee can. Twist the wire as shown. With the free end, form a handle.

B. Cut out a round piece of white paper a little smaller than the bottom of the can. Glue the paper to the inside bottom of the can.

C. Spread petroleum jelly over the paper. Why do you think you need to spread jelly on the paper?

D. Hang the can outdoors in an open area. A good place would be on a clothesline or a fence.

E. After 1 or 2 weeks, take the can indoors. Remove the paper circle from the can. Examine the paper with a hand lens.

Results

1. Did you find anything on the jelly-covered paper? If so, draw what you found.

2. Compare your findings with those of your classmates. Was there any difference? Make a list of what you found and what the others found.

Conclusion

Are there solid particles in the air you breathe? If so, where might they come from?

Using science ideas

Suppose you want to find the difference between pollution in the city and pollution in the country. Describe an activity you might do that would show this.

Water Pollution

What causes water pollution?

Most of the water on the earth is in the oceans. Because of the salt in the oceans, this water cannot be used for drinking. It also cannot be used in industry or in farming. People must depend on fresh water for their needs. Most fresh water comes either from under the ground or from lakes, rivers, and streams. It is important to take care of the limited supply of water.

Watering crops

How much water do you use each day? Some studies show that each person in the United States uses nearly 400 L a day. Some people have guessed that industries in the United States use about 10 billion L of water a day. Large amounts are also needed to water farmland in certain parts of the country. Most of this water comes from lakes, rivers, and reservoirs.

If the freshwater supply is polluted, there is less water left for people, farms, and industries. Polluted water means there is also less water for fishing and swimming.

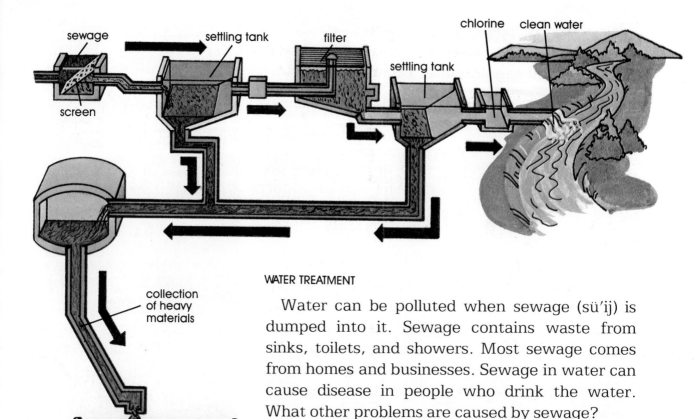

sewage · screen · settling tank · filter · chlorine · clean water · settling tank

collection of heavy materials

Sewage treatment plant

WATER TREATMENT

Water can be polluted when sewage (sü'ij) is dumped into it. Sewage contains waste from sinks, toilets, and showers. Most sewage comes from homes and businesses. Sewage in water can cause disease in people who drink the water. What other problems are caused by sewage?

Many large cities have sewage-treatment plants that remove many of the pollutants from water. The water must pass through several steps. Follow these steps in the drawing.

First, sewage that enters these plants must pass through screens. These screens filter and remove large objects. The water then passes to a settling tank. Light materials float to the top, where they are skimmed off. Heavier materials sink and are removed. The water is pumped through a filter and then to a second settling tank. Then it is treated with the chemical chlorine (klôr'ēn). The chlorine kills certain harmful living things in the water. After the water has been treated, it is returned to lakes, streams, rivers, and finally to the oceans.

Water can be polluted by fertilizers and chemical sprays. Many farmers use chemical fertilizers (fėr'tə lī zərz) on their crops. A **fertilizer** is a substance that helps plants grow. Chemical sprays are often used to kill insects and weeds that damage crops. Chemicals from the fertilizers and sprays soak into the soil when it rains. In time water carrying these chemicals drains into streams and rivers. The streams and rivers then empty into lakes and oceans. This is how these waters become polluted.

Fertilizers entering the water increase the growth of small plants called algae. When the algae die, they pile up on the bottoms of ponds and lakes. As the dead plants decay, they may use oxygen from the water. As the oxygen supply decreases, fish and other animals that get oxygen from the water may die. This kind of pollution is shown in the drawing.

EFFECT OF FERTILIZER RUNOFF

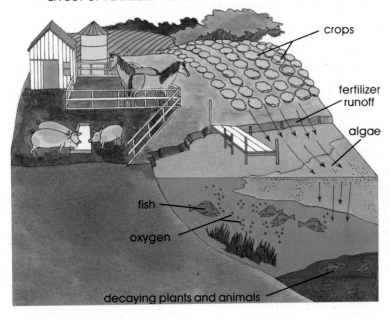

crops

fertilizer runoff

algae

fish

oxygen

decaying plants and animals

Algae covering water

Chemicals from insect and weed sprays can poison fish and other living things in the water. The sprays can even affect living things that live near the water. This happens through a food chain. For example, a small fish may take in the poison when it eats small plants. The small fish may be eaten by a larger fish. The larger fish may be eaten by a large bird. The poisons build up in the bird as it eats more fish. In time the bird dies from the poison.

POISON IN THE FOOD CHAIN

Runoff with poisonous materials

Pollution from fertilizers and insect sprays can be reduced by using less of these chemicals. Sometimes farmers plant shrubs and grasses near water. These plants help prevent soil erosion. In this way, soil carrying chemicals will not enter the water.

Taking water samples

Industries can also pollute water. When industries make products, they may dump liquid or solid wastes into bodies of water. Many of these wastes poison the water. The poison wastes make the water unsafe for drinking and swimming.

Many industries have built their own waste-treatment plants. These plants remove many harmful substances from water before it enters rivers, lakes, streams, or oceans.

Some industries also release hot water into streams and lakes. The dumping of heated material into water is called **thermal** (ther′məl) **pollution.** Hot water cannot hold as much oxygen as cold water. With lower amounts of oxygen, certain plants and animals cannot live in the water.

There are ways in which industries and power plants can stop thermal pollution. Instead of re-

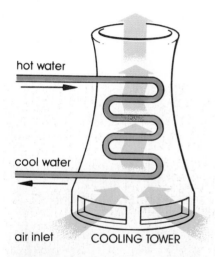

hot water

cool water

air inlet   COOLING TOWER

leasing heated materials into lakes and rivers, the heat can be released into the air. For example, some nuclear power plants have large cooling towers like the one shown. Hot water from the power plant is pumped to the cooling tower. In the tower, the hot water passes through coiled pipes. Cool air is then blown over the pipes. The air, which is now heated, is released through the top of the tower. The cooled water is returned to the power plant for reuse.

In recent years a new problem has developed. This problem is oil spills. Huge ships are used to carry oil across the oceans. Sometimes the tanks in these ships leak oil into the ocean. Another source of oil spills is offshore drilling for oil. Long stretches of beach have been damaged because of oil spills from these offshore wells. Fish and other wildlife have been killed by oil spills. The bird in the picture is being cleaned up after an oil spill. The people are tossing straw to stop the spread of oil.

Cooling tower

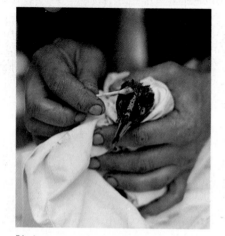

Bird rescued from oil spill

Cleanup after oil spill

Science & Technology

Scientists are working on ways to fight oil slicks. An oil spill often results in an oil slick, or layer of oil on top of the water. "Slickbusters" get to work at the scene. They gather information about how much oil has spilled. They report on the area's water temperature and currents. They may use computers to predict which way the slick will travel.

Special teams of workers also start the cleanup. Sometimes workers place pieces of absorbent material into the water. This material soaks up the oil. The picture shows workers gathering this material.

When a spill occurs in calm waters like rivers or lakes, workers set up booms. These are barriers that are placed around the oil to stop it from spreading. You can see a boom attached to a ship in the picture below. Skimmers are used to skim oil off the surface of the water. Pumps suck the oily water away. Can you suggest other ways to fight oil slicks?

Activity

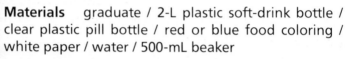

Does dilution help to reduce water pollution?

Materials   graduate / 2-L plastic soft-drink bottle / clear plastic pill bottle / red or blue food coloring / white paper / water / 500-mL beaker

Procedure

A. Use a graduate to measure 10 mL of water. Pour the water into a plastic pill bottle.

B. Add 1 drop of food coloring to the water in the pill bottle. Swirl the bottle gently to mix the color evenly. Hold a sheet of white paper behind the pill bottle. Observe how deep the color of the water is.

C. Using a 500-mL beaker, pour 1,000 mL of water into a plastic soft-drink bottle. (Fill the beaker twice.)

D. Add 1 drop of food coloring to the bottle. Swirl the bottle to mix the color evenly. Hold a sheet of white paper behind the bottle. Observe how deep the color of the water is.

E. Compare the color of the water that is in the two bottles.
   1. In which bottle is the color deeper?

F. Imagine that the food coloring is a harmful pollutant. Imagine that the pill bottle represents a small pond and the soft-drink bottle represents a lake.
   2. Predict whether the pollutant will do more harm in the pond or in the lake. Explain.

Conclusion

1. What is the difference between the effect of food coloring in the pill bottle and in the soft-drink bottle?
2. Compare the effect of the same amount of pollution in both a small and a large body of water.

Land Pollution

What causes land pollution?

There are several things that threaten the soil. One of the most serious is soil erosion. If soil erosion is not controlled, valuable land can be lost forever. The plants in the picture were planted along the road to prevent erosion of the hillside.

Soil can be polluted by toxic (tok'sik) wastes. **Toxic wastes** are wastes that are poisonous. These wastes may be produced by certain industries and then buried in the soil. Even toxic wastes stored in drums can reach the soil if these drums leak. The chemicals can stay in the soil a long time. They can harm or kill living things in the soil. They can even seep into water supplies.

Government and industries are working to clean up chemical dump sites. New ways to store and get rid of chemical wastes are being studied. The picture below shows workers testing drums for leakage. They are helping to prevent further land pollution.

Plants that prevent erosion

Drums of toxic wastes

Checking leaking drums

253

One of the ugliest kinds of pollution is litter. It is on city streets, country roads, and in fields and forests. People throw away huge amounts of trash.

Some forms of litter are more of a problem than others. Paper, cloth, cardboard, and wood are biodegradable (bī ō di grā′də bəl) materials. **Biodegradable materials** are materials that decay, or are broken down by living things. When materials decay, they break down into simpler materials. Small organisms in the soil break down biodegradable materials as they use them for food. These materials become part of the soil.

But not all materials are biodegradable. Plastic and aluminum are not broken down by living things. Materials that are not broken down by living things are **nonbiodegradable** (non bī ō di-grā′də bəl) **materials**. These materials litter the land long after they have been thrown away.

Finding Out

Which materials are biodegradable?

Collect small pieces of waste that your family might throw away. You might get pieces of paper or cardboard, aluminum foil, and plastic. Also collect some table scraps. Fill a plastic glass with soil to within one inch of the top. Now "bury" the small bits of waste at various depths in the soil. Place the materials close to the outer edge of the glass. Leave space between the materials. Pack the soil firmly and moisten it with water. Cover the glass with plastic wrap. Observe the glass every few days for two weeks. Which items changed? Which items stayed the same?

Laws have been passed in many areas to help stop litter. Most states fine people who are caught littering. Some states have even stopped the sale of throw-away bottles.

Pollution of air, water, and land is a problem that affects all people. Everyone must use the air, water, and land. Everyone can help to clean up the earth.

Ideas to Remember

▶ A renewable resource is one that can be replaced after it is used.

▶ Pollution is the presence of waste or other unwanted materials in a resource.

▶ The major cause of air pollution is the burning of fossil fuels by cars, trucks, homes, and factories.

▶ Air pollution can be reduced by the use of unleaded gas and antipollution devices on cars and smokestacks.

▶ Acid rain is rain with weak acids dissolved in it. It can harm or kill living things on land and in streams, lakes, and rivers.

▶ The major causes of water pollution are the dumping of sewage, chemicals, and heated material into water.

▶ The major causes of land pollution are careless dumping of litter and burial of harmful wastes in the soil.

▶ Laws are helping to control pollution of air, water, and land.

Reviewing the Chapter

SCIENCE WORDS

A. Write the letter of the term that best matches the definition. Not all the terms will be used.

1. Mixture of smoke and fog
2. Able to decay or break down
3. Substance that improves the growth of plants
4. Poisonous
5. Substances that cause pollution
6. Wastes from sinks, toilets, and showers
7. Dumping hot substances into water
8. Presence of waste or other unwanted materials in a resource
9. Useful material found in or on the earth
10. Resource that can be replaced

a. nonbiodegradable
b. thermal pollution
c. natural resource
d. renewable
e. sewage
f. pollution
g. smog
h. toxic
i. pollutants
j. fertilizer
k. biodegradable
l. carbon dioxide

B. Identify each of the following.

1. It is formed when chemicals combine with water vapor in the air. It can take the nose off a statue. It can kill the fish in a lake. What is it?
2. It could be plastic. It could be aluminum. It does not decay. What is it?

UNDERSTANDING IDEAS

A. A *cause* makes things happen. An *effect* is what happens. For each pair of sentences, write which is the cause and which is the effect.

1. a. A picnic area is littered with non-biodegradable materials.
   b. A family leaves aluminum cans and plastic bags at a picnic area.
2. a. Fertilizer runoff pollutes a stream.
   b. Algae cover the surface of a stream.
3. a. A city is covered with smog.
   b. Calm, moist air becomes trapped near the ground and does not move.

B. The drawing below shows at least five examples of pollution. Describe each of the types of pollution shown.

USING IDEAS

Think of three ways that you and your family pollute the air, water, and land. Suggest three ways you can help stop this pollution.

THINKING LIKE A SCIENTIST

Answer the following questions. You may be able to answer some of the questions just by thinking about them. To answer other questions you may have to do some research.

1. Suppose nonbiodegradable wastes from a chemical plant or paper mill were accidentally dumped into a lake. Suppose the same amount of wastes was dumped into a bay near the ocean. Which body of water is more likely to be permanently polluted? Why?

2. What parts of North America are most likely to be affected by acid rain? Explain your answer.

3. On an average day in Yellowstone National Park, campers produce about 24,500 kg of trash. What kinds of trash do you think cause the greatest disposal problems? Explain your answer.

Chapter 11

Changes in the Weather

People often talk about the condition of the atmosphere in a place. You may talk about it every day. This popular topic is the weather. What is the weather like in the picture?

When people talk about weather, they usually discuss the changing conditions of the atmosphere. The atmosphere is the layer of air that surrounds the earth. In just a few hours the weather shown in the picture may be very different. This is because conditions in the atmosphere can change rapidly.

In this chapter you will learn what causes weather and why weather changes. You will also learn about some unusual kinds of weather.

How Weather Begins

What causes uneven heating of the atmosphere?

How does weather begin? It begins with energy from the sun. You have learned that energy from the sun is called solar energy. It is this energy that causes weather.

What happens to the sun's energy as it enters the atmosphere? Some of it is reflected, or bounced back, into space by clouds, dust, and air particles. A small amount is absorbed, or taken in, by the atmosphere. Absorbed solar energy changes to heat energy. So only a small amount of the atmosphere is heated directly by the sun.

Some of the sun's energy does pass through the air and reach the earth. This energy is absorbed by land and water surfaces and changes to heat. This warms the earth's surface. Heat from the earth's surface then warms the air above it. You can see that the atmosphere gets most of its energy secondhand.

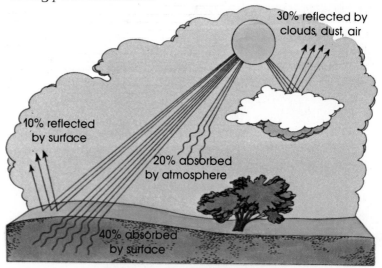

WHAT HAPPENS TO SOLAR ENERGY

Weather is caused by the uneven heating of the atmosphere. The air is heated unevenly because the earth's surface is heated unevenly. Why does this happen? There are several reasons. One reason is due to the round shape of the earth. It causes different parts of the earth to receive different amounts of solar energy.

Look at the drawing. The rays of the sun strike the equator directly. When the sun's rays strike the earth directly, the earth's surface is heated the most. Look at the areas north and south of the equator. In these places the sun's rays strike the earth's surface at a slant. When the rays strike the surface at a slant, the surface is heated less.

You can see why the earth is heated more at the equator than at the poles. Where would the atmosphere be colder, over the poles or over the equator? Why?

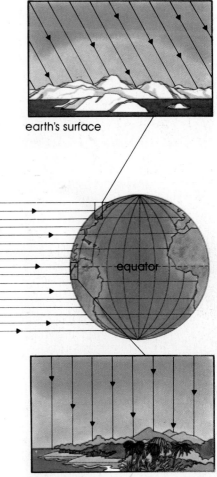

earth's surface

sun

equator

earth's surface

Another reason that the earth's surface is heated unevenly can be seen in pictures taken from a plane. Such pictures show places covered by white snow and dark soil. They show green fields and forests, blue water, and red deserts. These different-colored surfaces absorb different amounts of energy from the sun. The amount of solar energy that they reflect is also different.

Light-colored surfaces reflect much of the sun's energy that strikes them. Dark-colored surfaces absorb much of the sun's energy that strikes them. Which gets warmer, a light-colored surface or a dark-colored surface? What color clothing is best to wear on a hot summer day? Why?

The more solar energy a surface absorbs, the more the surface warms the air above it. Do you think that snow reflects, or absorbs, most of the solar energy that strikes it? Would dark soil absorb, or reflect, more solar energy? Would the air above dark soil be warmed more, or less, than the air above snow? You can see that differences in the color of the earth's surface cause uneven heating of the earth's atmosphere.

There is another factor that causes the earth's surface to heat unevenly. About three-fourths of the earth is covered by water. Water and land areas absorb solar energy at different rates.

Land and water heat up at different rates. During the day, the sun shines and the land heats up

faster than the water. So the air over the land becomes warmer than the air over the water. While the land heats up faster than the water, it also loses heat faster. At night, when there is no sunlight, the warm land cools quickly. So the air over the land becomes cooler. The water holds heat and stays warm at night. What would the air over the water be like at night?

Very little heat from the earth's surface and atmosphere escapes into space. This is because clouds, dust, and air particles trap the heat. This is an example of the greenhouse effect. In Chapter 8 you learned how the greenhouse effect can be used to heat buildings. On a large scale, the greenhouse effect keeps the earth warm.

How do materials differ in the ways they heat and cool?

Materials 6 paper cups / metric ruler / scissors / dark-colored soil / light-colored sand / water / 3 thermometers / lamp

Procedure

A. Cut the tops off three paper cups so that the remaining part is about 4 cm deep. Fill each cup with one of the following materials: dark-colored soil, light-colored sand, and water.

B. Place the cups together as shown. Put a thermometer into each cup. The bulb of the thermometer should be covered by about 0.5 cm of sand, soil, or water. Rest the top of each thermometer on a paper cup that has been turned upside down.

C. Copy this chart. Record the starting temperature in each cup.

1. Do you think the materials will heat at different rates? Explain your answer.

D. Place a lamp so that its light bulb is about 15 cm from the tops of the cups. Turn on the lamp. After 5 minutes read and record the temperature in each cup.

2. Which material was heated the most? Which was heated the least?

3. Do you think the materials will cool at different rates if you turn off the lamp? Explain your answer.

E. Turn off the lamp. After 5 minutes read and record the temperature in each cup.

4. Which material cooled the least?

Conclusion

How does this activity help to explain the uneven heating of the earth?

Material	Starting temp.	Temp. after 5 min of heating	Temp. after 5 min of cooling
Soil			
Sand			
Water			

Air Pressure and Winds

What causes winds?

Air is made up of particles of matter. Like all matter, air has mass. The mass of the atmosphere above the earth pushes down on the surface. This causes air pressure. The pressure of air changes from day to day and from place to place. The temperature of the air affects the pressure of the air.

When air is heated, it expands. This means that the particles in air move farther apart. When this happens, the air becomes less dense. So there are fewer air particles over a certain part of the earth's surface. This lowers the air pressure in that place.

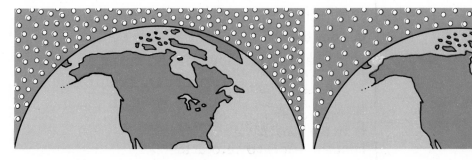

Before heating (higher pressure)   After heating (lower pressure)

Usually when temperature increases, air pressure decreases. Think about equal volumes of warm air and cold air. Would the cold air have higher, or lower, air pressure than the warm air?

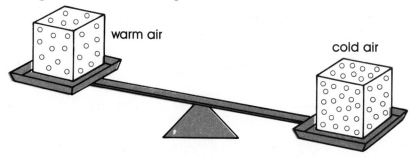

warm air   cold air

The amount of water in the air also affects the air pressure. The more water vapor there is in air, the lower the air pressure. This may seem strange to you. But keep in mind that water vapor is a gas. Water vapor is less dense than air. So 1 L of water vapor has less mass than 1 L of air. Usually the more water vapor in air, the lower the air pressure.

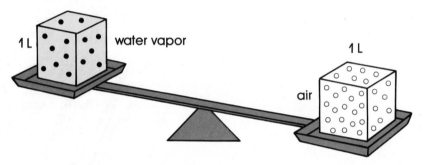

Differences in air pressure cause air to move. This movement of air is wind. Winds may be gentle breezes, or they may be strong gusts. The greater the difference in air pressure from one place to another, the greater the strength of the wind. Small differences in air pressure bring gentle breezes. Air always moves from regions of high pressure, called highs, to regions of low pressure, called lows.

There are different groups of winds. Some winds are local winds. Local winds are caused by local differences in pressure. For example, there are differences in air pressure over land and water. These differences cause winds to change direction along coastal regions.

During the day the air over the land is heated more than the air over the water. So the pressure of the air over the land is lower. The cooler, high-pressure air over the water blows toward the land. It moves under the warm, low-pressure air and pushes it up. This movement of air from water to land is called a **sea breeze.** On a summer day at the beach, you can often feel cool breezes blowing from the sea to the land.

At night the air over the land becomes cooler than the air over the water. So the pressure of the air over the land is higher. This air blows toward the water. It pushes up the warm, low-pressure air over the water. This movement of air from land to water is called a **land breeze.**

Sea and land breezes are local winds. But the earth has large regions of high and low pressure. Air moves from the high-pressure regions to the low-pressure regions. This movement of air, along with the rotation of the earth, creates wind belts, shown in the drawing. These wind belts, which circle the earth, are called global winds. Global winds are another group of winds.

GLOBAL WIND BELTS

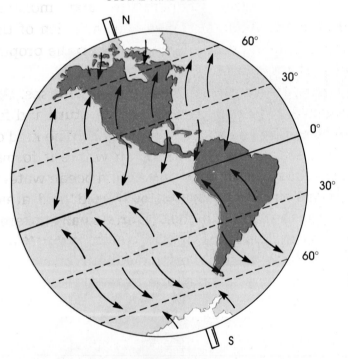

The global winds in each belt blow steadily in the direction shown by the arrows. The winds are named for the direction from which they come. Most of the United States lies within a global wind belt called the westerlies. Because of the direction in which these global winds blow, much of the weather in the United States moves from west to east across the country.

Air Masses and Weather

What are the four kinds of air masses?

Have you ever noticed how hot and humid it can be on a summer day? Then, the very next day, the air is cool and dry. This type of change in the weather is caused by the movement of air masses. An **air mass** is a large body of air that has about the same temperature and moisture throughout. When air stays over a region of the earth for a long time, the air takes on the properties of that region.

There are four basic kinds of air masses. Air masses are named for their temperature and for the amount of moisture they contain. The kind of air mass that forms depends on where it forms. Cold, wet air masses form over cold ocean waters. Cold, dry air masses form over cold land areas near the poles. These regions are usually covered by snow and ice.

Warm, wet air masses form over oceans near the equator. Where do warm, dry air masses form? What kind of air mass would form in each place shown on page 269 and this page?

The map shows the six major areas where air masses that affect North America form. It shows the kind of air mass that forms over each area and the path it often follows. During winter a cold, dry air mass will bring clear but very cold weather. In summer a warm, wet air mass will mean hot, humid weather. How long any kind of weather remains in an area depends on how fast an air mass is moving.

MAJOR AIR MASSES OF NORTH AMERICA

When Air Masses Meet

How do cold fronts and warm fronts differ?

You have learned that air masses move. As one air mass moves away from a region, another air mass moves in. The place where two air masses meet is called a **front.** Changes in weather take place at a front.

Fronts are named for the kind of air mass moving into a region. The drawing shows what happens when a cold air mass moves into a warmer air mass. The place where these air masses meet is a **cold front.**

As the dense, cold air mass moves forward, it remains close to the ground. It moves under the less dense, warm air mass. This forces the warm air to rise quite rapidly. As the warm air is forced up, it cools. Water vapor in the air condenses. The water vapor changes to tiny drops of liquid water. These drops form clouds. The clouds that form along a cold front are often dark towering clouds.

movement of cold air

cold air mass

cold front

warm air mass

movement of warm air

Cold front

Thunderstorm

Brief but heavy rain may occur along cold fronts. And wind speed may increase a great deal. Thunderstorms are common along cold fronts. Sometimes very wet, warm air is pushed up by a cold front. This can form a line of thunderstorms ahead of the front. Under certain conditions, tornadoes (tôr nā′dōz) can form along with a line of thunderstorms. A tornado is the most violent kind of storm.

Tornadoes are narrow, funnel-shaped spirals of air. Wind speeds in a tornado may be as much as 800 km/h. Tornadoes hang from the bottom of

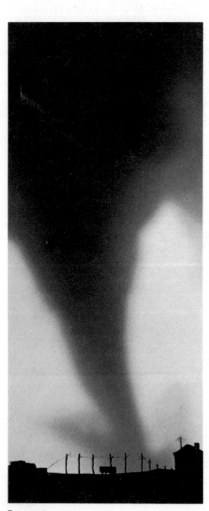

Tornado

272

storm clouds. They move in a twisting path. From time to time, they touch the ground. When they do, they can destroy buildings, uproot trees, and carry cars many meters through the air.

During winter, a blizzard (bliz′ərd) may form along a cold front. Blizzards occur when there are large differences in pressure between two air masses. Blizzards are snowstorms in which temperatures are below freezing and winds are very high.

After a cold front passes, the temperature in the region drops. The sky usually clears and fluffy white clouds may be seen. Why does the temperature drop after a cold front passes?

Now look at the drawing that shows a warm front. A **warm front** is the place where a moving warm air mass meets a colder air mass. The dense, cold air mass remains close to the ground. As the less dense, warm air mass moves forward, it slowly slides up and over the cold air mass. As it

Blizzard

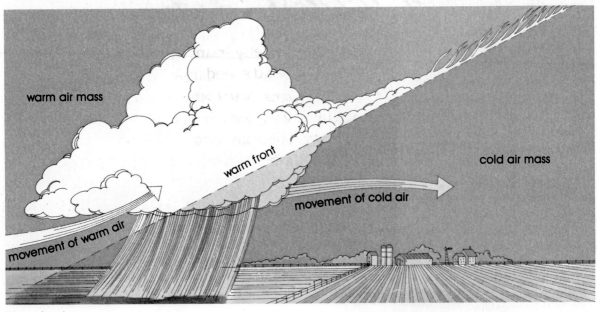

warm air mass

warm front

cold air mass

movement of cold air

movement of warm air

Warm front

273

slowly rises, the warm air cools. Water vapor in the warm air condenses. High thin, feathery clouds may form. They are a sign that a warm front is coming.

A warm front passes through a region more slowly than does a cold front. As the warm front moves, thick low clouds may form ahead of it. Steady, light rain may fall for a day or more. When the warm front passes, the temperature rises and the sky slowly clears.

Science & Technology

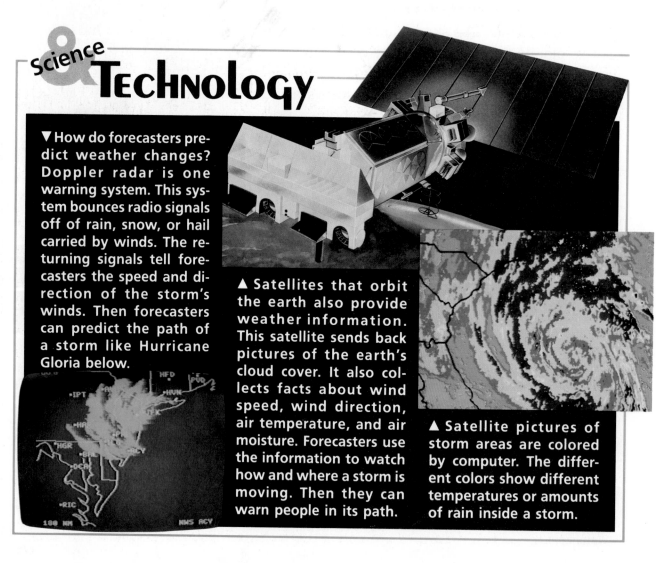

▼ How do forecasters predict weather changes? Doppler radar is one warning system. This system bounces radio signals off of rain, snow, or hail carried by winds. The returning signals tell forecasters the speed and direction of the storm's winds. Then forecasters can predict the path of a storm like Hurricane Gloria below.

▲ Satellites that orbit the earth also provide weather information. This satellite sends back pictures of the earth's cloud cover. It also collects facts about wind speed, wind direction, air temperature, and air moisture. Forecasters use the information to watch how and where a storm is moving. Then they can warn people in its path.

▲ Satellite pictures of storm areas are colored by computer. The different colors show different temperatures or amounts of rain inside a storm.

How does the weather change?

Materials   thermometer / barometer

Procedure
A. Scientists observe changes in the conditions of the air. These changes help scientists understand and predict weather. You can study the weather. First make a chart on paper. Include columns for such things as the day, temperature, and air pressure.

B. Write in your chart what day it is.

C. Read a thermometer that is in a shady place outside. Record the temperature in your chart.

D. Read a barometer. A barometer is an instrument that measures air pressure. Most barometers have an indicator. It helps you determine whether the air pressure has risen, fallen, or remained steady since the last reading. Line up the indicator with the barometer needle. Write in your chart whether the air pressure is rising, falling, or steady. Changes in air pressure indicate changes in weather.

E. Look at the cloud cover. Write in your chart whether it is clear, partly cloudy, or cloudy. Also indicate the direction the wind is coming from.

F. Write in your chart the weather conditions. You might use terms such as *rainy, clear,* or *hazy.*

G. Repeat steps **B** through **F** at the same time each day for 1 week.

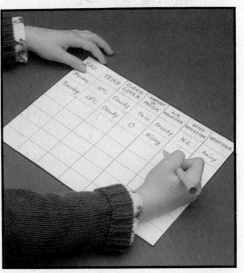

Results
1. On what day was the temperature the highest? On what day was it the lowest?
2. How did the barometer change?

Conclusion
Based on the week's weather changes and on today's weather, what do you think the weather will be tomorrow?

Clouds

How are cloud types related to weather?

There are many types of clouds. You have learned that different types of clouds form along cold fronts and warm fronts. Clouds are named for their shapes. The type of cloud that forms depends on the conditions of the atmosphere. So the type of cloud that you see depends on the weather.

The large fluffy white clouds often seen during fair weather are called **cumulus** (kyü′myə ləs) **clouds.** *Cumulus* means "heap." These clouds are flat on the bottom. Their rounded tops can billow high into the sky.

The thin, wispy clouds that look like feathers or curls of hair are called **cirrus** (sir′əs) **clouds.** *Cirrus* means "curl." Cirrus clouds are the highest clouds. The air high in the sky is very cold. So cir-

Cumulus clouds

Cirrus clouds

rus clouds are usually made up of tiny ice crystals. You often see cirrus clouds in a blue sky. They are sometimes a sign that a warm front is moving in and that the weather will soon change.

Thick low clouds that cover the sky are called **stratus** (strā′təs) **clouds.** *Stratus* means "layer." These sheetlike clouds are a sign of rainy weather. Fog is a stratus cloud near the ground.

Stratus clouds

Finding Out

What weather forecasts can you make?

Make a chart like the one shown. For the next 7 days, observe the clouds. Try to identify the types of clouds you see. Find out the temperature at the time you make your observation. What is the weather like? Record the information in your chart. Using what you know about clouds and fronts, try to forecast the weather for the next day. Predict how the temperature and other weather conditions will change. The next day look at your forecast to see how accurate it is.

Date	Cloud Type	Time and Temp.	Forecast

Altocumulus clouds

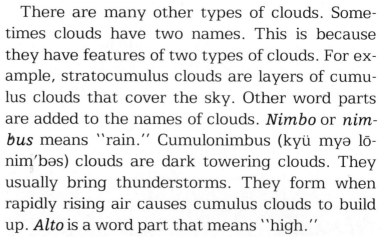

There are many other types of clouds. Sometimes clouds have two names. This is because they have features of two types of clouds. For example, stratocumulus clouds are layers of cumulus clouds that cover the sky. Other word parts are added to the names of clouds. *Nimbo* or *nimbus* means "rain." Cumulonimbus (kyü myə lō-nim′bəs) clouds are dark towering clouds. They usually bring thunderstorms. They form when rapidly rising air causes cumulus clouds to build up. *Alto* is a word part that means "high."

Look at the clouds shown on these two pages. Read the name of each type of cloud. See if you can tell why each cloud was given that name.

Stratocumulus clouds

Cumulonimbus clouds

278

Nimbostratus clouds

Ideas to Remember

▶ The earth's surface and atmosphere are heated unevenly. Weather is caused by the uneven heating of the atmosphere.

▶ Weather is related to air pressure. Cold, dry air has the highest pressure. Warm, wet air has the lowest pressure.

▶ An air mass is a large body of air that has about the same temperature and moisture throughout. The kind of air mass present determines the weather.

▶ Differences in air pressure cause winds. Sea and land breezes are local winds.

▶ Global winds cause weather to move from west to east across the United States.

▶ Weather changes take place at fronts. A front is the place where two air masses meet.

▶ The type of cloud that forms depends on the weather.

Reviewing the Chapter

SCIENCE WORDS

A. Identify each of the following.

1. It is a type of cloud. Its name means "curl." It forms high in the sky. It is mostly made up of tiny ice crystals. What is it?
2. It is a type of cloud. Its name means "layer." It is sheetlike. It is a sign of rainy weather. What is it?
3. It is a type of cloud. Its name means "heap." It has rounded tops that can billow high into the sky. It is often seen during fair weather. What is it?

B. Copy the sentences below. Use science terms from the chapter to complete each sentence.

1. When a warm air mass moves into a cold air mass, a/an _____ forms.
2. The movement of air from water to land is called a/an _____.
3. A large body of air that has about the same temperature and moisture throughout is called a/an _____.
4. When a cold air mass moves into a warm air mass, a/an _____ forms.
5. The movement of air from land to water is called a/an _____.
6. The place where two air masses meet is called a/an _____.

UNDERSTANDING IDEAS

A. Look at the drawings on the next page. Write the kind of air mass that would form over each place shown in the drawings.

B. Look again at the drawings on the next page. Suppose the air mass that formed over the place in drawing 1 moved into the air mass that formed over the place in drawing 3. What kind of front would form? Describe how air masses move at this kind of front. What weather changes might occur?

C. Describe three factors that cause the uneven heating of the earth's atmosphere.

1   2   3

USING IDEAS

1. Because the moon has no atmosphere, it has no weather. Explain why this is a true statement.
2. When weather announcers predict the temperature range for the next day, they often say, "Daytime temperatures will be cooler for places along the shore." Why is this statement true?

THINKING LIKE A SCIENTIST

Answer the following questions. You may be able to answer some of the questions just by thinking about them. To answer other questions you may have to do some research.

1. Suppose two unpolluted freshwater lakes are located 1 mile apart. Both lakes have the same volume of water. One lake is shallow and the other lake is deep. Which lake would freeze first in the winter? Explain your answer.
2. While at the beach in Rhode Island, a child released a helium balloon into the air. The balloon contained a note with her name and address on it. She watched the balloon disappear out over the Atlantic Ocean. She hoped that the balloon would travel to England. Weeks later she received a letter from a man who had found the deflated balloon in Pittsburgh, Pennsylvania. Explain how this might have happened.
3. Plains states, such as Kansas and Arkansas, have suffered from droughts that have turned huge areas into swirling dust bowls. Why are the plains states more likely to have droughts than states such as Oregon and Washington?
4. What causes sunburn? Why do snow skiers often get sunburn on their faces?

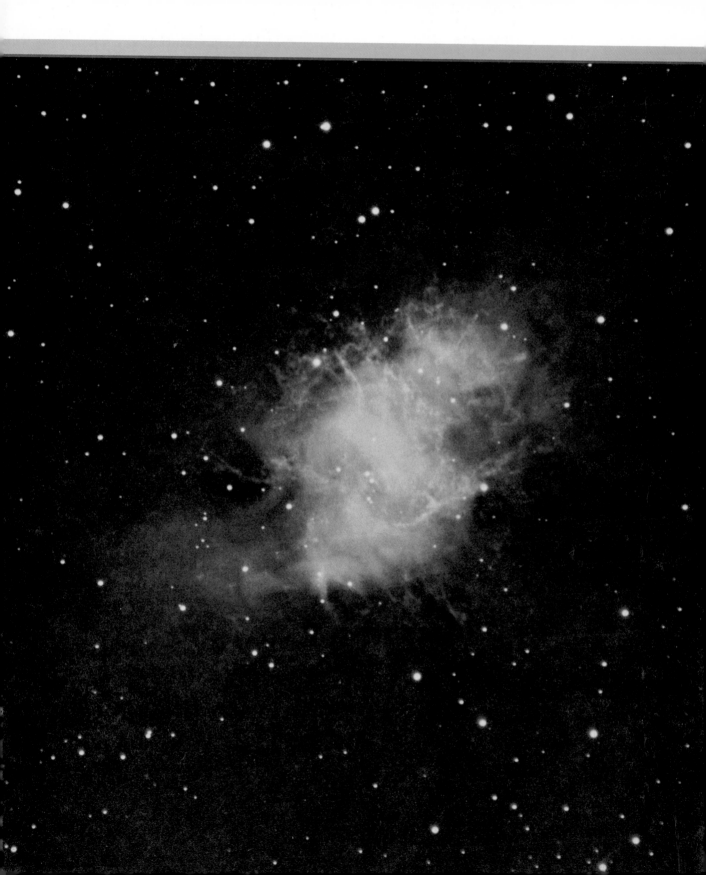

Chapter 12

Beyond the Solar System

Have you ever looked into the night sky and wondered how far it is to the edge of space? On a clear night you can see thousands of stars. Are there any stars so far away you cannot see them?

People have always been interested in space. What do you think this picture shows? It is a cloud of dust and gas in space. Scientists think it was left when a star exploded in the year 1054.

Objects like this are of great interest to people who study space. Scientists are trying to find out what lies beyond the solar system. They are also interested in finding out how far space extends.

In this chapter you will see how to measure distances to objects in space. You will learn about the life stages of a star. You will also find out how stars are grouped in patterns.

Distances in Space

What is a light-year?

You know that the sun and nine planets make up most of the solar system. The sun is at the center of this system. But do you really have any idea of how large the solar system is? It may help you get an idea of the distances between bodies in space if you study the paths of the space probes. A **space probe** is an unmanned spacecraft that collects information about planets and stars.

The "map" below shows the path of the Voyager 2 spacecraft. Voyager 2 will explore four planets before leaving the solar system. When was this space probe launched? How long did the trip from the earth to Jupiter take? When did Voyager 2 reach Saturn? How long will it take Voyager 2 to get from the earth to Neptune?

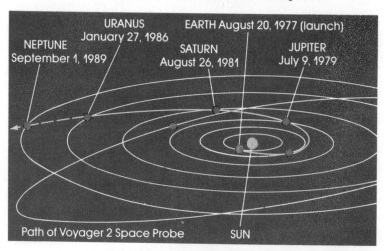

NEPTUNE September 1, 1989
URANUS January 27, 1986
SATURN August 26, 1981
EARTH August 20, 1977 (launch)
JUPITER July 9, 1979

Path of Voyager 2 Space Probe   SUN

Spacecraft travel much faster than any object travels on earth. For example, in a car on a highway, you might travel about 88 km/h. By the time it reached Saturn, Voyager 2 had an average speed of over 64,000 km/h.

It took Voyager 2 about 12 years to travel from the earth to Neptune. This gives you an idea of how large the distances are between planets in the solar system. But remember that the solar system is only a tiny speck in a larger family of stars in space. Look at the "map" below of the path of the Pioneer 10 space probe. Pioneer 10 was launched in 1973. After it left Jupiter in 1973, it crossed the orbit of Uranus in 1979. It crosses Pluto's orbit in 1987. Finally, it will leave the solar system and travel to other stars.

The "map" shows the number of years it will take Pioneer 10 to reach certain stars. The nearest star beyond the sun is Proxima Centauri (prok'sə mə sen tôr'ī). Suppose you could travel in a space probe. It would take you over 26,000 years to reach Proxima Centauri. How many years will it take Pioneer 10 to reach Lambda Serpens? How many years will it take to reach Altair? How many years will it take to reach the last star shown on the "map"? Many millions of stars are even farther away from the earth than are the stars shown.

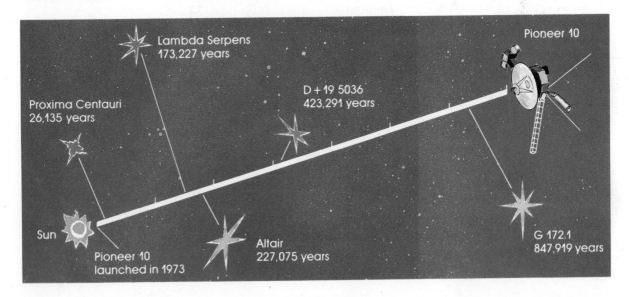

For centuries people have wondered about the size of the universe (yü'nə vërs). The **universe** includes all of space and all the matter and energy in it. People have wondered how far out space goes. They have wondered *where* it ends and even *if* it ends.

Astronomer looking through telescope

The study of the universe and all the objects in it is a science called **astronomy** (ə stron'ə mē). Astronomy includes the study of stars, planets, moons, and other objects in space. It is one of the oldest sciences. Scientists who study the universe are called **astronomers** (ə stron'ə mərz).

In the picture above, the Italian astronomer Galileo is shown with his telescope. The scene may have occurred in the early 1600s. A modern telescope is shown on page 287.

Sacramento Peak Observatory

You have learned that distances between certain bodies in the universe are very great. How do astronomers work with such great distances? Units such as meters and kilometers are used to measure much shorter distances. A larger unit is needed to measure distances in space.

Astronomers use the speed of light in measuring distances in space. Light travels great distances in a short time. For example, light from the sun reaches the earth in about 8 minutes. Light travels 300,000 km in 1 second (km/s). This is equal to 1,080,000,000 km/h. How much faster is this than a car on a highway? To find out, divide 1,080,000,000 by 100, which is about the speed of a car on a highway (100 km/h).

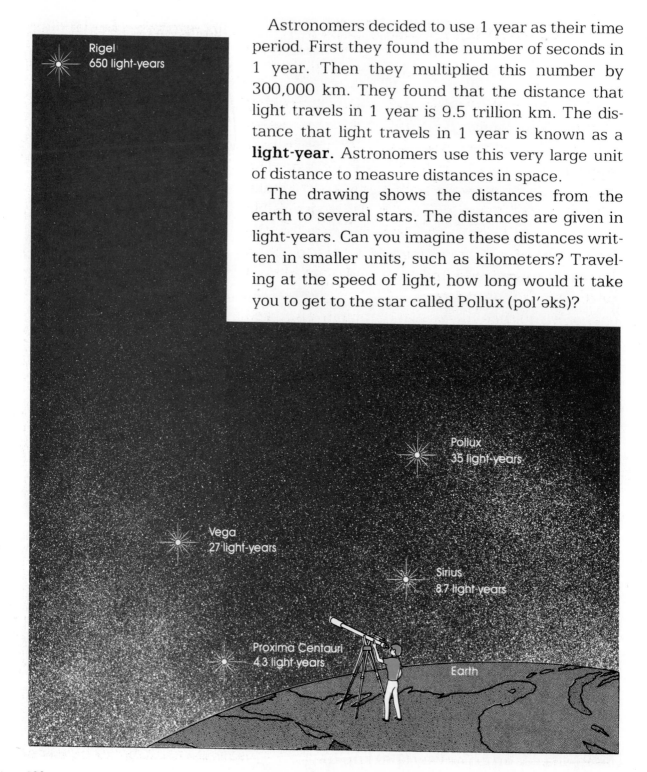

Astronomers decided to use 1 year as their time period. First they found the number of seconds in 1 year. Then they multiplied this number by 300,000 km. They found that the distance that light travels in 1 year is 9.5 trillion km. The distance that light travels in 1 year is known as a **light-year.** Astronomers use this very large unit of distance to measure distances in space.

The drawing shows the distances from the earth to several stars. The distances are given in light-years. Can you imagine these distances written in smaller units, such as kilometers? Traveling at the speed of light, how long would it take you to get to the star called Pollux (pol'əks)?

Rigel
650 light-years

Pollux
35 light-years

Vega
27 light-years

Sirius
8.7 light-years

Proxima Centauri
4.3 light-years

Earth

Characteristics of Stars

How are stars different from each other?

You may think all stars look alike. By looking closely you might observe that some seem brighter than others. You may even notice that some appear to be slightly different in color. The great distances between stars and the earth make it hard to see all the differences. The most visible difference is brightness. The measure of the brightness of a star as seen from the earth is known as **magnitude** (mag′nə tüd). In the picture which star is the brightest?

The magnitude of a star depends on three things. The first is the star's distance from the earth. Suppose two stars are exactly alike except for their distance from the earth. The one that is closer will appear brighter. It will have a greater magnitude. You can compare the magnitude of a star to the brightness of the headlights of a car. The closer the car is, the brighter its headlights will seem. The closer a star is to the earth, the brighter the star will appear.

The second thing that affects the magnitude of a star is size. Stars differ greatly in size. Some stars are very small. Many of these stars are smaller than the earth. The sun, with a diameter of 1,392,000 km, is a medium-sized star. There are stars that have a diameter 10 to 100 times that of the sun. Supergiant stars have a diameter 100 to 1,000 times that of the sun.

The third thing that affects the magnitude of a star is temperature. Stars differ greatly in temperature. The temperature of a star also determines its color. Look at the drawing that shows star temperature and color. Notice that red stars are the coolest stars. Which stars are the hottest?

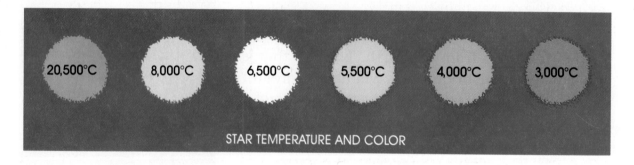

20,500°C   8,000°C   6,500°C   5,500°C   4,000°C   3,000°C

STAR TEMPERATURE AND COLOR

Suppose that two stars are the same distance from the earth. They are also the same size. All that differs is their temperature. One is blue and one is red. Which will appear brighter? The blue star will seem brighter because it is hotter. It will have a greater magnitude.

A star's magnitude, then, depends on its distance from the earth, its size, and its temperature. All three things must be considered. Remember that when scientists speak of magnitude, they mean the brightness of a star as it is seen from the earth.

What things affect brightness of light?

Materials   3 identical flashlights labeled *X*, *Y*, and *Z* / cardboard / scissors / tape / meterstick

Procedure

A. Cut three circles of cardboard so that each will cover the end of a flashlight. Cut a hole 1 cm in diameter in the center of each circle. Tape the circles to three flashlights labeled *X*, *Y*, and *Z*.

B. Mark three positions on the floor. Position 1 is 1 m away from a wall. Position 2 is 10 m away. Position 3 is 20 m away.

C. You will need three of your classmates to help you complete this activity. Give each student a labeled flashlight. Have the students stand in a row at position **1**.

D. After the room is darkened, have the students turn on their flashlights. Ask them to focus the light on the wall, to the side of their classmates.
  1. How would you describe the brightness of each flashlight?

E. Have the student with flashlight *X* stay at position 1. Have the student with flashlight *Y* move to position 2. Have the student with flashlight *Z* move to position 3.
  2. Which flashlight looks brightest? Dimmest?

F. Cut a cardboard circle with a 2-cm hole in the center. Cut another circle with a 3-cm hole in the center. Replace the circles on flashlights *Y* and *Z* with these new circles.

G. Have the three students stand in a row at position 3 and turn on the flashlights.
  3. Which flashlight looks brightest? Dimmest?

Conclusion

What two things affect how bright the flashlights look?

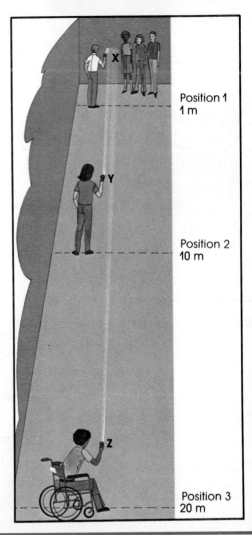

Position 1
1 m

Position 2
10 m

Position 3
20 m

The Life of a Star

What are the life stages of a star?

You may be surprised to know that stars have life stages. New stars are being "born" and old stars are "dying." Of course, the life and death of stars does not happen overnight. Changes in stars take place over billions of years. The drawings show the stages in the life of a typical star. Not all stars will go through every stage. As you read, look at the drawings.

1. A star is formed from dust and gas in space. A cloud of dust and gas found in space is called a **nebula** (neb'yə lə). The dust and gas in such clouds come together because of gravitational attraction. A great amount of matter must collect for a new star to form. There must be about as much matter as there is in the sun. As the matter in the nebula presses together, it gets hot.

2. Just before a new star is "born," it has a red glow. As matter continues to press together, the star's temperature rises. Finally, the

Horsehead Nebula

nebula

292

"fuel" of which stars are made begins to "burn." But it is not burning like a fire. Instead, hydrogen atoms combine to form helium atoms, giving off energy. A star can be described as a ball of burning hydrogen gas. At this point, a new star is born.

3. Most young stars are very hot. They are blue or blue-white. As more of a star's hydrogen fuel is used up, it becomes cooler. It may turn white. When even more hydrogen is used up, the star cools more and turns yellow. Most "middle-aged" stars, like the sun, are yellow. As it cools even more, a star may become orange or red. Look at the drawing on page 290. How does it help to explain changes in the color of a star?

4. A star beginning "old age" often swells up to form a **red giant**. A red giant is a star that may be many times larger than the sun. The temperature of a red giant is lower than that of the sun. Some scientists believe that the sun will enter this stage millions of years from now.

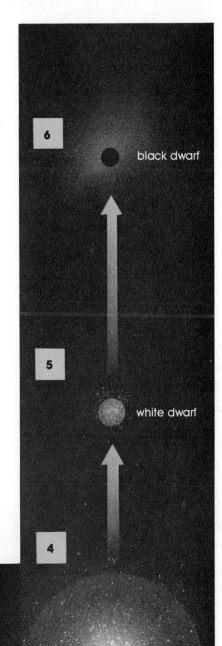

6 black dwarf

5 white dwarf

4

red giant

5. After a while a red giant begins to collapse into a smaller star. It becomes hotter and appears white in color. A star at this stage is called a **white dwarf.** It may be about as large as the earth. Because it is smaller than most stars, a white dwarf does not appear bright. The drawing of the life stages of a star on page 293 shows a white dwarf.

6. Once most of a star's fuel is gone, it will enter the last stage of its life. The star will become a **black dwarf.** In this stage the star has no heat or light. It is a cold, dense object in space.

Not all stars follow these stages. Stars that collapse into the white dwarf stage sometimes explode and become very bright. An exploding star of this type is called a **nova.** After the explosion the star will slowly shrink and grow dim. Sometimes a very large star may explode violently. Then it is called a **supernova.** The Crab Nebula shown on pages 282–283 is a supernova.

SUPERNOVA   NEUTRON STAR

BLACK HOLE

Stars that explode into supernovas sometimes collapse into very dense stars called **neutron stars.** A neutron star is much smaller than a white dwarf, even though it has more matter packed into it.

Some scientists think that the gravitational pull of a neutron star can be so great that the star disappears. When this happens, a black hole forms. A **black hole** is a region in space that was once occupied by a star. Some people believe that the gravity of a black hole is so great that not even light can escape. The drawing above shows how a black hole might look.

Families of Stars

What are the shapes of galaxies?

By this time you probably know that there is gravity everywhere in the universe. Each body in space attracts every other body. Because of gravity, no bodies are all alone in space. Instead, bodies in space collect in families. The sun is one of billions of stars that form the family called the Milky Way. A large group of stars and other bodies in space is called a **galaxy** (gal'ək sē). The Milky Way is a **spiral** (spī'rəl) **galaxy.** This type of galaxy is shaped like a flat disk, or wheel, with curved arms coming out from the center.

Sun

Milky Way

The Milky Way is about 100,000 light-years from edge to edge. The solar system is about one third of the way from the outer edge of the Milky Way. The sun is believed to be one of about 200 billion stars in the Milky Way. Can you find the sun in the drawing of the Milky Way on page 296?

Many scientists believe that all the objects in the Milky Way revolve around its center. This means that the sun and its planets are moving around the center of the Milky Way. The Milky Way is so large that it takes the sun 250 million years to go once around. It is possible that the sun is just now returning to the place where it was before dinosaurs were on the earth.

Science & Technology

▶ Astronomers use telescopes to find out about distant objects in space. Radio telescopes pick up radio waves from outer space. The telescope's giant dish collects and focuses the radio waves. Other parts of the telescope use these waves to produce signals. A computer then uses the signals to draw a picture of the source of the radio waves.

◀ A radio telescope was used to produce this map of a quasar (kwā′ sar). Scientists think that quasars are high-energy galaxies. One quasar releases as much energy as 10 trillion suns. Quasars are very far away. Light coming from them takes 12 billion years to reach the earth. When you see light from a quasar, you are looking back into the early days of the universe. Other distant objects in space called pulsars also give off radio waves. Try to find out what a pulsar is and how it got its name.

All galaxies are not spiral-shaped. Two other types of galaxies have been discovered. One of these is the **elliptical** (i lip′tə kəl) **galaxy.** An elliptical galaxy is like a spiral one, but it does not have arms. There are more elliptical galaxies than spiral galaxies. But the elliptical galaxies are not as large or as bright. Most of the stars in elliptical galaxies are very old.

Another kind of galaxy is called an irregular (i reg′yə lər) galaxy. An **irregular galaxy** does not have a definite shape or size. Some scientists believe that this type of galaxy may have formed when two or more galaxies bumped into one another.

ELLIPTICAL GALAXY (top); SPIRAL GALAXY (bottom)

Spiral galaxy

Many astronomers believe that entire galaxies are moving. They think that galaxies are moving toward the outer edges of the universe. The galaxies seem to be moving away from each other. The belief that galaxies are moving is part of a theory that suggests that the universe is expanding. No one seems to know why the universe is expanding. No one knows if it will ever stop expanding. What is your theory about the universe?

MOVEMENT OF GALAXIES

How can you make
a model of the moving galaxies?

Balloon size	Distance between dots (in mm)			
	V to W	V to X	V to Y	V to Z
Small				
Medium				
Large				

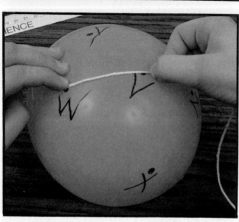

Materials round balloon / 10-cm twist-tie / felt-tip pen / string / metric ruler

Procedure

A. Copy the data chart. Blow up a round balloon to a small size. Tightly twist a twist-tie around the neck of the balloon so that the air does not escape. The balloon represents the universe.

B. Use a felt-tip pen to mark five dots on the balloon. Label the first dot *V*. Add dots *W, X, Y,* and *Z* to form a square, with the *V* dot in the center. Make each of these dots about the same distance from *V*. The dots represent the galaxies.

C. Use string to measure the distance from *V* to each of the other dots. Find these distances in millimeters by placing the measured string against a metric ruler. Record these distances in the chart.

D. Untie the twist-tie. Blow up the balloon to a medium size. Twist the twist-tie around the neck of the balloon. Repeat step **C**.
  1. How have the distances between dots changed?
  2. Find the difference between the measurements on the small balloon and the medium balloon.

E. Untie the twist-tie. Blow up the balloon to a large size. Twist the twist-tie around the neck of the balloon. Repeat step **C**.
  3. How have the distances between dots changed?
  4. Find the difference between the measurements on the medium balloon and the large balloon.

Conclusion

1. How is the expanding balloon like the universe?
2. If dot *V* represents the Milky Way and the other dots represent other galaxies, what is happening to the other galaxies?

Star Patterns

What is a constellation?

People have always been interested in the objects they could see in the sky. For centuries people have gazed into the night sky and wondered about stars. They have wondered about such things as what stars were made of and how big they were. As people watched, they noticed that stars seemed to form groups. People observed that even though the stars seemed to change position, the groups stayed together.

Ancient people saw patterns in these groups of stars and gave them names. Today we call these star patterns **constellations** (kon stə lā'shənz). One of the best-known constellations is the Big Dipper. Another is Scorpio (skôr'pē ō), shown on page 289. Have you ever seen these constellations? Can you name other constellations?

Finding Out

Why do stars seem to move?

You may know that the stars seem to move in the sky. But you do not see them moving. They seem to move because the earth moves. You can show how the stars seem to move. You will need a black umbrella and a star chart. Use chalk to draw a few familiar constellations on the underside of the opened umbrella. Be sure to draw the North Star at the point where the handle connects with the ribs of the umbrella. Slowly turn the handle of the umbrella counterclockwise. This shows how the stars seem to move in the sky as the earth turns.

GREAT BEAR

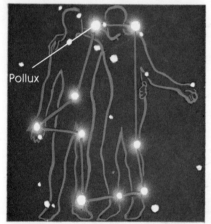

Pollux

TWINS

The constellations helped people keep track of certain stars in the sky. People could watch the movements of these stars. They used these star movements to measure time and the seasons.

How did the constellations first get their names? Years ago ancient people named many constellations for people or animals. Some examples are the Great Bear, the Little Bear, and Draco (the Dragon). These names are still used today.

Some constellations are shown on this page. The drawings show the main stars in the constellations. They also show the figure that each star pattern looks like. The main stars in a constellation have names. For example, Sirius (sir'ē-əs) is part of the Big Dog. Sirius is also the brightest star in the sky. Vega (vē'gə) is a star in Lyra (lī'rə). Lyra is a constellation that is the shape of a lyre, a type of harp. Pollux is part of the constellation called the Twins. See if you can find some of these stars in the drawings of the constellations. Do the constellations really look like the things for which they were named?

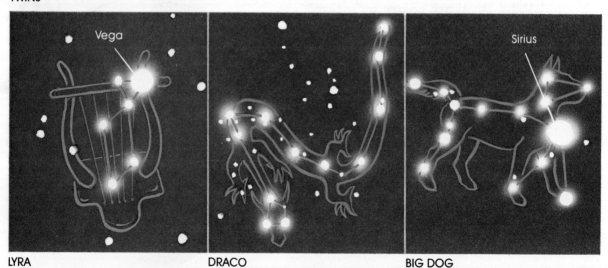

Vega

Sirius

LYRA   **DRACO**   **BIG DOG**

Ideas to Remember

▶ Astronomy is the study of the universe and all the objects in it. Scientists who study the universe are called astronomers.

▶ The distance to objects in space is measured in light-years. A light-year is the distance light travels in 1 year.

▶ Magnitude is a measure of the brightness of a star as seen from the earth. Magnitude depends on the distance of a star from the earth. Magnitude also depends on the size and the temperature of a star.

▶ The color of a star and its temperature are related. The coolest stars are red; the hottest are blue.

▶ New stars are always forming and old ones are dying. During its life a star may change color, temperature, and size.

▶ A galaxy is a group of billions of stars. A galaxy may be spiral, elliptical, or irregular in shape.

▶ A constellation is a group of stars that seem to form a pattern. Ancient people named constellations for familiar objects.

Reviewing the Chapter

SCIENCE WORDS

A. Use all the terms below to fill in the blanks.

astronomers   astronomy   light-year   universe

Space and all the matter and energy in it is called the __1__. The study of the stars, planets, moons, and other objects in space is called __2__. Scientists who do this study are called __3__. To measure distances in space, scientists use a unit called a/an __4__.

B. Write the letter of the term that best matches the definition. Not all the terms will be used.

1. A large group of stars and other bodies in space
2. An exploding star
3. Region in space once occupied by a star
4. Last stage in the life of a star
5. Pattern of stars
6. Measure of the brightness of a star as seen from the earth
7. Galaxy shaped like a wheel with arms coming out of the center
8. Cloud of dust and gas in space
9. A very dense star
10. Star much larger than the sun

a. magnitude
b. elliptical galaxy
c. black dwarf
d. constellation
e. neutron star
f. galaxy
g. black hole
h. red giant
i. nebula
j. nova
k. spiral galaxy
l. irregular galaxy

UNDERSTANDING IDEAS

A. List three characteristics that determine the magnitude of a star.

B. The pictures on the next page show some of the stages in the life of a star. Answer the questions.

1. Is the star in picture 1 cooler or hotter than the star in picture 3?
2. Is the star in picture 4 cooler or hotter than the star in picture 2? Which of these two stars is the oldest?
3. Which picture shows the oldest star?
4. Which picture shows the youngest star?

USING IDEAS

1. Choose your favorite constellation. Find out the story behind its name. Draw the constellation.

2. Make up your own constellation. Write a story telling how it got its name.

THINKING LIKE A SCIENTIST

Answer the following questions. You may be able to answer some of the questions just by thinking about them. To answer other questions you may have to do some research.

1. Why didn't scientists consider using the distance that sound travels in a year to measure distances in space?

2. Scientists have never observed a black hole. They only have indirect evidence that black holes exist. For example, scientists have observed stars rotating around what seems to be an empty region in space. How does this indirect evidence show that black holes exist?

Science in Careers

Many people are concerned about the condition of the world around them. **Soil conservationists** help farmers make the best use of land without damaging it. If a farmer has a problem with soil erosion, the soil conservationists can help solve it.

As you know, fossil fuels are an important source of energy. So the **petroleum geologist** (pe trō′lē əm jē ol′ə jist) has an important job. This person is a scientist who looks for new sources of oil. The petroleum geologist is usually one of a team of people who carry out this task.

Some people are always seeking answers to questions about the universe. Such people may one day want a career in astronomy.

Most people think of **astronomers** as stargazers. But astronomers of today spend little time gazing at the sky through a telescope. Most of their time is spent examining photographs and studying the information gained through research. Some astronomers work in observatories. An observatory is a building with special equipment for studying objects in space. Almost all astronomers do research or are teachers in colleges.

Astronomers

Soil conservationist

People in Science

RACHEL CARSON
(1907–1964)

Rachel Carson was a biologist and a science writer. In her most famous book, *Silent Spring*, Carson warns about DDT, a chemical that is used to kill insects that feed on crops. She points out that DDT pollutes the environment in a way that affects many living things, including people. She explains how DDT poisons the food supply of animals. As a result of *Silent Spring*, many laws were passed that changed the ways in which DDT could be used. Carson worked for the U.S. Fish and Wildlife Service for many years.

Bird egg damaged by DDT

Developing Skills

WORD SKILLS

Many English words come from Latin, Greek, and other languages. If you know the meanings of words in other languages, you can often understand the meaning of English words. The table lists some word parts that come from other languages and gives their meanings.

Use the table to help you write a definition for each of the following words. You can do this by breaking each word into parts. For example, the word *geothermal* is made up of these parts: *geo-* + *therm* + *-al.* Check your definitions in a dictionary.

Word part	Meaning
astro-	star, heavenly body
bio-	life, of living things
geo-	earth
inter-	among, between
tele-	over a long distance
mass	lump
naut	sailor
stella	star
therm	heat
-al	of, like
-ar	of, relating to
-logy	science of
-scope	for seeing

1. geothermal
2. astronaut
3. interstellar
4. biomass
5. telescope
6. geology

READING A MAP

Maps can give you many types of information. For example, road maps can help you find your way to a certain place. Look at the map on the next page. It shows the United States with numbers along part of its coastline. Each number shows the chance that a hurricane will occur there. The higher the number shown, the greater the chance that a hurricane will occur. Use the map to answer the following questions.

1. Which state contains the section of coast where there is the greatest chance of a hurricane?

2. Which state has the greater chance of a hurricane, North Carolina or Louisiana?
3. Which state has the lesser chance of a hurricane, Maine or Georgia?
4. Make a map of your school that a new student could use. Give your map to someone who is not familiar with your school to see how well you made your map. What symbols did you use in your map? How many classrooms are there in your school?

HURRICANE MAP

New Hampshire
Rhode Island
Massachusetts
Connecticut
Maine

New York

New Jersey
Delaware
Maryland

Virginia

North Carolina

South Carolina

Georgia

Mississippi

Alabama

Texas

Louisiana

Florida

USING THINKING SKILLS

Hurricanes cause millions of dollars' worth of damage nearly every year. Part of the reason for this is that many buildings are built along coastlines. Think about this as you answer the following questions.

1. Should the building of homes along coastlines be limited? Should this building be stopped? Explain your answer.

2. What are some other ways that the damage caused by hurricanes can be reduced?

Unit Four

Discovering the Human Body

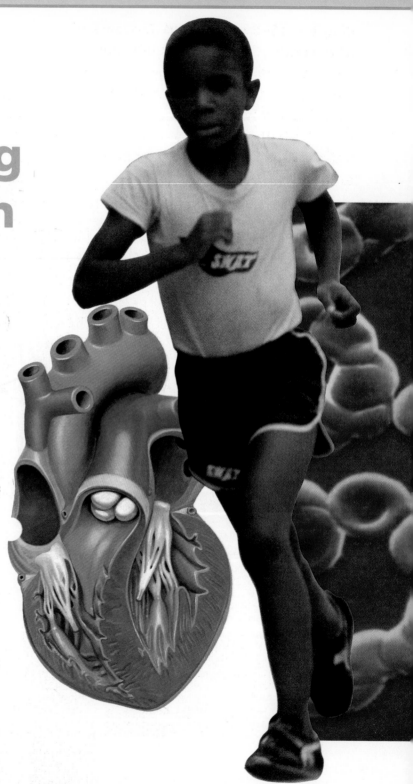

Chapter 14–Transport Systems of the Body Your heart pumps blood to all parts of your body. Below are some blood cells as they look under a microscope. Your blood is part of one transport system in your body. You will learn in this chapter about the body's three transport systems.

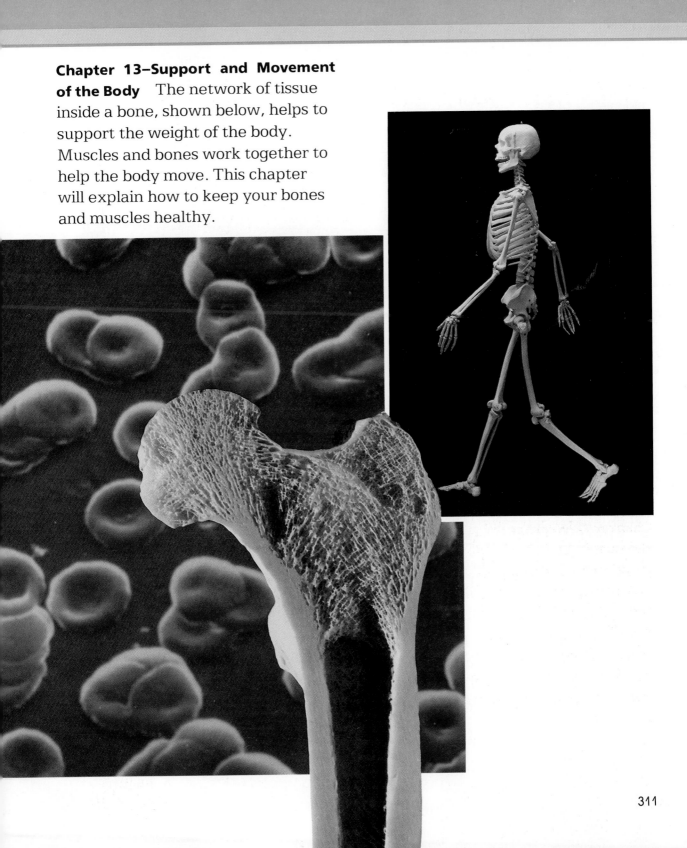

Chapter 13–Support and Movement of the Body   The network of tissue inside a bone, shown below, helps to support the weight of the body. Muscles and bones work together to help the body move. This chapter will explain how to keep your bones and muscles healthy.

Support and Movement of the Body

Have you ever played volleyball? Have you ever thought about how your body moves when you run or jump up to hit the ball? Every time your body moves, dozens of muscles and bones are put into action. Muscles and bones work together to move your whole body when you play volleyball. And muscles and bones work together to move your fingers, hand, and arm when you write.

In this chapter you will learn about bones and muscles. You will learn what they look like and how they work together. You will also learn how to keep them healthy.

Your Body's Framework

What jobs does the skeleton do?

You may know that some animals have soft bodies. Many of them live in water. The water helps support their bodies. Some animals have a hard outer covering that supports and protects their bodies. Still other living things have bones inside their bodies. All of these bones together make up the skeleton. The **skeleton** (skel'ə tən) is the system of bones that supports and protects the body and the organs inside it. The skeleton is also called the skeletal (skel'ə təl) system. What parts of the human skeleton can you name?

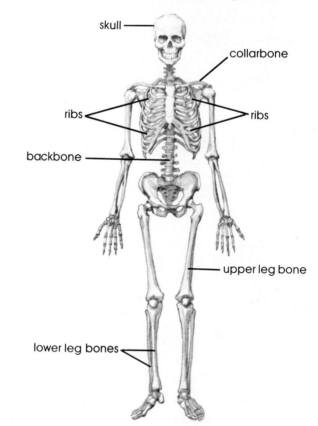

THE HUMAN SKELETON

The skeleton of your body can be compared with the steel framework of a building. The picture shows a skyscraper being built. The steel beams give the building its shape and support.

The skeletal system forms the framework of the body. It supports the body and gives it shape. But it does other jobs, too. Some parts of the skeleton protect soft parts of the body. For example, the brain, heart, and lungs are protected by the skeleton.

The skeleton is different from the framework of a building in an important way. The steel framework of a building cannot move. But the skeleton can move. It can move because muscles are attached to the bones of the skeleton. Muscles make the bones move.

Many parts of the skeleton help support and protect the body. In fact, the skeleton has 206 bones that help it do its jobs. There are two kinds of bones in the head. They are the bones of the face and the bones that protect the brain. These bones are joined together and form the **skull.**

BONES OF THE SKULL

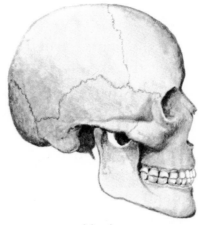

front view   side view

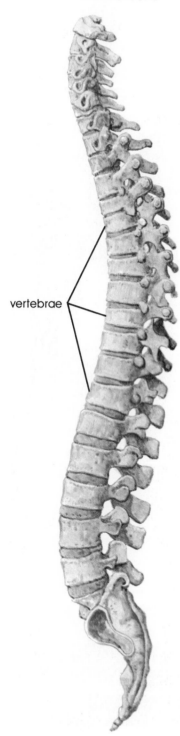

vertebrae

The skeleton in the middle part of the body is made up of the backbone and ribs. You have learned that the backbone is made of many small bones called vertebrae. Run your finger along your backbone. Can you feel the vertebrae? These bones protect many nerves in your back. They also help support your body.

Some of the bones of your backbone are attached to ribs. There are 12 pairs of ribs. The ribs protect organs inside the body. Look at the drawing below. Which organs do the ribs protect?

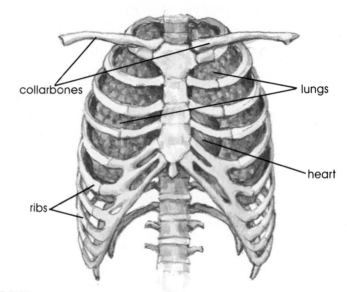

collarbones

lungs

heart

ribs

THE RIBS

The shoulders, arms, hips, and legs are also parts of the skeleton. The shoulders are made of flat bones. These are the collarbones and the shoulder blades. Find the collarbones in the drawing above. Can you find these bones in your body?

The hips are made of bones in the shape of a bowl. The bowl shape of these bones helps support and protect the organs inside the body. Find these bones in the drawing on the next page.

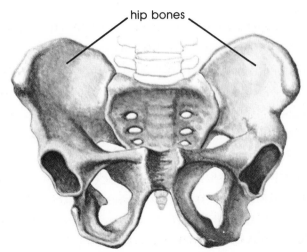
hip bones

ARM BONES

LEG BONES

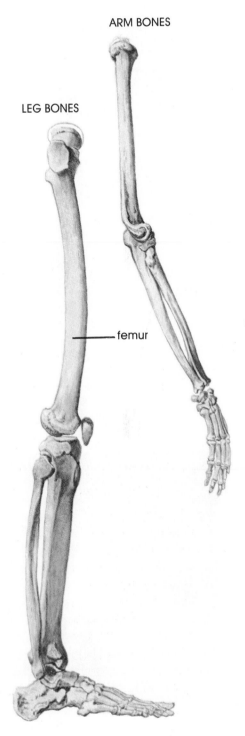
femur

Long bones make up the arms and legs. The center of these bones contains a soft material called **bone marrow.** Refer to the drawing below. You may have seen bone marrow inside round bones of beef. The bone marrow inside of some bones produces new blood cells. This is another important job of the skeletal system.

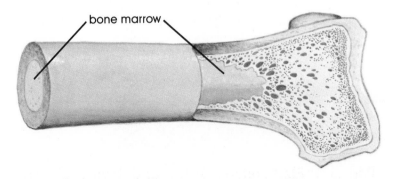
bone marrow

The drawing on the right shows the bones in the arm and the leg. Compare these bones. Notice that the leg bones are longer and heavier than the bones in the arm. The strength of the leg bones allows them to hold the body upright when walking or running. The long bone in the thigh is called the **femur** (fē′mər). It is the longest and heaviest bone in the body.

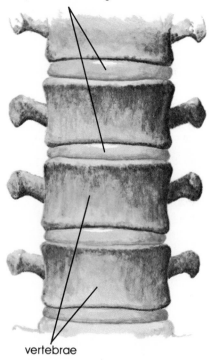

pads of cartilage

vertebrae

When you were born, most of your skeleton was made of a soft, bonelike material that bends. This material is called **cartilage** (kär′tə lij). As you grow older, much of this cartilage changes to hard bone. Not all the cartilage in the body changes to bone. Feel your ears and the tip of your nose. These parts are made of cartilage.

Cartilage is found in other places in your body. The backbone is made of many small bones. Nerves travel out from between these bones. If the bones were able to rub against one another, they would also rub against the nerves. This would be painful. But there are pads of cartilage between the bones. These pads keep the bones from rubbing against the nerves and against other bones. Cartilage pads are also found at the ends of the long bones in your arms and legs. The pads act as cushions, or shock absorbers.

Science & TECHNOLOGY

Sometimes cartilage or bones in the knee are damaged or injured. When surgery is needed, the doctor makes several small cuts in the knee. An arthroscope (är′ thrō skōp), a thin metal tube, is put into one hole. It has a light and a camera lens on one end. It sends pictures to a TV screen. The doctor watches the screen to see what is going on inside the knee. Through another hole the doctor inserts surgical tools. He or she uses the tools to repair the damage. When an arthroscope is used, the patient recovers in only 2 weeks. Recovery from open-knee surgery takes 2 months.

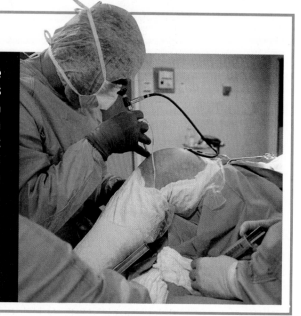

Where Bones Meet

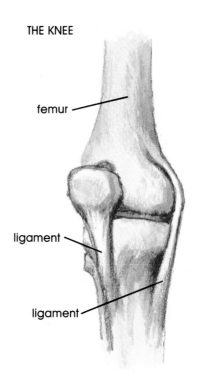

What are four kinds of joints?

You know that parts of your skeleton can move. They can move because of the way bones are joined together. The place where two or more bones are joined together is called a **joint.** Most joints in the body allow the body to move. Bones are held together at joints by strong cords of tissue called **ligaments** (lig′ə mənts). The drawing on the right shows ligaments in the knee joint.

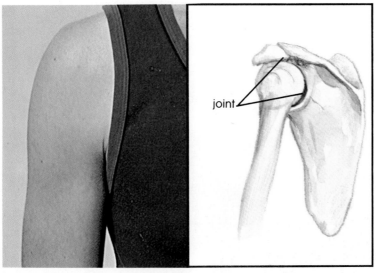

Ball-and-socket joint of the shoulder

Move your arm around. How many different ways does it move? Your arm can move in many directions. The kind of joint that allows the most movement of bones is a **ball-and-socket joint.** Part of this joint is formed by a round knob at the end of one bone. The knob fits into a hollow cavity, or socket, at the end of another bone. The drawing above shows the ball-and-socket joint that connects the upper arm to the shoulder.

319

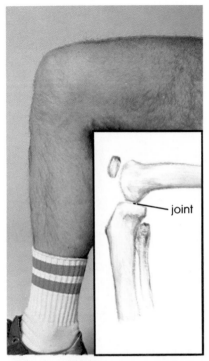

Hinge joint of the knee

A ball-and-socket joint allows bones to move in many directions. But some bones can only move back and forth. This is because they are connected by another kind of joint. A **hinge joint** allows bones to move back and forth. Your knee is a hinge joint. Move the bottom part of your leg. How is this movement different from the way your upper arms can move? Where else do you have a hinge joint?

Turn your head from side to side. Your skull is attached to your backbone by a pivot joint. This joint is between the first two vertebrae. A **pivot joint** allows for movement from side to side.

You have learned that the bones of the skull are joined together. But the bones of the skull cannot move. The kind of joint between bones that cannot move is called a **fixed joint.**

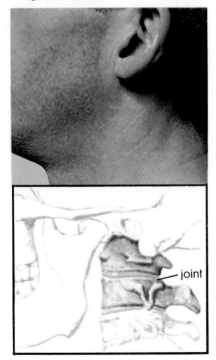

Pivot joint of the neck

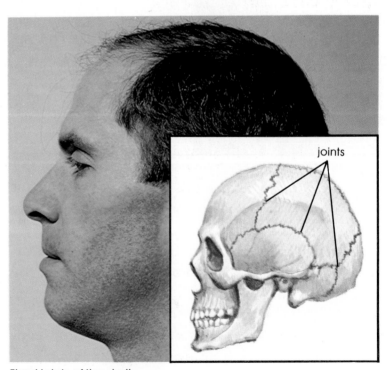

Fixed joints of the skull

Muscles Move Bones

How do muscles move bones?

You have learned that bones form the framework of your body. You also know that bones move. Bones are able to move because muscles move them. The whole skeletal system is covered with muscles. Muscles are made of soft but strong tissue. The muscles in the body make up the muscular system. You have more than 600 muscles. The drawing shows the muscles of someone who is running.

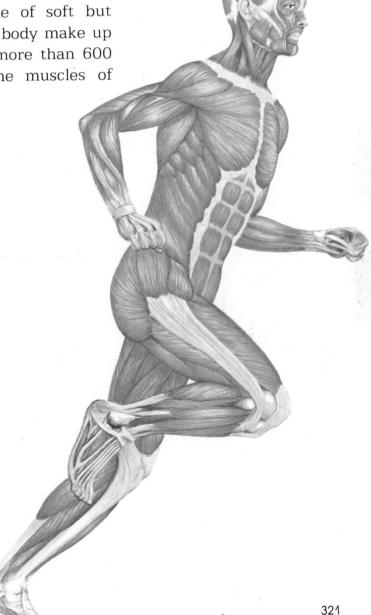

Muscles are attached to bones by tough cords called **tendons** (ten'dənz). You can feel tendons in your hand and wrist. You can also feel the big tendon that connects the large muscle in the calf of your leg to your heel. The drawing below shows this tendon.

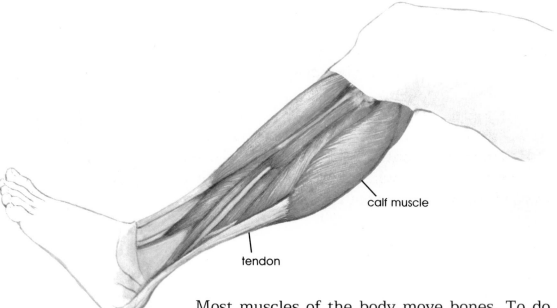

calf muscle

tendon

Most muscles of the body move bones. To do this, the muscles must contract. When a muscle contracts, the muscle becomes shorter and thicker. Muscles also relax. When a muscle relaxes, the muscle becomes longer and thinner. Muscle is the only kind of tissue that can contract and relax. The contracting and relaxing of muscles causes them to move.

Most muscles that move bones work in pairs. One muscle pulls a bone in one direction. The other muscle of the pair pulls the bone in the opposite direction. Muscles can only pull. They cannot push. To make a bone move, one muscle shortens, or contracts. This pulls the bone and moves it. The other muscle of the pair relaxes.

You can observe how pairs of muscles contract and relax to move a bone in your body. Place your left hand over the muscle on the top of your upper right arm. Move the lower half of your right arm upward, as shown in the drawing below. You should feel the muscle in your right arm bulge. This muscle bulges because it is contracting. As it contracts, it pulls the bones in your lower arm upward. Now feel the muscle on the underside of your right arm. This muscle should feel soft. It is soft because it is relaxed.

Now lower your arm. Again feel the pair of muscles on the top and underside of your upper arm. Which one contracts? Which one relaxes? The drawings show what these muscles look like as you raise and lower your arm.

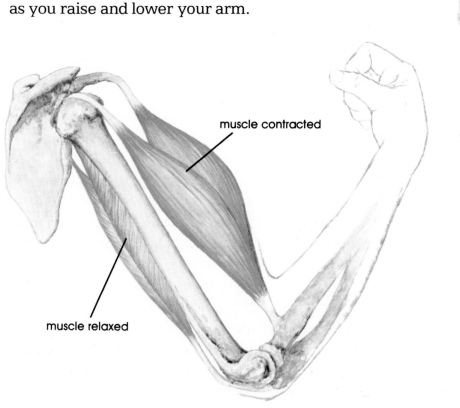

muscle
contracted

muscle
relaxed

muscle contracted

muscle relaxed

How muscles move bones of the lower arm

What happens when muscles become tired?

Materials clock or watch with second hand

Procedure

A. Copy a paragraph from any page in this book. Then move the fingers of your writing hand quickly, as though you were playing a piano. Keep moving your fingers until your fingers or arm become tired. Now copy the same paragraph again. Compare the way your handwriting looks in the two samples.

  1. Was it harder to write when your fingers were tired?

  2. How do your two handwriting samples differ?

B. While seated, raise one leg as shown. Record the time you begin. Keep your leg raised until it becomes tired. Record the time you put your leg down. Rest for 30 seconds.

  3. How long did you keep your leg raised?

C. Repeat step **B** at once.

  4. How long did you keep your leg raised this time?

  5. How do the results for step **B** compare with these results?

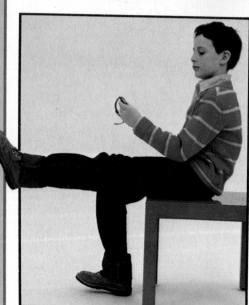

Conclusion

1. How do tired muscles affect how well you can do a task?

2. How do tired muscles affect how long you can do a task?

Using science ideas

Repeat steps **B** and **C** five times in a row. Graph your results. Suppose someone rides a bicycle every day for an hour. Hypothesize how this might affect that person's results for steps **B** and **C**?

Two Groups of Muscles

What are two groups of muscles?

You can control some of the muscles in your body. You can control muscles that help you walk, run, sit down, get up, or jump. The muscles that you can control are in a group called **voluntary muscles.** These muscles are attached to your bones. Voluntary muscles contract and relax to move bones. The pictures show some of the many activities that are possible because of voluntary muscles.

Muscles that you cannot control are in a group called **involuntary muscles.** You need these muscles to stay alive. Suppose you had to control your heartbeat. You would have to think about moving your heart muscle every moment of your life. Other involuntary muscles are in the stomach and intestines. They move food through these parts of the body. Involuntary muscles also move blood through the blood vessels. They even cause you to blush or to turn pale.

Do your eyes have both voluntary and involuntary muscles?

Look at your eyes in a mirror and try to keep from blinking. Blink your eyes four times in a row. What kind of muscle allows you to blink? Now look in the mirror at the pupils of your eyes. The pupils are the dark circular openings in the center of the eyes. They control the amount of light that enters the eyes. Observe the size of your pupils. Now use your hands to cover your eyes for one minute. Remove your hands and quickly note the size of your pupils. What happens to the size of your pupils as you continue to look in the mirror? Why do you think this happens?

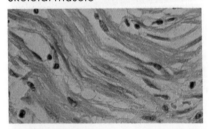

Skeletal muscle

Smooth muscle

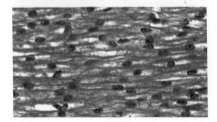

Heart muscle

There are three kinds of muscles. Most muscles that move bones are made of long fibers. These are voluntary muscles called **skeletal muscles.** The first picture shows what skeletal muscle looks like under a microscope.

The involuntary muscles that make up most body organs are another kind of muscle. They are called **smooth muscles.** These muscles make up the inside of the blood vessels, stomach, intestines, and other body organs. Smooth muscles, as seen through a microscope, are shown in the second picture.

A third kind of muscle is found in the heart. This special kind of muscle, called **heart muscle,** is also involuntary. The third picture shows heart muscle as it appears under a microscope. The heart is the hardest-working muscle in the body. It beats between 2 billion and 3 billion times during an average lifetime.

Bone and Muscle Injuries

What are some common injuries of bones and muscles?

Even though bones are strong, they can be damaged. Have you ever had a broken bone? Because most young people are very active, many of them break bones. A crack or a break in a bone is called a **fracture** (frak'chər). There are different kinds of fractures.

Usually when a bone breaks it does not push through the muscle and skin. This is called a **simple fracture.** Sometimes the broken end of a bone pushes through the muscle and skin. This is called a **compound fracture.** Look at the drawing of a compound fracture. Compare it with the drawing of a simple fracture. Why do you think there is a great danger of infection with a compound fracture?

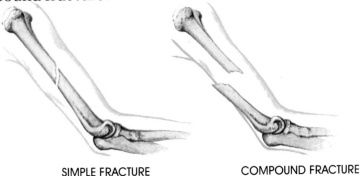

SIMPLE FRACTURE   COMPOUND FRACTURE

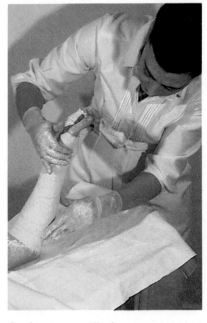

Cast being applied

Because bones contain living tissue, they can repair themselves. The parts of broken bones are put back in place, or set, by a doctor. Then the broken parts will grow back together. A cast holds the broken bones in place. The picture shows a cast being put on a broken arm.

Proper way to lift a heavy object

328

The ligaments that connect bones can also be injured. A **sprain** is an injury in which a ligament is stretched or torn. This happens when a joint is forced to move in a way other than the way it normally moves. Football players often suffer torn ligaments of the knee joint when they are hit from the side. Ankle and wrist sprains are also a result of torn or stretched ligaments.

Sometimes muscles are injured. Some muscle injuries are caused by overuse of a muscle. A muscle **strain** is an injury caused by overstretching a muscle or tendon. Muscle strain often results when someone lifts a heavy object in the wrong way. The pictures show the correct way to lift a heavy object.

Did you ever wake up in the middle of the night with a cramp in your leg or foot? A **cramp** is a sudden strong contraction of a muscle. It can be very painful. But it does not usually last long. Often you can help get rid of a cramp by rubbing the muscle.

Care of Bones and Muscles

How can you keep bones and muscles healthy?

There are three important things you can do to keep your bones and muscles healthy. You can eat a proper diet. You can get enough of the right kind of exercise. And you can get enough rest.

Eating a proper diet means eating the foods needed for healthy bones and muscles. There are four main groups of foods that make up a proper diet. The meat group contains protein foods needed for cell growth and to make new cells. The dairy group includes foods that contain minerals that make bones hard. The foods in the fruit and vegetable group contain needed vitamins. The bread and cereal group foods provide energy needed for muscles to move bones.

Meat group

Dairy group

Fruit and vegetable group

Bread and cereal group

What happens to bones when minerals are removed from them?

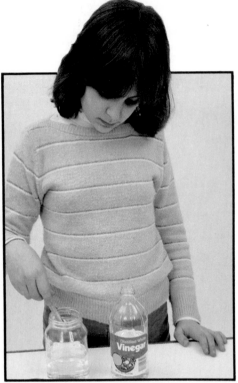

Materials chicken leg or thigh bone / jar with lid / vinegar / paper towels

Procedure

A. Remove all the meat from a chicken bone. Wash the bone in water and then dry it with a paper towel. Feel the bone. Then gently try to bend the bone.

    1. Does the bone feel hard or soft?

    2. Does the bone bend?

B. Half fill a jar with vinegar. Place the bone in the jar and place a lid tightly on it. Allow the bone to remain in the vinegar for 5 days. Vinegar removes minerals from bone.

C. After 5 days, remove the bone from the jar. Wash the bone in water and then dry it with a paper towel. Feel the bone. Gently try to bend the bone.

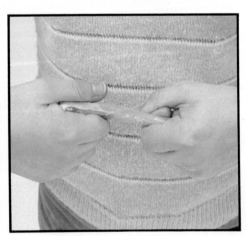

Results

1. How does the bone feel now compared with the way it felt in step **A**?

2. Does the bone bend?

Conclusion

1. If you did not eat foods containing minerals, what would your bones be like?

2. How would a lack of minerals affect the ability of your skeleton to support your body?

Using science ideas

Find out why you need vitamin D for strong bones and teeth. Also find out why this vitamin is often called the sunshine vitamin.

In addition to a proper diet, exercise is important for the growth and development of muscles. When muscles are not used, they shrink. This means they become smaller and weaker. Exercise keeps muscles strong.

While your muscles need exercise, they also need rest and sleep. As you exercise, your cells break down digested food to give you energy. As this happens, waste products are produced. These wastes build up in your muscles. When you rest or sleep, your muscles can relax and get rid of waste materials. Rest also keeps your muscles from being overused.

Ideas to Remember

▶ The skeletal system forms the framework of the body and protects soft body parts.

▶ Most joints allow the body to move. The main kinds are ball-and-socket joints, hinge joints, and pivot joints. Fixed joints do not allow movement.

▶ Bones are moved when muscles contract and relax.

▶ Skeletal muscle is voluntary muscle. Smooth muscle and heart muscle are involuntary muscle.

▶ Injuries to the skeletal system include fractures and sprains.

▶ Injuries to the muscular system include strains and cramps.

▶ Muscles and bones can be kept healthy with proper diet, exercise, and rest.

Reviewing the Chapter

SCIENCE WORDS

A. Use all the terms below to complete the sentences.

simple fracture   skull   compound fracture
bone marrow   skeleton   cartilage

    The system of bones that supports and protects the body and the organs inside it is the __1__. The bones of the face are part of the __2__. New blood cells are made by a soft material called __3__. Pads of __4__ prevent the small bones of the back from rubbing together. A break in a bone in which the broken end pushes through muscle and skin is a/an __5__. A break in a bone in which this does not happen is called a/an __6__.

B. Write the letter of the term that best matches the definition. Not all the terms will be used.

1. Attaches muscles to bone
2. Injury that is caused by overstretching a muscle or tendon
3. The place where two or more bones are joined together
4. Any crack or break in a bone
5. Muscle that you can control
6. Holds bones together at a joint
7. Muscle that you cannot control
8. Sudden strong muscle contraction
9. Injury in which a ligament is torn or stretched

  a. involuntary muscle
  b. sprain
  c. cramp
  d. ligament
  e. fracture
  f. skull
  g. strain
  h. tendon
  i. bone marrow
  j. voluntary muscle
  k. joint

USING IDEAS

A. Identify each of the following.

1. It is a kind of muscle. It makes up the hardest working muscle in the body. What is it?
2. It is a kind of muscle. It makes up the inside of the blood vessels, stomach, and other organs. What is it?
3. It is a kind of muscle. It is muscle that moves bones. What is it?

B. Write the name of each kind of joint shown in the drawings below.

1

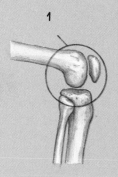

2

3

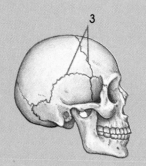

4

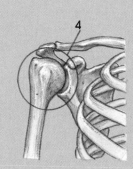

C. Name the four food groups.

1. Identify three different foods in each group.
2. Describe how the foods in each food group help to keep your bones and muscles healthy and working in the proper way.

UNDERSTANDING IDEAS

1. Prepare three menus—one for breakfast, one for lunch, and one for dinner. Be sure each meal includes foods from all four food groups.

2. Use a reference book to find out what type of injury a dislocated bone is. Write a brief description of this injury and the type of treatment that is given.

THINKING LIKE A SCIENTIST

Answer the following questions. You may be able to answer some of the questions just by thinking about them. To answer other questions you may have to do some research.

1. On the top of a newborn baby's head there is a soft spot called a fontanel. If you touch gently on the spot, you can feel the baby's heartbeat. A fontanel is an opening in the baby's skull. As the baby grows, the bones of the skull grow together and close. Why, do you think, do babies have fontanels?

2. Did you know that you are slightly taller in the morning than you are at night? Why is this so? (HINT: Think about the cartilage found between the vertebrae in your backbone.)

3. Put your right elbow on your desk. Use your right hand to lift a book off the desk. Your arm is working like a simple machine. Which simple machine is it working like? Explain your answer.

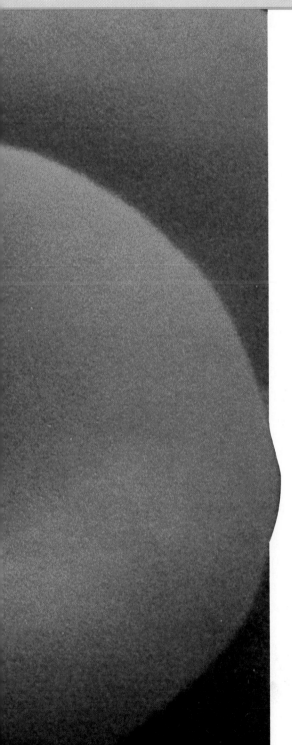

Chapter 14

Transport Systems of the Body

These red blood cells are part of a transport system. The heart and blood vessels transport blood throughout the body. The red blood cells carry oxygen to other body cells that need it. Your lungs are part of another transport system. This system helps your body use oxygen in the air.

In this chapter you will learn about the three main transport systems of the body. You will learn about the structures of these systems and how they work. You will also learn about some of the diseases that affect these systems.

The Circulatory System

What are the two jobs of the circulatory system?

The **circulatory** (sėr′kyə lə tôr ē) **system** is one of the body's transport systems. It carries needed materials, such as food and oxygen, to the cells of the body. It also carries away waste products. Another important job of the circulatory system is to protect the body from disease. The circulatory system has three main parts that help it perform its jobs. These parts are the blood, the heart, and the blood vessels.

How much blood is in the body? An average adult's body contains 5 L of blood. Blood is a liquid with solid parts floating in it. The liquid part of the blood is called **plasma** (plaz′mə). Plasma is yellowish in color and is mostly water. It contains digested food materials and waste products. Plasma makes up over half of the blood.

There are three different kinds of solid parts in the blood. The first solid part of the blood is the **red blood cells.** Red blood cells pick up oxygen in the lungs and carry it to all the cells of the body. Red cells can do this because they contain a special chemical called hemoglobin (hē′mə glō bən). The hemoglobin in red blood cells contains iron and makes blood look red. Red blood cells also pick up carbon dioxide from the cells and carry it to the lungs. Then this waste gas is breathed out.

A red blood cell looks something like a doughnut without a hole. This shape is shown in the picture. A red blood cell is very small. A single drop of blood contains about 5 million red blood cells.

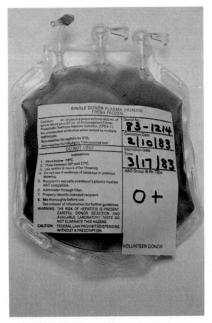

Container of plasma

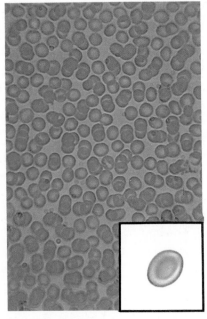

Red blood cells

White blood cells are the second solid part of the blood. They help the body fight infection. Some white blood cells are shown in the picture. White blood cells do not contain hemoglobin. Although they are called white cells, they really have no color. White blood cells change shape as they move. Sometimes they even squeeze through the walls of blood vessels. They move out into infected parts of the body, where they destroy bacteria and other harmful things. White blood cells surround and digest the bacteria.

Have you ever had a cut or scratch that bled? A cut will bleed for a short time. But usually the bleeding soon stops. The **platelets** (plāt′lits), the third solid part of the blood, stop the bleeding. Platelets cause the blood to thicken and clot. The drawing below shows this process.

Platelets are not whole cells. They are parts of cells that form clots of blood. These blood clots

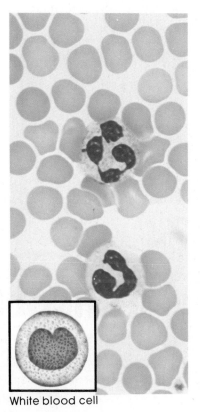

White blood cell

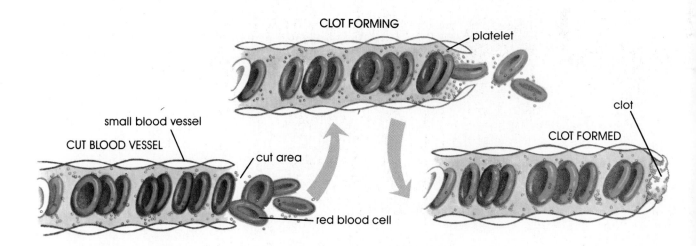

CLOT FORMING

platelet

small blood vessel

CUT BLOOD VESSEL

cut area

clot

CLOT FORMED

red blood cell

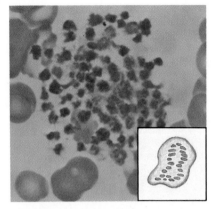

Platelets

keep the wound from bleeding while the cut heals. Like white blood cells, they have no color. They are much smaller than red blood cells. Look for the platelets in the picture to the left. Without platelets to control bleeding, a person could bleed to death from a cut.

Science & TECHNOLOGY

▶ An artificial heart replaces the two lower chambers of a person's natural heart. In 1982, the first permanent artificial heart was placed in a human being, Dr. Barney Clark. The Jarvik-7 heart, made of plastic and aluminum, runs on electricity. One patient has lived over a year with this type of artificial heart.

◀ A temporary artificial heart, called the Pennsylvania State heart, was first used in 1985. It is similar to the Jarvik-7. But its design helps to prevent blood clots. The Penn State heart is used to keep the patient alive until a donor heart can be found.

There are some problems with the use of artificial hearts. Since tubes must pass through the skin, infection is a danger. Also, the hearts can cause blood clots and strokes. Patients must be connected to machines at all times. Why do you think people disagree on whether artificial hearts should be used?

Circulation of Blood

How does blood move through the body?

The second main part of the circulatory system is the heart. The heart is a strong, hollow muscle about the size of a fist. It is located in the center of the chest. As long as you are alive, your heart never stops working. A normal heart beats about 70 to 80 times per minute.

There are four cavities, or hollow chambers, in the heart. Each upper chamber of the heart is called an **atrium** (ā′trē əm). There is a right atrium and a left atrium. Blood collects in these thin-walled chambers. Each lower chamber of the heart is called a **ventricle** (ven′trə kəl). There is a right ventricle and a left ventricle. Ventricles have thick, muscular walls. They are the pumping chambers of the heart. Between each upper and lower chamber is a flap of tissue. This tissue acts as a valve. The valve keeps the blood from flowing backward. The drawing at the top of the page shows the heart chambers and valves.

There are three kinds of blood vessels: arteries, veins, and capillaries. An **artery** (är′tər ē) is a blood vessel that takes blood away from the heart. It usually carries blood that is rich in digested food and oxygen. A **vein** (vān) is a blood vessel that carries blood back to the heart from the body cells. This blood usually carries only waste products. A **capillary** (kap′ə ler ē) is a tiny blood vessel that connects an artery and a vein. Capillaries allow digested food, oxygen, and wastes to pass directly between the blood and the cells.

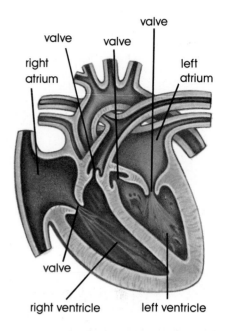

INSIDE THE HEART

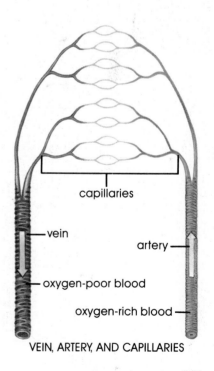

VEIN, ARTERY, AND CAPILLARIES

The drawing shows the path of blood through the circulatory system. Refer to the drawing as you read the steps.

1. Begin in the left atrium. The blood has just left the lungs. It has a rich supply of oxygen.

2. Blood passes from the left atrium through a valve into the left ventricle. From here the blood is pumped into a large artery.

3. The large artery branches into smaller and smaller arteries. These arteries go to all parts of the body.

4. Blood from the arteries enters the capillaries. Digested food and oxygen in the blood pass through the capillary walls into the cells.

5. Carbon dioxide and waste products from the cells pass through the capillary walls into the blood.

6. From the capillaries blood enters the smallest veins. The blood flows from the smallest veins into larger and larger veins.

7. Blood passes into the largest of the veins.

8. The largest veins return blood that is poor in oxygen to the right atrium.

9. Blood passes from the right atrium through a valve to the right ventricle. Then the blood is pumped into a large artery to the lungs.

10. In the lungs the blood loses carbon dioxide and picks up a fresh supply of oxygen.

11. Oxygen-rich blood from the lungs returns through veins to the left atrium.

12. The whole cycle begins again.

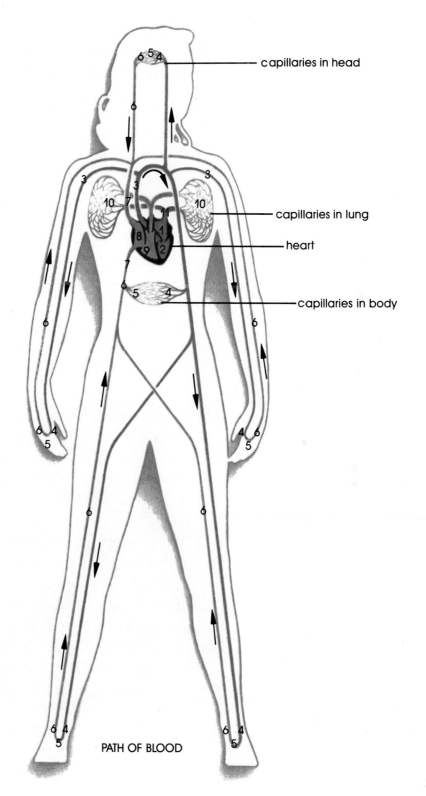

capillaries in head

capillaries in lung

heart

capillaries in body

PATH OF BLOOD

Diseases and Care of the Circulatory System

What are some circulatory problems?

Severe cuts can cause a loss of blood. No one can afford to lose large amounts of this substance. The best way to stop bleeding is to apply direct pressure to the wound. A clean cloth should be used to apply the pressure. To prevent infection, the wound should be covered with a bandage. A large, deep cut should be checked by a doctor.

Blood can also be lost in a nosebleed. The best way to stop a nosebleed is to hold the head straight and pinch the nostrils together. Sometimes a severe nosebleed must be treated in a doctor's office or a hospital.

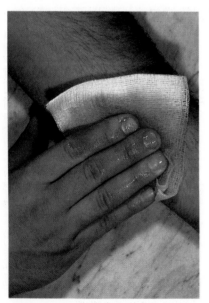

Applying direct pressure

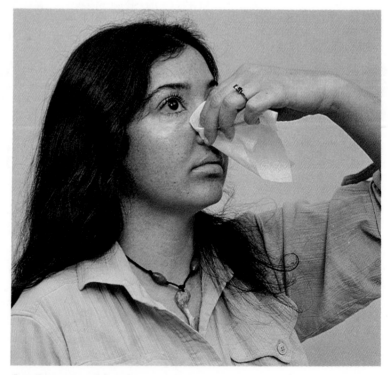

Treating a nosebleed

Each of the three main parts of the circulatory system can become diseased. For example, fat may build up in the walls of arteries. The inside of the arteries may then become clogged. The clogging of an artery is similar to the clogging of a water pipe with minerals. The drawings show how clogged arteries and clogged pipes are alike.

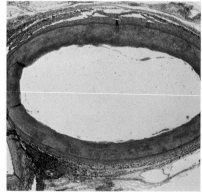
Normal artery

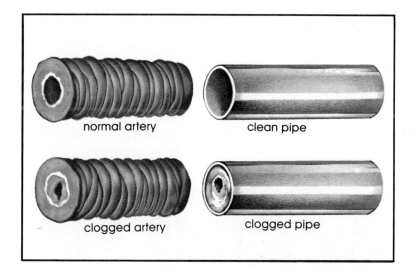
normal artery   clean pipe

clogged artery   clogged pipe

Clogged artery

Heart attack is a common heart problem. It occurs when the supply of blood to part of the heart is cut off. Usually the blood cannot reach the heart because the arteries that carry blood to the heart are clogged. If the blood supply is cut off too long, the heart can be permanently damaged. A person can die from a heart attack. It is a leading cause of death in the United States.

High blood pressure is another serious problem. Blood flowing through the arteries presses against the artery walls. This pressure is called the blood pressure. It can be measured with a special device. The picture shows a person having his blood pressure tested. Sometimes the blood

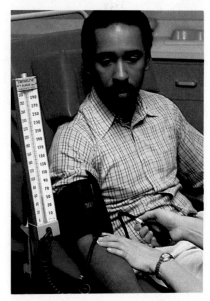
Taking blood pressure

pressure is too high. This causes the heart to work harder than it should. High blood pressure can often be controlled with certain kinds of medicine.

People can usually enjoy long, healthy lives if they take care of themselves. People who are very overweight and those who smoke are more likely to get circulatory system diseases. Eating foods that contain certain animal fats increases a person's risk of getting heart and blood vessel diseases. These fats build up in the blood and can clog the arteries. Exercise may reduce the level of fats in the blood. So it is helpful to exercise, to eat low-fat foods, and to avoid becoming overweight.

Checking weight

Low-fat foods

Exercise

Exercise is also good for the heart itself. Like other muscles, the heart benefits from exercise. Making the heart work harder with exercise helps to make it stronger. Exercise such as swimming, jogging, and jumping rope is good for the heart.

How does exercise affect the pulse rate?

Materials stopwatch or watch with second hand

Procedure

A. Work with a partner. Sit quietly and find your pulse as shown. Hold your index finger and middle finger against your wrist at the base of the thumb. Press firmly. Make sure you can feel the pulse.

B. Take your pulse for 15 seconds. Have your partner tell you when 15 seconds has passed. Multiply the number by 4. Record your pulse.
   1. What was your pulse rate?

C. Take and record your pulse rate two more times. Find and record the average rate. (Add the three readings and divide by 3.)
   2. What was your average pulse rate?

D. Jog in place for 1 minute. Take your pulse rate.
   3. What is your pulse rate after jogging?

	1	2	3	Average
Pulse rate while sitting				
Pulse rate after jogging				

E. Take and record your pulse rate after jogging two more times. Be sure there is a rest period before each 1-minute period of jogging.

F. Take your pulse 30 seconds, 1 minute, and 2 minutes after you stop jogging. Record these pulse rates on the back of your chart.

Conclusion

1. How is your average sitting pulse rate different from your average jogging pulse rate?
2. The pulse is the beating of the arteries with each heartbeat. What causes the pulse rate to change when you exercise?
3. What happened to your pulse rate 30 seconds after you stopped jogging? Why?

The Respiratory System

How does air move in and out of the lungs?

A healthy person can live several weeks without food. It is also possible for a healthy person to live a few days without water. But a person can live only a few minutes without air. A constant supply of air is necessary for life.

When you breathe, air enters your body through your respiratory (res′pər ə tôr ē) system. The **respiratory system** is another transport system of the body. It works closely with the circulatory system to put to use the oxygen in the air you breathe.

Receiving oxygen

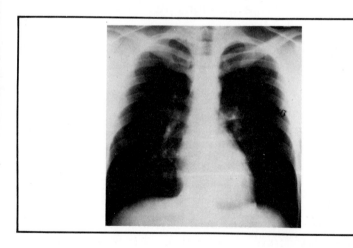

Living cells need oxygen from the air in order to use digested food from the blood. In each body cell, oxygen combines with digested food to release energy. Carbon dioxide and water are also given off. This process is called respiration. The respiratory and circulatory systems work together during the process of respiration.

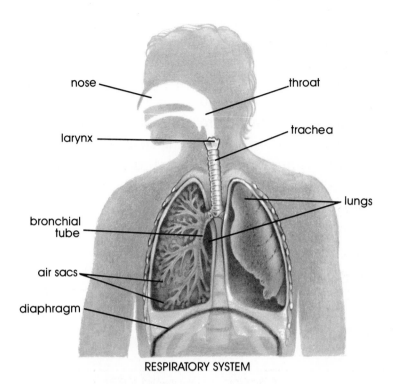

RESPIRATORY SYSTEM

The drawing shows the respiratory system. The steps below tell how oxygen in the air travels from outside the body to the cells inside the body.

1. When a person breathes in, air enters the nose. From the nose the air travels to the throat. The air then enters a soft tube with rings of cartilage around it. This tube is the windpipe, or **trachea** (trā′kē ə). The voice box, or **larynx** (lar′ingks), is at the top of the trachea. Air passing through the larynx lets a person make sounds for speaking or singing.

2. The trachea divides into two tubes. These tubes are called the **bronchial** (brong′kē əl) **tubes.** They lead to the lungs.

3. The lungs are made of spongy tissue. In the lungs the bronchial tubes divide many times into smaller branches. The smallest branch is thinner than a human hair.

4. At the ends of the tiny branches in the lungs are the air sacs. The air sacs look something like a bunch of grapes. They have very thin walls. Each sac is surrounded by a capillary. Gases can pass from the sacs into the capillaries and from the capillaries into the sacs.

5. Every time a person breathes in, the air sacs fill with air. Oxygen from the air leaves the air sacs and enters the blood through capillaries.

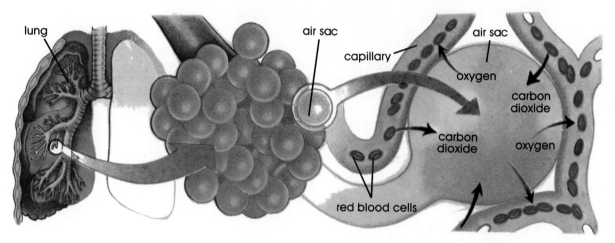

INSIDE THE LUNGS

Oxygen that is brought to the body cells by the blood is used to break down digested food. In the process, energy is released and waste products, such as carbon dioxide, are produced. Carbon dioxide passes into the blood and is carried to the lungs. In the lungs, carbon dioxide passes from the capillaries into the air sacs. When a person breathes out, carbon dioxide passes from the air sacs into the bronchial tubes. From there it goes to the outside air.

The **diaphragm** (dī′ə fram) is a thick sheet of muscle at the bottom of the chest cavity. It moves down when a person breathes in. This movement spreads the ribs and allows the lungs to expand.

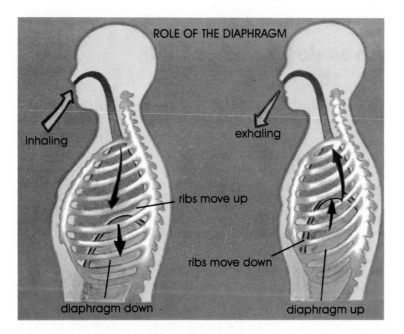

ROLE OF THE DIAPHRAGM

inhaling

exhaling

ribs move up

ribs move down

diaphragm down

diaphragm up

This process is called **inhaling** (in hāl'ing). When a person breathes out, the diaphragm moves up and the ribs come together. This movement pushes air out of the lungs. This process is called **exhaling** (eks hāl'ing). The drawings help show how air enters and leaves the lungs.

Finding Out

How does the diaphragm help to fill up the lungs?

You will need a 2-L plastic bottle, two balloons, scissors, and 2 rubber bands. Cut the bottle in half. Place one of the balloons through the opening of the bottle. Stretch the balloon opening over the bottle opening. Hold the balloon in place with a rubber band. Think of this balloon as the lungs. Cut the neck off the other balloon. Stretch this balloon across the bottom of the bottle. Hold the balloon in place with a rubber band. Think of this balloon as the diaphragm. Pull down on the stretched balloon. What happens to the balloon in the bottle? Explain how this action is like that of the lungs and the diaphragm.

How much air do your lungs hold?

Materials large empty plastic milk jug with cap / plastic dishpan / rubber tubing / drinking straw / masking tape / grease pencil / graduate

Procedure

A. Work with a partner. Place a piece of masking tape on a plastic milk jug from top to bottom as shown.

B. Fill the jug with water. Screw the cap on the jug. Fill a dishpan about one third full of water. Place the jug upside down in the water. Carefully remove the cap. Do not let air bubbles enter the jug.

C. Ask your partner to hold the jug so that it does not tip over. Place one end of the tubing inside the jug. Put a straw in the other end of the tubing. Take a deep breath and blow through the straw.
   1. What happens to the water in the jug?
   2. Where did the air in your lungs go?

D. While the neck of the jug is still underwater, replace the cap on the jug. Do not let any water out of the jug.

E. Remove the jug from the dishpan. Turn the jug right side up. Mark the level of water on the tape.

F. Use a graduate to fill the jug with water.
   3. How much water did you add?

G. The amount of water you just added to the jug is equal to the amount of air you blew into the jug.
   4. How much air did you blow into the jug?

H. Repeat steps **B–F** two more times. Take an average of the three volumes of air collected.
   5. What was the average volume of air blown into the jug?

Conclusion
How much air do your lungs hold?

Diseases and Care of the Respiratory System

What are some common respiratory diseases?

Think back to the last time you had a cold. Colds are one of the most common diseases of the respiratory system. Colds are easily spread from one person to another. Every time a person sneezes or coughs, germs are sprayed into the air. People nearby may breathe in the germs. When you cough or blow your nose, germs may be spread to your hands. What can you do to help prevent the spread of colds?

Ragweed—a plant that causes allergies

Do you know someone who has allergies? An allergy is a strong reaction to a substance that is not normally in the body. Plant pollen and dust are such substances. They often enter the body through the respiratory system. These materials can cause sneezing, headaches, or difficult breathing. Many people are allergic to the pollen of ragweed, shown in the picture.

Warning labels on cigarettes

Bronchitis (brong kī′tis) is another respiratory disease. In this disease the bronchial tubes become red and swollen. Sometimes bronchitis can lead to other diseases of the lungs.

Another disease of the respiratory system is lung cancer. Lung cancer has several causes. One cause is breathing polluted air. Another cause is smoking cigarettes. The pictures show a lung from a person who did not smoke and a lung from a smoker. Which would you rather have in your body? Over half the people with lung cancer smoked cigarettes. Because of the dangers of smoking, every package of cigarettes must carry a warning label.

Exercising for good health

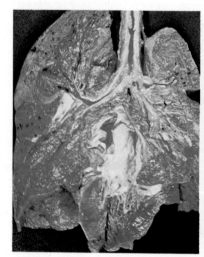

Healthy lung

Smoker's lung

Regular exercise is needed for a healthy respiratory system. When strenuous exercise is done, the diaphragm becomes stronger. A stronger diaphragm allows a person to take in more air. With more air in the lungs, more oxygen can be sent to the body cells. Then the cells can work better to release energy from digested food.

The Excretory System

What waste products are removed by the excretory system?

The **excretory** (eks′krə tôr ē) **system** is the transport system that removes waste products from the body. Waste products are the unwanted materials left over from life processes such as respiration. Living things will die if they do not get rid of waste products.

Many body parts get rid of waste products. The kidneys are among the main organs of the excretory system. But the lungs and the skin may also be thought of as parts of the excretory system.

The lungs get rid of one main waste product. This product is carbon dioxide. They also get rid of some moisture. These materials leave the body each time a person exhales. You may be surprised to learn that the skin is also a part of the excretory system. One layer of the skin contains sweat glands. Find them in the drawing. When a person sweats, water leaves the body through pores. This water contains many waste materials. Sweating gets rid of extra water and wastes.

Replacing lost fluids

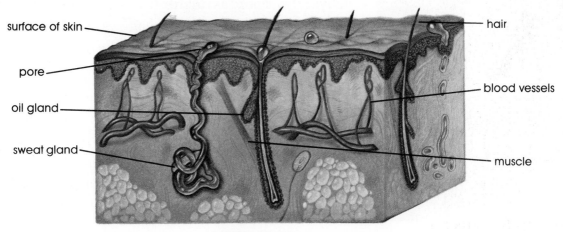

surface of skin

pore

oil gland

sweat gland

hair

blood vessels

muscle

LAYERS OF SKIN

Most of the waste water in the body is removed by the kidneys. Normally a person has two kidneys. They are located in the lower back, one on each side of the backbone. The drawing below shows the parts of the excretory system.

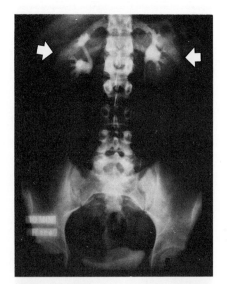

X ray of kidneys

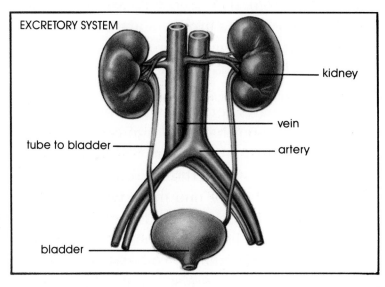

EXCRETORY SYSTEM

kidney

vein

tube to bladder

artery

bladder

All the blood passes through the kidneys. As it does, the kidneys take out waste materials and excess water. These dissolved wastes and excess water are taken through small tubes to the bladder for storage. Finally, the water and wastes leave the body as **urine** (yŭr′ən). Urine is water with wastes and salts dissolved in it. Solid human waste is removed from the body by the large intestine, which is part of the digestive system.

If the kidneys become diseased, they may stop working properly. Harmful waste products will then build up in the body. People with diseased kidneys can use a special machine to remove wastes from the blood. A person using one of these machines is shown in the picture. These machines have saved many lives.

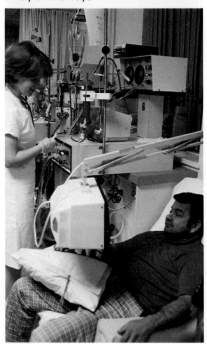

Person using kidney machine

To keep the excretory system healthy, a person should drink several glasses of water each day. The water will replace water that is lost when waste products are removed. Water can be supplied to the body by various foods. It is found in such foods as milk, soup, and juice, as well as in juicy fruits and vegetables.

Ideas to Remember

▶ The transport systems of the body are the circulatory system, the respiratory system, and the excretory system.

▶ The blood, the heart, and the blood vessels are parts of the circulatory system.

▶ The circulatory system carries digested food and oxygen to cells and carries away wastes. It also protects the body from disease.

▶ The nose, the trachea, the bronchial tubes, the lungs, and the air sacs are parts of the respiratory system.

▶ The respiratory system brings oxygen into the body and removes carbon dioxide and some water.

▶ The parts of the excretory system include the kidneys, the skin, and the lungs.

▶ The excretory system gets rid of waste products.

Reviewing the Chapter

SCIENCE WORDS

A. Identify each of the following.

1. It is a type of blood vessel. Its walls are thin. It carries blood from the body cells back to the heart. What is it?
2. It is a thick sheet of muscle. It is found at the bottom of the chest cavity. It helps in breathing. What is it?
3. It is one of the body's transport systems. It carries food and oxygen to the cells. It defends the body against disease. What is it?

B. Write the letter of the term that best matches the definition. Not all the terms will be used.

1. Lower chamber of the heart
2. Windpipe
3. Cell that helps in clotting
4. Waste formed of water and dissolved salts
5. Thick-walled blood vessel
6. Cell shaped like a doughnut without a hole
7. Process of breathing out
8. Upper chamber of the heart
9. Voice box
10. Smallest blood vessel

a. capillary
b. inhaling
c. red blood cell
d. atrium
e. larynx
f. exhaling
g. trachea
h. ventricle
i. urine
j. platelet
k. artery
l. white blood cell

UNDERSTANDING IDEAS

A. Make a chart like the one shown. Write each science term under the correct heading of the chart.

kidneys   air sacs   bronchial tubes   skin
trachea   atrium   diaphragm   lungs
bladder   nose   ventricle   artery

Circulatory system	Respiratory system	Excretory system

B. Write the correct term for each number in the diagram. Then describe the process of respiration.

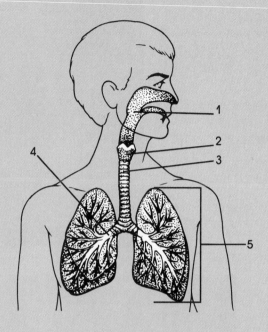

USING IDEAS

Do some research at the library on the effects of pollution on health. Write a report about how air pollution harms the circulatory and respiratory systems.

THINKING LIKE A SCIENTIST

Answer the following questions. You may be able to answer some of the questions just by thinking about them. To answer other questions you may have to do some research.

1. Oxygen-rich blood is red in color. Oxygen-poor blood appears slightly bluish. Suppose you saw a person begin to turn a bluish color around the lips. What would this indicate?

2. Why do people who smoke often have a more difficult time breathing when they exercise than do people who do not smoke?

Science in Careers

There are many careers available in the health field. An **emergency medical technician** (EMT) is a public-health worker. EMTs usually work in teams on rescue squads. They give aid in many situations. They give on-the-scene treatment to victims of automobile accidents, heart attacks, near drownings, and poisonings. This type of emergency treatment saves thousands of lives each year. An EMT must have at least an 80-hour basic course. The need for additional training varies.

Dietitians (dī ə tish' ənz) provide an important health service. Some dietitians work in schools or in businesses. They plan menus so that meals have the proper amounts of foods from each food group. Many dietitians plan special diets for people in hospitals and nursing homes.

Physical therapists help people with diseases or injuries of muscles, bones, joints, or nerves. They test the strength of muscles and develop treatment programs, such as special exercises. They help disabled people adjust to physical problems.

Emergency medical technicians

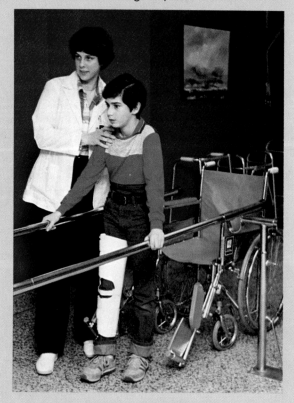

Physical therapist

People in Science

WILLIAM DeVRIES
(1943-   )

Dr. DeVries is the skillful young surgeon who placed the first permanent artificial heart into the chest of a human being. Dr. DeVries prepared over 3 years for the task. He practiced the operation 200 times on sheep and calves.

Dr. DeVries enjoys the challenge of surgery. "You have to pay attention to a million different things at once," he says. "You know you're doing something really important."

Dr. DeVries and his staff placing artificial heart in patient

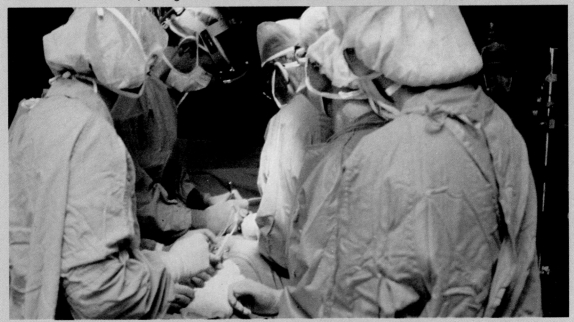

Developing Skills

The table lists some word parts that come from other languages and gives their meanings. Use the table to help you write a definition for each of the following words. You can do this by breaking each word into parts. For example, the word *hemophilia* is made up of these parts: *hemo-* + *philia*.

1. hemophilia
2. cardiology
3. leukocyte
4. bronchitis
5. erythrocyte
6. hemostasis
7. cardiograph
8. transport

Word part	Meaning
bronch-	bronchial tubes
cardio-	heart
erythro-	red
hemo-	blood
leuko-	white
trans-	across, to the other side
-cyte	cell
-graph	instrument that writes or records
-itis	swelling of
-logy	science of
-philia	tending toward
-port	to carry
-stasis	stopping, slowing

READING A BAR GRAPH

A bar graph can be used to compare facts. Look at the bar graph on the next page. The graph compares facts about heart disease in 7 different years. It shows how many people died from heart disease in the years 1920 to 1980. The numbers show how many deaths there were for every 100,000 Americans. For example, the number 163 means that 163 out of every 100,000 Americans died of heart disease. Use the bar graph to answer the following questions.

1. During which year did the most people die of heart disease?

2. During which year did the fewest people die of heart disease?

3. In general, how did the number of Americans that died from heart disease change from 1920 to 1980?

4. How did the number of Americans that died from heart disease change from 1960 to 1980?

5. During which year did more people die of heart disease–1970 or 1980?

6. How many more people per 100,000 died of heart disease in 1960 than in 1940?

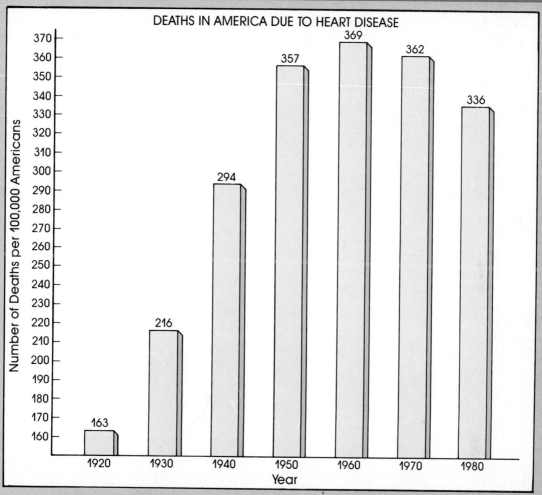

DEATHS IN AMERICA DUE TO HEART DISEASE

Number of Deaths per 100,000 Americans vs. Year

- 1920: 163
- 1930: 216
- 1940: 294
- 1950: 357
- 1960: 369
- 1970: 362
- 1980: 336

USING THINKING SKILLS

Heart disease is one of the biggest killers of Americans today. One method of treating people with severe heart disease is to perform a heart transplant. Another method is to give the person an artificial heart. Think about this as you answer the following questions.

1. One problem with depending on heart transplants is a shortage of heart donors. A long search is usually needed before the right heart is found for a person who needs one. How do you think doctors should decide who gets a specific heart? Explain your answer.

2. There are many problems with using an artificial heart. For one thing, people with artificial hearts have not lived for long periods of time. People who have artificial hearts have to be connected to many pieces of equipment. Should doctors continue to use artificial hearts? Explain your answer.

Study Guide

Reading your book will help you learn more about the world around you. Your book will provide answers to many questions you may have about living things, the earth, space, matter, and energy.

On the following pages you will find questions from each lesson in your book. These questions will help test your understanding of the terms and ideas you read about. You will also find information about metric measurement.

There are three sections for each chapter. You can answer questions in the first section, "Lesson Questions," by using the information you read in each chapter. Careful reading will help answer these questions.

The second section is called "Problem Solving." These questions are more challenging. The answer may not be found just by reading the lesson. You may have to think harder.

The third section is called "Skills." In this section you will be asked to read tables and graphs.

Units of Measurement 364

Chapter 1 **Activities of Green Plants** 366

Chapter 2 **Animals Without a Backbone** 368

Chapter 3 **Animals With a Backbone** 370

Chapter 4 **Living Communities** 372

Chapter 5 **Building Blocks of Matter** 374

Chapter 6 **Physical Changes in Matter** 376

Chapter 7 **Understanding Electricity** 378

Chapter 8 **Sources of Energy** 380

Chapter 9 **Changes in the Earth** 382

Chapter 10 **Cleaning Up the Earth** 384

Chapter 11 **Changes in the Weather** 386

Chapter 12 **Beyond the Solar System** 388

Chapter 13 **Support and Movement of the Body** 390

Chapter 14 **Transport Systems of the Body** 392

Units of Measurement

Two systems of measurement are used in the United States, the metric system and the English system. Feet, yards, pounds, ounces, and quarts are English units. Meters, kilometers, kilograms, grams, and liters are metric units. Only metric measurements are used in science. The following tables list some metric and English units. The tables show what each unit is approximately equal to in the other system. The metric mass/English weight relationships hold true for objects on the earth.

MEASUREMENT	METRIC UNITS (symbol)	EQUAL TO IN ENGLISH UNITS (symbol)
Length	1 millimeter (mm)	0.04 inch (in.)
	1 centimeter (cm)	0.4 inch (in.)
	1 meter (m)	39.4 inches (in.) or
		1.1 yards (yd)
	1 kilometer (km)	0.6 mile (mi)
Mass (weight)	1 gram (g)	0.035 ounce (oz)
	1 kilogram (kg)	2.2 pounds (lb)
Volume	1 liter (L)	1.06 quarts (qt)

MEASUREMENT	ENGLISH UNITS (symbol)	EQUAL TO IN METRIC UNITS (symbol)
Length	1 inch (in.)	2.5 centimeters (cm) or
		25 millimeters (mm)
	1 foot (ft)	30.5 centimeters (cm)
	1 yard (yd)	0.91 meter (m)
	1 mile (mi)	1.6 kilometers (km)
Weight (mass)	1 ounce (oz)	28.4 grams (g)
	1 pound (lb)	0.45 kilogram (kg)
Volume	1 quart (qt)	0.95 liter (L)

Chapter 1

Activities of Green Plants

LESSON QUESTIONS

Plants and Animals Are Alike (pp. 4–5)

1. What is a cell?
2. Describe four life processes.

Transporting Materials (pp. 6–11)

1. How do green plants get the materials they need to make food?
2. What are root hairs? Why are root hairs important?
3. Describe a plant stem.
4. What structures in a leaf are used by the plant to make food?

Food Making in a Leaf (pp. 12–15)

1. What is photosynthesis?
2. How is chlorophyll different from a chloroplast?
3. Describe how food is made by a plant.

Using the Energy in Food (pp. 16–17)

1. What is respiration?
2. What happens during respiration?

Producing New Plants (pp. 18–23)

1. What is reproduction?
2. Identify the parts of the flower shown below.
3. What is pollination?
4. Describe two ways flowers may be pollinated.
5. How does fertilization take place in a plant?
6. Define the term *germination*.

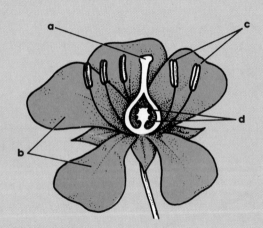

PROBLEM SOLVING

Use after page 11.
Gardeners sometimes dig around the base of a plant to loosen the soil. How does this benefit the plant?

Use after page 17.
Certain plants can be grown in rich, moist soil in sealed glass containers called terrariums. Plants grown in this way do not need to be watered. How can the plants carry on photosynthesis and respiration in the closed containers?

Use after page 23.
Many people are allergic to pollen dust. They might sneeze, have itchy noses, or have trouble breathing. How does pollen get into these people's lungs? During which seasons are the people more likely to be bothered by the allergy? During which seasons are they less likely to be bothered?

Reading a Map

A map can contain many types of information. The map shown here indicates different plant regions in the world. Use the map to answer the following questions.

1. What six regions are shown on this map?

2. On which continents can the mountain and tundra region be found?

3. Which regions can be found in Australia?

4. Which regions can be found in Africa?

5. Can the desert region be found in South America?

PLANT REGIONS

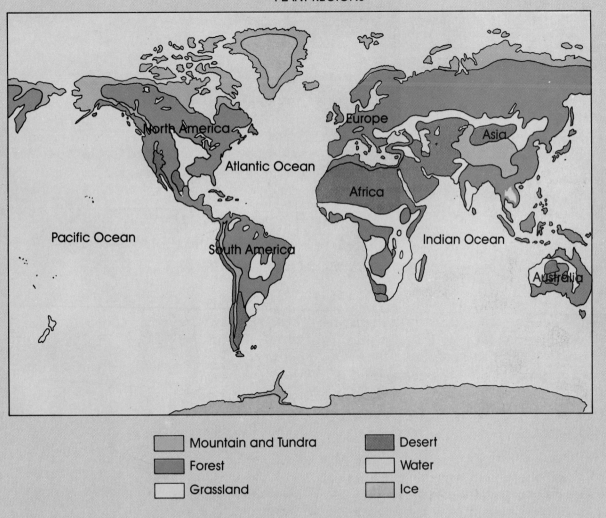

Mountain and Tundra

Forest

Grassland

Desert

Water

Ice

Chapter 2

Animals Without a Backbone

LESSON QUESTIONS

Classifying Living Things (pp. 28–29)
1. How do scientists classify animals?
2. Describe two large groups of animals.

Sponges (pp. 30–31)
1. Describe the structure of a sponge.
2. Describe the skeleton of a sponge.

Animals with Stinging Cells (pp. 32–33)
1. Name two animals with stinging cells.
2. Describe the body of a typical animal with stinging cells.
3. How does an animal with stinging cells use its stinging cells?

Worms (pp. 34–38)
1. Name three groups of worms.
2. Describe two types of flatworms.
3. Describe the structure of an earthworm. To which group of worms do earthworms belong?

Animals with Spiny Skin (pp. 39–40)
1. What is a spiny-skinned invertebrate called?
2. How does a starfish get food?

Animals with a Soft Body (pp. 41–44)
1. What is an invertebrate with a soft body called?
2. Name three types of animals with a soft body.
3. Describe the structure of a clam.

Animals with Jointed Legs (pp. 45–53)
1. What is an arthropod?
2. Describe the structure of an arthropod.
3. Name four groups of arthropods. Give an example of each group.
4. Describe the three parts of an insect body.
5. Describe three different types of special mouth parts found in insects.

PROBLEM SOLVING

Use after page 33.
When jellyfish die and wash up onto the shore, they disappear much faster than do fish that die and wash up onto the shore. Why, do you think, does this happen?

Use after page 38.
A storybook for little children contained the following paragraph.

Little Wendell Worm was crawling happily through the desert, searching for a new place to make a nest in the sand. He had been moving along at a fast pace when suddenly he looked up and spotted a fat robin. "Oh, no!" squeaked Wendell. "I'm in trouble now!" And he dashed over to a bush and hid under a large green leaf.

What is scientifically wrong in this?

Use after page 44.
If animals were classified simply on appearance, the jellyfish, octopus, and squid might all be grouped together. Why aren't these animals in the same group?

Use after page 53.
Most invertebrates live in water. Most arthropods do not. What parts of their bodies enable arthropods to live on land?

Reading a Circle Graph

Look at these circle graphs. A circle graph is a good way to show how something is divided. The large circle graph shows how animals are divided, or classified, into major animal groups. It gives the number of different kinds of animals in each group. The smaller circle graph shows the major groups of vertebrates and gives the number of kinds in each.

Use the circle graphs to answer these questions.

1. Which is the largest major group of animals? Which is the smallest major group?

2. How many kinds of echinoderms are there? How many kinds of arthropods are there?

3. Which is the smallest group of vertebrates? The largest?

4. How many more kinds of worms are there than kinds of reptiles?

NUMBER OF KINDS OF ANIMALS IN MAJOR ANIMAL GROUPS

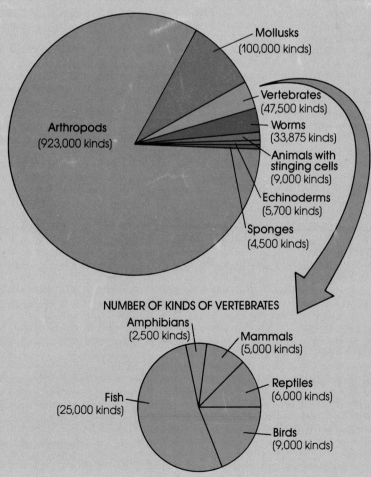

Mollusks
(100,000 kinds)

Vertebrates
(47,500 kinds)

Worms
(33,875 kinds)

Animals with
stinging cells
(9,000 kinds)

Echinoderms
(5,700 kinds)

Sponges
(4,500 kinds)

Arthropods
(923,000 kinds)

NUMBER OF KINDS OF VERTEBRATES

Amphibians
(2,500 kinds)

Mammals
(5,000 kinds)

Fish
(25,000 kinds)

Reptiles
(6,000 kinds)

Birds
(9,000 kinds)

Chapter 3

Animals With a Backbone

LESSON QUESTIONS

Fish (pp. 58–60)
1. What is a cold-blooded animal?
2. Identify the parts of the fish below.
3. How do fish get oxygen?

Amphibians (pp. 61–62)
1. What is an amphibian? Give two examples of amphibians.

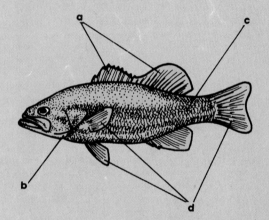

2. Describe how most adult amphibians breathe.
3. Describe the stages of growth in a frog.

Reptiles (pp. 63–66)
1. What is a reptile? Give two examples of reptiles.
2. How do alligators differ from crocodiles?
3. How do snakes eat?

Birds (pp. 67–70)
1. What is a warm-blooded animal?
2. Describe the characteristics of birds.
3. Describe how the structure of their bones and feathers helps birds to fly.

Mammals (pp. 72–75)
1. What is a mammal?
2. How do mammals differ from other vertebrates?
3. Describe how mammals differ from each other.

PROBLEM SOLVING

Use after page 60.
Do you think it is possible to catch fish through a hole in a frozen lake? Explain your answer in scientific terms.

Use after page 62.
Scientists can draw conclusions about what an animal eats by looking at where it lives and what it looks like. What conclusions can you make about what a tadpole eats and what a frog eats?

Use after page 71.
You can tell something about how a bird flies by looking at its wings and the size and shape of its body. Think about a sparrow, a chicken, a hawk, a duck, an ostrich, a hummingbird, and a goose. Which of these birds can soar for long periods of time? How do the wings of these birds compare to their body size? Which of the birds can travel long distances? How do the wings of these birds compare to their body size? Which birds do not fly very well? How do the wings of these birds compare to their body size?

SKILL

Reading a Table

Tables can be used to show and compare information. This table gives you the names of different animal groups and the names of different animals and their young. Use the table to answer the following questions.

1. What is a female hog called?
2. What is a group of lions called?
3. What is a young kangaroo called?
4. Which animals in the table travel in groups called herds?
5. Which of the male animals are called bulls?
6. What is a young seal called? What is a young turkey called?

NAMES FOR ANIMAL GROUPS, ANIMALS, AND THEIR YOUNG

Animal	Group	Adult Male	Adult Female	Young
antelope	herd	buck	doe	kid
bear	sloth	boar	sow	cub
cat	clowder	tom	puss	kitten
cattle	herd or drove	bull	cow	calf
deer	herd	buck	doe	fawn
elephant	herd	bull	cow	calf
goose	flock or gaggle	gander	goose	gosling
hog	herd or drove	boar	sow	shoat or piglet
kangaroo	troop or mob	buck	doe	joey
lion	pride	lion	lioness	cub
rabbit	warren	buck	doe	kit or kitten
seal	herd or trip	bull	cow	pup or whelp
turkey	flock	tom	hen	poult
whale	herd	bull	cow	calf

Chapter 4

Living Communities

LESSON QUESTIONS

The Living and Nonliving World (pp. 82–83)

1. What is your environment?
2. What is ecology?
3. Describe a large ecosystem and a small ecosystem.

Living Things in Ecosystems (pp. 84–90)

1. Describe a community that might be found in a park near your school.
2. Describe the habitat of each animal shown below.

3. How is a niche different from a habitat?

Changes in Populations (pp. 91–94)

1. What factors might affect the birth rate of a population?
2. Give an example of a predator and an example of its prey.

Changes in Communities (pp. 95–100)

1. What things might cause major changes in whole communities?
2. Describe the stages of succession in the forest below.

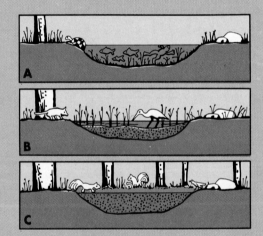

PROBLEM SOLVING

Use after page 90.

People design tools to help them solve problems. The ax and the machete are two tools that people have invented to be used in different ecosystems. Where is each tool used? How does each tool help to solve a problem?

Use after page 94.

Sometimes scientists disagree about how to handle increasing populations of animal pests such as gypsy moths. In the caterpillar stage they cause widespread damage to trees. Insecticides are often used to try to control the caterpillars. But many scientists argue that leaving the caterpillars alone is the best solution. How could this problem be solved? What is the scientists' hypothesis?

SKILL

Reading a Line Graph

Some line graphs contain only one line. Other line graphs, like the one shown here, contain two lines. This line graph compares the population of a group of lynx with the population of a group of rabbits. As you can see, the graph compares these populations over 90 years. Use the graph to answer the following questions.

1. During which year was the rabbit population the greatest?

2. During which year was the lynx population the greatest?

3. During which year was the rabbit population the lowest?

4. During which year was the lynx population the lowest?

5. What happened to the lynx population every time the rabbit population increased?

6. What happened to the lynx population every time the rabbit population decreased?

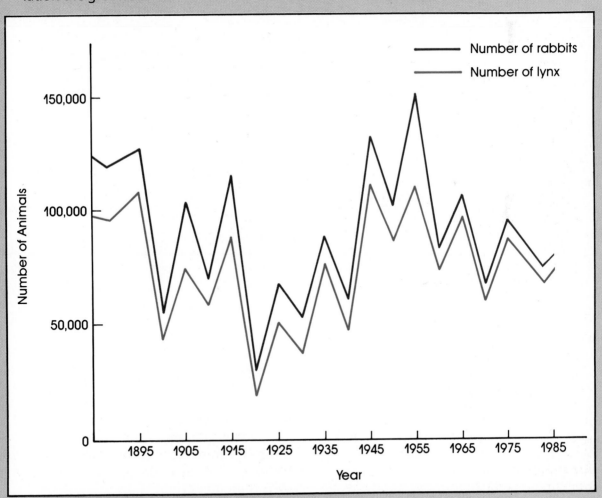

Chapter 5

Building Blocks of Matter

LESSON QUESTIONS

Studying Matter (pp. 112–115)

1. What is matter?
2. How do scientists study matter? What have they learned?
3. What is indirect evidence? How is indirect evidence used to study matter?

The Atom (pp. 116–117)

1. What is an atom?
2. Identify the parts of this atom.

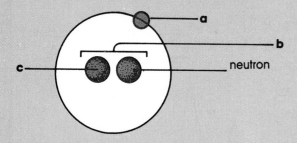

Elements (pp. 118–121)

1. What is an element? Name three elements.
2. How do elements differ?
3. What element has the symbol Hg? What element has the symbol C? What is the symbol for iron?

Molecules and Compounds (pp. 122–129)

1. How is a compound different from an element?
2. What is a molecule?
3. Identify the parts of the water molecule shown below.
4. What is the formula for the molecule shown below the water molecule?

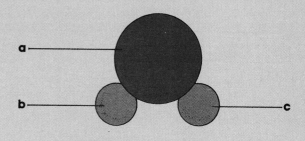

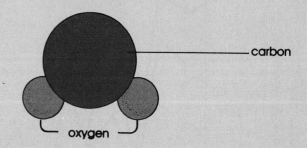

PROBLEM SOLVING

Use with page 115.
Long ago, scientists used indirect evidence to conclude that the earth is round. Today, we have direct evidence of this. What is this direct evidence?

Use with page 121.
Scientists throughout the world use the same names and symbols for the elements. Why is this important?

Reading a Bar Graph

This bar graph shows the density of different elements. Use the graph to answer the following questions.

1. What is the most dense element shown?

2. What is the least dense element shown?

3. Which elements shown are more dense than silver?

4. How much more dense is mercury than carbon?

5. Topaz is a mineral with a density of about 3.6. Which of the elements in the table are more dense than topaz? Which are less dense?

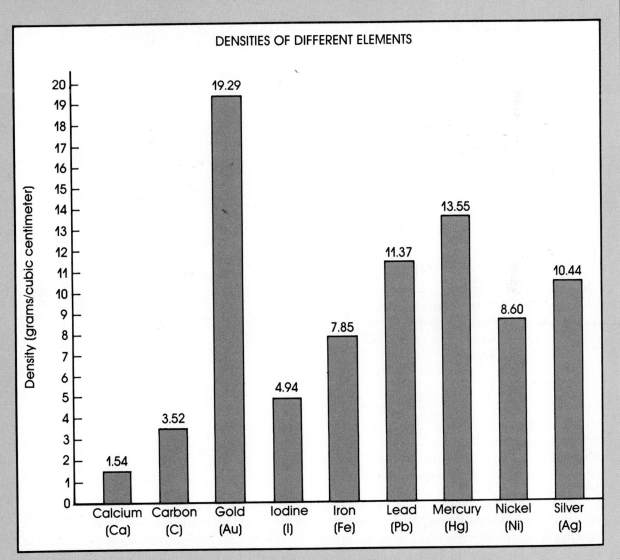

DENSITIES OF DIFFERENT ELEMENTS

Chapter 6

Physical Changes in Matter

LESSON QUESTIONS

Physical Properties (pp. 134–135)

1. What is a physical property? Give two examples of physical properties.
2. What is density? How is the density of a material determined?

Physical Changes (pp. 136–141)

1. What is a physical change? Give two examples of physical changes.
2. What are the three states of matter?
3. How do the particles that make up a gas differ from the particles that make up a solid?
4. What is a melting point? How does melting point differ from boiling point?
5. How is energy involved in changes of state?

Mixtures (pp. 142–144)

1. What is a mixture? How is a mixture different from a compound?
2. Give two examples of mixtures.

Two Kinds of Mixtures (pp. 145–148)

1. How is a solution different from a suspension?

2. How is a solute different from a solvent?
3. What factors might affect how fast a solute dissolves?
4. Explain why a chalk-and-water mixture is not a solution.

Another Kind of Change (pp. 149–150)

1. What is a chemical change?
2. Which of the following is an example of a fast chemical change? Which is an example of a slow chemical change?

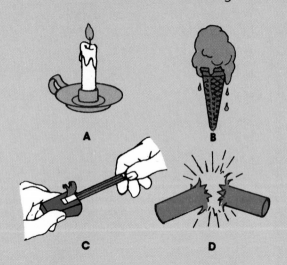

PROBLEM SOLVING

Use after page 141.

How are liquids like honey, tree sap, tar, and glue different from liquids like water, milk, and orange juice? Explain the difference in terms of the movement of particles.

Use after page 148.

Two boys decide to paint their bicycles. They have four unmarked cans of paint. Two of the cans have water as a basic ingredient. The other two cans have oil. The boys mix two cans. How will they know if they have mixed a can of paint containing water with a can containing oil?

Use after page 150.

What physical changes and chemical changes take place to make a bowl of hot buttered popcorn?

Reading a Pictograph

A pictograph uses pictures or symbols to show information. This pictograph uses thermometers to show the freezing points of different types of matter. Use it to answer the following questions.

1. Which of the types of matter shown has the highest freezing point?

2. Which has the lowest freezing point?

3. Which has the higher freezing point—sodium or sulfur?

4. How much higher is the freezing point of lead than iodine?

5. Which of the materials shown would be a solid at room temperature (22°C)?

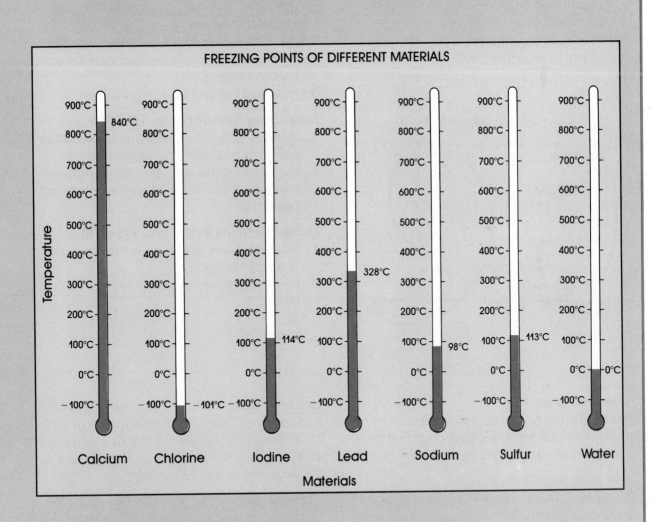

FREEZING POINTS OF DIFFERENT MATERIALS

Chapter 7

Understanding Electricity

LESSON QUESTIONS

Electricity (pp. 156–158)
1. How is the movement of electrons related to electricity?
2. How is electricity like a tug-of-war?

Kinds of Electricity (pp. 159–162)
1. What is static electricity? Give an example of static electricity.
2. What is current electricity?
3. How does a conductor differ from an insulator? Give an example of each.

Electric Circuits (pp. 163–166)
1. What is a circuit?
2. Identify these two types of circuits.

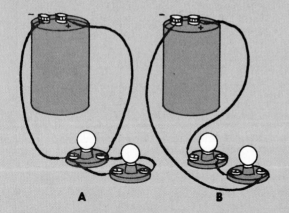

Producing Electricity (pp. 167–170)
1. How can a magnet be used to produce electricity?
2. How is electricity produced by a generator?
3. What is an electric cell? Describe two types of electric cells.

Using Electricity (pp. 171–172)
1. Describe three ways you use electricity.
2. How can electricity be changed to mechanical energy?
3. How does a light bulb produce light?

Measuring Electricity (pp. 173–174)
1. What is power? In what units are small amounts of electric power measured?
2. In what units do power companies measure how much electricity a person uses?

Using Electricity Safely (pp. 175–176)
1. How do fuses and circuit breakers protect against fire?
2. Describe three safety rules for using electricity.

PROBLEM SOLVING

Use after page 158.
Static electricity can be a nuisance. For one thing, it makes clothes stick together in a clothes dryer. How does this occur?

Use after page 170.
Many electric companies are working hard to produce solar-powered generators. How might a solar-powered generator work?

Use after page 174.
Suppose your electric company charges 10 cents for every kilowatt-hour of electricity. How much would you owe if you used a 200-watt motor for 10 hours?

Use after page 176.
Why are houses safe places to be during a lightning storm?

SKILL

Reading a Bar Graph

Some bar graphs can be used to compare two things at the same time. This bar graph compares the amount of energy different countries or regions produce with the amount they use. Use the graph to answer the following questions.

1. Which country or region uses the most energy? Which uses the least?

2. Which country or region produces the most energy? Which produces the least?

3. Which countries or regions produce more energy than they use?

4. Which countries or regions use more energy than they produce?

5. Which countries or regions use more energy than the United States and Canada do?

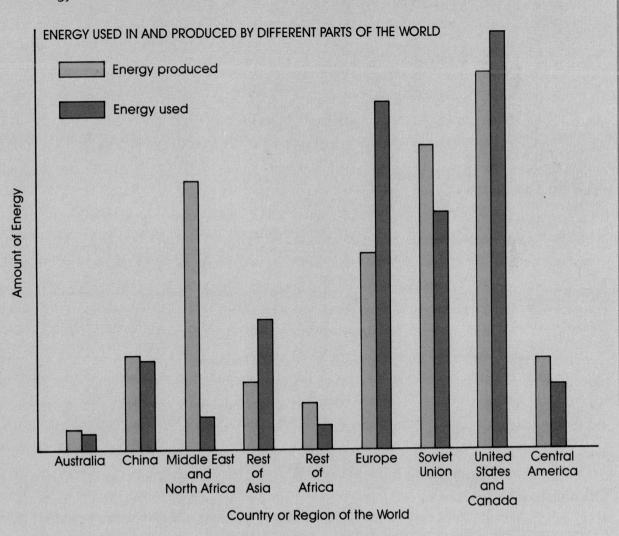

ENERGY USED IN AND PRODUCED BY DIFFERENT PARTS OF THE WORLD

Energy produced

Energy used

Amount of Energy

Australia China Middle East and North Africa Rest of Asia Rest of Africa Europe Soviet Union United States and Canada Central America

Country or Region of the World

Chapter 8

Sources of Energy

LESSON QUESTIONS

Energy from Fossil Fuels (pp. 182–185)

1. What is a fossil fuel? Give two examples of fossil fuels.
2. How did fossil fuels form?
3. Describe how fossil fuels are used to produce electricity.

Energy from Atoms (pp. 186–189)

1. What is nuclear fission?
2. What is nuclear fusion?
3. How is nuclear energy used to produce electricity?
4. What are some problems that occur with using nuclear energy?

Energy from the Sun (pp. 190–194)

1. Explain why the inside of a closed car parked in direct sunlight becomes warm.
2. What is a solar collector?
3. How can a solar cell be used to produce electricity? Where can solar cells be used?

Energy from Water (pp. 195–196)

1. How is electricity produced in a hydro-electric power plant?
2. How can the tides be used to produce electricity?

Energy from Heat in the Earth (pp. 197–198)

1. What is geothermal energy?
2. How is geothermal energy used to produce electricity?

Energy from the Wind (pp. 199–200)

1. How can the wind be used to produce electricity?
2. What are some problems with using wind energy?

Energy from Living Things (pp. 201–203)

1. What is biomass?
2. Give an example of bioconversion.
3. Describe two ways energy can be produced by using biomass.

PROBLEM SOLVING

Use after page 189.
Energy from nuclear fusion can come from combining the nuclei of two hydrogen atoms. What common substance on earth contains hydrogen atoms? Why would fusion be a good alternative to fossil fuels?

Use after page 194.
What advantages are there to having solar collectors on orbiting satellites?

Use after page 198.
Geothermal energy plants are almost always found near active volcanoes, where the heat is close to the surface. What else must be present in these areas to produce geothermal energy?

Use after page 200.
People found wind energy to be very useful for more than 1000 years. Why isn't this form of energy used more often today?

Use after page 203.
Scientists warn that fossil fuels will be used up in the near future. Why, then, don't we return biomass into the ground so that it can change into coal, oil, or gas?

SKILL

Reading a Pictograph

Obviously, the amount of sunshine a place gets determines whether solar energy can be used there. This information can be shown with a pictograph such as the one you see here. It shows what chance there is of having a sunny day in different cities. Use the pictograph to answer the following questions.

1. In which city is there the greatest chance of having a sunny day?
2. In which city is there the least chance of having a sunny day?

3. In which of these cities is there a greater than 50 percent chance of having a sunny day? Less than a 50 percent chance?
4. Suppose you wanted to build a solar energy plant. Your research indicates that you must build the plant in a city in which there is at least a 70 percent chance of sunshine. In which of these cities could you build your plant—Boston, Seattle, Miami, or Sacramento?

CHANCE OF SUNSHINE IN DIFFERENT CITIES

City		Chance
Boston	☀☀☀☀☀☀	60%
Indianapolis	☀☀☀☀☀☀	57%
Juneau	☀☀☀☀	32%
Miami	☀☀☀☀☀☀☀☀	73%
Oklahoma City	☀☀☀☀☀☀☀	68%
Phoenix	☀☀☀☀☀☀☀☀☀	86%
Reno	☀☀☀☀☀☀☀☀☀	81%
Sacramento	☀☀☀☀☀☀☀☀	79%
Seattle	☀☀☀☀☀	49%

Chapter 9

Changes in the Earth

LESSON QUESTIONS

Weathering Changes the Land (pp. 214–217)

1. What is weathering?
2. What is physical weathering? Give two examples of physical weathering.
3. How can water cause weathering?

Another Kind of Weathering (pp. 218–219)

1. How is chemical weathering different from physical weathering?
2. How does chemical weathering form limestone caves?
3. Describe how chemical weathering breaks up rocks that contain iron.

Water Changes the Land (pp. 220–225)

1. What is erosion?
2. Describe how water is an agent of erosion.
3. Describe two ways water erosion can be prevented.

4. How are erosion and deposition related?
5. What is a delta? How is a delta formed?

Ice Changes the Land (pp. 227–230)

1. Describe how glaciers weather land.
2. How do glaciers change the shape of valleys?

Wind Changes the Land (pp. 231–233)

1. How are sand dunes formed?
2. Identify this method of preventing erosion. Explain why it is helpful.

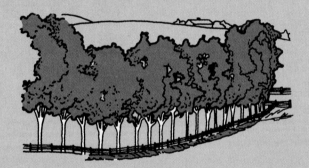

PROBLEM SOLVING

Use after page 219.

Which do you think would be damaged by chemical weathering faster—statues in Washington, D.C., or statues in Egypt? Explain your answer.

Use after page 230.

Describe two ways in which glaciers might have helped make farming in New England difficult.

Use after page 233.

The Rocky Mountains are steep, tall mountains. The Appalachian Mountains, in the eastern part of North America, are not as tall or as steep as the Rocky Mountains. The Appalachian Mountains are generally more rounded off than the Rocky Mountains. How could weathering help explain these differences? Which of these mountain ranges is probably older? Explain your answer.

Reading a Diagram

Diagrams can show you many types of information. A series of diagrams can be used to compare how things change over a period of time. The diagrams you see here show how the delta of a river changed over 500 years. Study the diagram. Then do the following.

1. Describe how the delta changed from 1488 to 1688.

2. Describe how the delta changed from 1688 to 1956.

3. Describe how the delta changed from 1956 to 1986.

CHANGES IN A RIVER DELTA

1488
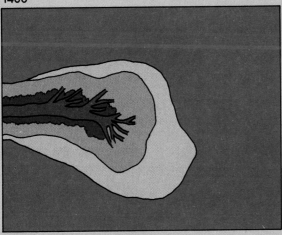

1688
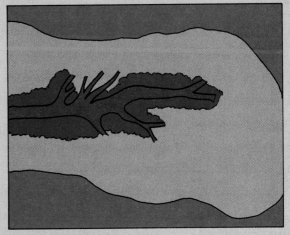

1956
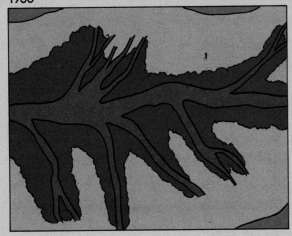

1986

Cleaning Up the Earth

LESSON QUESTIONS

Natural Resources (pp. 238–239)
1. What is a natural resource? Give two examples of natural resources.
2. What is a renewable resource? Give two examples of renewable resources.
3. How does pollution affect resources?

Air Pollution (pp. 240–244)
1. Use the graph below to identify the gases that make up air.
2. What is acid rain? How does acid rain affect land and water?

Water Pollution (pp. 245–252)
1. How do people depend on clean water?
2. Describe how a sewage-treatment plant is used to clean water.
3. How does water polluted by fertilizer affect living things?
4. What is thermal pollution? How does thermal pollution affect living things?

3. How does smog occur?
4. Describe two methods that are being used to reduce air pollution.

Land Pollution (pp. 253–255)
1. Describe how toxic wastes pollute the land.
2. Distinguish between biodegradable and nonbiodegradable materials. Give two examples of each.

THE PARTS OF AIR

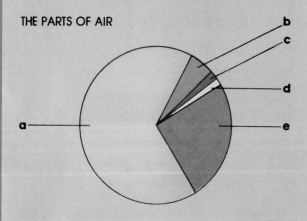

a   b   c   d   e

PROBLEM SOLVING

Use after page 239.
Sometimes natural resources are destroyed by careless human beings. Forest fires are often caused by carelessness. How can forest fires be prevented?

Use after page 252.
Scientists are constantly searching for new and better ways to clean up oil spills. One scientist has developed a strain of super-bacteria that eat oil. It has been shown that these bacteria can eat an entire 40-liter oil spill in 6 hours. What advantages does this method have? What problems could come from using these bacteria?

SKILL

Reading a Map

This map shows the number of toxic dump sites in every state. Use the map to answer the following questions.

1. In which state are the most toxic dump sites found?

2. In which states are the fewest sites found?

3. How many sites are found in Michigan?

4. Which states have more sites than Texas does?

5. New England consists of Maine, New Hampshire, Vermont, Massachusetts, Connecticut, and Rhode Island. How many sites are found in New England?

TOXIC DUMP SITES BY STATE

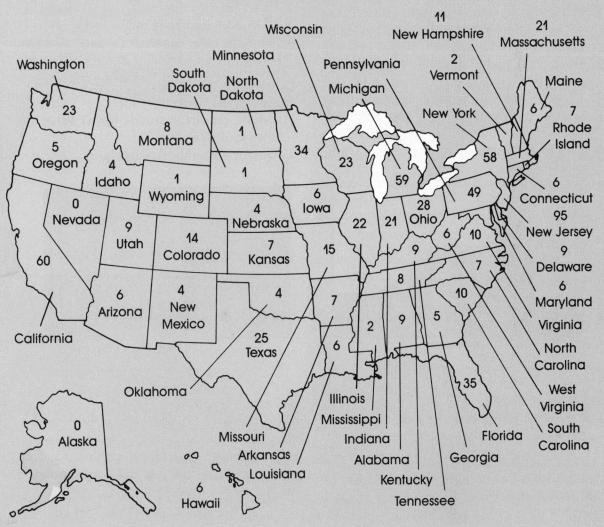

Chapter 11

Changes in the Weather

LESSON QUESTIONS

How Weather Begins (pp. 260–264)
1. How does weather begin?
2. What happens to solar energy in the atmosphere?
3. Describe three reasons why the earth heats unevenly.

Air Pressure and Winds (pp. 265–268)
1. What happens to air pressure when the air is heated? What happens when it is cooled?
2. How does water vapor affect air pressure?
3. Describe how air pressure causes wind.
4. Describe how warm air and cold air move in each picture.
5. Describe the movement of the earth's global winds.

Air Masses and Weather (pp. 269–270)
1. Define the term air mass.
2. Describe the four basic kinds of air masses.

When Air Masses Meet (pp. 271–275)
1. What is the place where two air masses meet called?
2. Describe the weather along a cold front.
3. How do blizzards form?
4. Describe the weather along a warm front.

Clouds (pp. 276–278)
1. Describe a cumulus cloud.
2. Where do cirrus clouds form? What do they look like?
3. Describe a nimbostratus cloud.

sea breeze

land breeze

PROBLEM SOLVING

Use after page 268.
Is it possible to have a sea breeze and a land breeze at a lake? Explain your answer.

Use after page 275.
Why can cold fronts cause special problems for people who are fishing from small boats?

Use after page 278.
Airport traffic controllers inform pilots about the "cloud ceiling" before takeoffs and landings. What do you think a cloud ceiling is? What do you think a ceilometer measures?

Reading a Weather Map

A weather map gives information about the weather in a region on a certain day. A weather map for the United States is shown here. The symbols on the map are explained in the boxes below the map. The numbers next to the cities are temperature readings in degrees Celsius.

Use the weather map to answer these questions.

1. Name two cities in which it rained.

2. What kinds of clouds were over Dallas? Over Atlanta?

3. Describe the cloud cover that was over Los Angeles and Atlanta.

4. What kind of front was east of Miami?

5. What was the temperature in New York? In St. Louis?

6. Name a city in which it snowed.

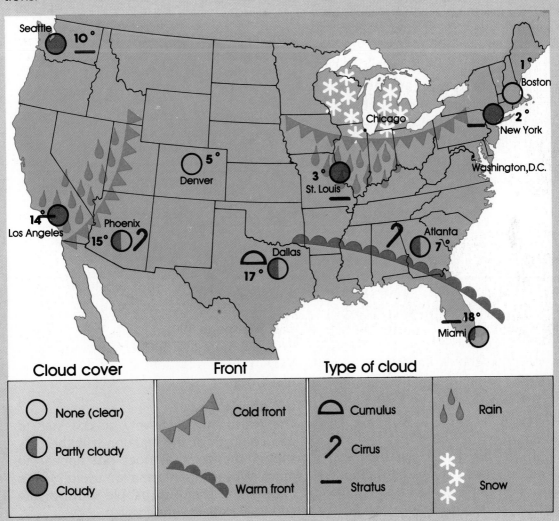

Cloud cover	Front	Type of cloud	
None (clear)	Cold front	Cumulus	Rain
Partly cloudy		Cirrus	
Cloudy	Warm front	Stratus	Snow

Chapter 12

Beyond the Solar System

LESSON QUESTIONS

Distances in Space (pp. 284–288)

1. Which is closer to the earth–Pluto or Proxima Centauri (the nearest star)?
2. What is the study of the universe called? What are scientists who study the universe called?
3. What is a light-year? If you could travel at the speed of light, how long would it take you to reach a place that is 60 light-years away?

Characteristics of Stars (pp. 289–291)

1. What is magnitude? What does the magnitude of a star depend on?
2. Which star is hotter–a blue star or a red star?

The Life of a Star (pp. 292–295)

1. What is a nebula?
2. Describe a middle-aged star. Give an example of a middle-aged star.
3. What is a red giant?
4. How does a nova differ from a super-nova?
5. How do scientists believe a black hole forms?

Families of Stars (pp. 296–300)

1. Describe the Milky Way galaxy. Where is the sun located in the galaxy?
2. Describe three kinds of galaxies.

Star Patterns (pp. 301–302)

1. What is a constellation?
2. Describe three constellations.

PROBLEM SOLVING

Use after page 288.
Several space probes containing information about Earth have been launched. It is hoped that the information will tell whoever finds the probes about our planet. What three pieces of information about Earth do you think should be included on a space probe traveling beyond our solar system?

Use after page 291.
Photographs of the sun show that it is brighter at the center than at the edges. What conclusion can you draw from this information?

Use after page 295.
What do you suppose it would be like to enter a black hole?

Use after page 300.
Why is it more difficult to observe the Milky Way in cities today than it was during colonial times?

Use after page 302.
The North Star is a very special star to people north of the equator. It is the only star in the sky that does not appear to move. Why is this information useful? Is this information useful to people south of the equator? Explain your answer.

SKILL

Reading a Map

Maps can be used to show many things on the earth. This map shows constellations as seen from the earth. Use the map to answer the following questions.

1. Which constellation is called the Big Dipper?

2. Which constellation is to the right of Ursa Minor?

3. What stars are found in Draco?

4. In which constellation is the star Alcor?

5. What is another name for Polaris?

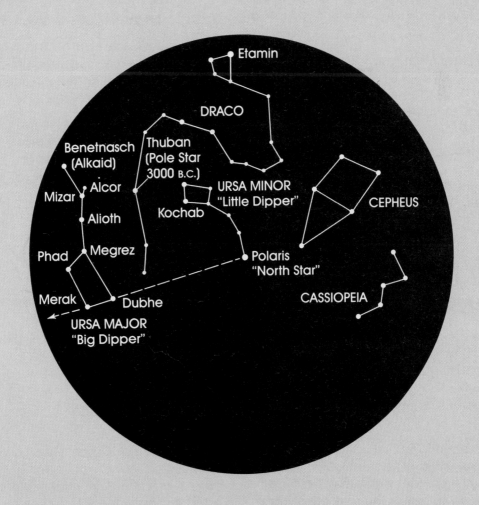

Chapter 13

Support and Movement of the Body

LESSON QUESTIONS

Your Body's Framework (pp. 314–318)
1. What is the skeleton? What is the function of the skeleton?
2. Describe the inside of a bone.
3. What is cartilage? Where is cartilage found? Why is it important?

Where Bones Meet (pp. 319–320)
1. What is a joint? Describe four types of joints.
2. What is the function of a ligament?

Muscles Move Bones (pp. 321–324)
1. Describe how muscles are attached to bones.
2. How do muscles move bones?

Two Groups of Muscles (pp. 325–326)
1. What are voluntary muscles? Where are voluntary muscles found?
2. What are involuntary muscles? Where are they found?
3. Describe three kinds of muscles.

Bone and Muscle Injuries (pp. 327–328)
1. Describe two types of fractures.
2. How is a sprain different from a strain?
3. What is a muscle cramp?

Care of Bones and Muscles (pp. 329–331)
1. What are the four main groups of foods that make up a proper diet?
2. Why is exercise important in caring for your bones and muscles?

PROBLEM SOLVING

Use after page 320.
Is there any advantage in having hinge joints at knees and elbows? What would the movement of legs and arms be like if ball-and-socket joints were at knees and elbows?

Use after page 326.
When you are cold your muscles contract and you shiver. Your teeth may even chatter. What do you think the purpose of these movements is? Are they voluntary or involuntary movements?

Use after page 328.
A broken bone in a child heals faster than a broken bone in an adult. Why, do you think, does this happen?

Use after page 331.
What would happen to astronauts on long space missions if they did not exercise? Design a piece of exercise equipment that could be used by astronauts in the weightless environment of space.

Reading a Food Label

Many packaged foods have a nutrition panel on their label or box. These nutrition panels show how much of each nutrient is in a certain amount of food. Nutrients are materials that are needed for good health.

Use the nutrition panels to answer these questions.

1. What does *U.S. RDA* mean?
2. How much magnesium does each cereal provide?
3. What is the amount of carbohydrates in 1 oz of each cereal?
4. How much fat is in ½ cup of whole milk?
5. Which cereal provides more vitamin C? How much more?
6. Both cereals provide less than 2 percent of which nutrient?
7. How much vitamin A is provided by one serving of each cereal with whole milk? How much vitamin A is still needed to have 100 percent of the U.S. RDA?
8. For cereal *A*, which nutrients are supplied by the cereal alone?

CEREAL A

NUTRITION INFORMATION PER SERVING
SERVING SIZE: 1 OZ (28.4 g)

	CEREAL A	
	1 OZ (28.4 g)	WITH ½ CUP WHOLE MILK
CALORIES	110	190
PROTEIN	2 g	6 g
CARBOHYDRATE	25 g	30 g
FAT	0 g	5 g
SODIUM	75 mg (265 mg per 100 g)	135 mg (90 mg per 100 g)

PERCENTAGE OF U.S. RECOMMENDED DAILY ALLOWANCES (U.S. RDA)

	CEREAL A	
	1 OZ (28.4 g)	WITH ½ CUP WHOLE MILK
PROTEIN	2	10
VITAMIN A	25	30
VITAMIN C	25	25
THIAMIN	25	30
RIBOFLAVIN	25	35
NIACIN	25	25
CALCIUM	*	15
IRON	10	10
VITAMIN D	10	25
VITAMIN B₆	25	25
FOLIC ACID	25	25
PHOSPHOROUS	4	15
MAGNESIUM	4	8
ZINC	2	6
COPPER	2	2

*CONTAINS LESS THAN 2 PERCENT OF THE U.S. RDA OF THIS NUTRIENT.

CARBOHYDRATE INFORMATION

	CEREAL A	
	1 OZ (28.4 g)	WITH ½ CUP WHOLE MILK
STARCH AND RELATED CARBOHYDRATES	10 g	10 g
SUCROSE AND OTHER SUGARS	15 g	20 g
TOTAL CARBOHYDRATES	25 g	30 g

CEREAL B

NUTRITION INFORMATION PER SERVING
SERVING SIZE: 1 OZ (28.4 g)

	CEREAL B	
	1 OZ (28.4)	WITH ½ CUP WHOLE MILK
CALORIES	110	180
PROTEIN	2 g	6 g
CARBOHYDRATE	24 g	30 g
FAT	0 g	5 g
SODIUM	350 mg (1235 mg per 100 g)	410 mg (275 mg per 100 g)

PERCENTAGE OF U.S. RECOMMENDED DAILY ALLOWANCES (U.S. RDA)

	CEREAL B	
	1 OZ (28.4 g)	WITH ½ CUP WHOLE MILK
PROTEIN	8	10
VITAMIN A	25	30
VITAMIN C	28	25
THIAMIN	25	30
RIBOFLAVIN	25	35
NIACIN	25	25
CALCIUM	*	15
IRON	10	10
VITAMIN D	10	25
VITAMIN B₆	25	25
FOLIC ACID	25	25
PHOSPHOROUS	2	15
MAGNESIUM	*	4

*CONTAINS LESS THAN 2 PERCENT OF THE U.S. RDA OF THESE NUTRIENTS.

CARBOHYDRATE INFORMATION

	CEREAL B	
	1 OZ (28.4 g)	WITH ½ CUP WHOLE MILK
STARCH AND RELATED CARBOHYDRATES	22 g	22 g
SUCROSE AND OTHER SUGARS	2 g	8 g
TOTAL CARBOHYDRATES	24 g	30 g

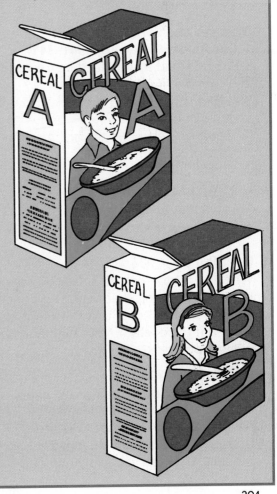

Chapter 14

Transport Systems of the Body

LESSON QUESTIONS

The Circulatory System (pp. 336–338)

1. What are the three main parts of the circulatory system?
2. Describe the three solid parts that make up blood.
3. What causes blood to clot?

Circulation of Blood (pp. 339–341)

1. Describe the four chambers of the heart.
2. What are the three kinds of blood vessels? How do they differ?

Diseases and Care of the Circulatory System (pp. 341–345)

1. How should a nosebleed be treated?
2. What is a heart attack?
3. What is high blood pressure? How does it affect the body?
4. Describe two ways to care for your circulatory system.

The Respiratory System (pp. 346–350)

1. What is the function of the respiratory system?
2. Describe the passageway from the mouth to the lungs.
3. What happens to air inside the lungs?
4. How do the lungs expand?

Diseases and Care of the Respiratory System (pp. 351–352)

1. What are allergies? How do allergies affect the body?
2. Name two things that can cause lung cancer.

The Excretory System (pp. 353–355)

1. What is the function of the excretory system?
2. What waste products do the lungs get rid of?
3. Describe how the kidneys function.

PROBLEM SOLVING

Use after page 338.
When a doctor orders a blood test on a patient, one thing that might be done is a white blood cell count. What might be indicated if the doctor finds a high number of white blood cells?

Use after page 345.
In China and other countries, people eat mostly fish, rice, and vegetables. Fewer people living in these countries have clogged arteries than do people living in America. How can you explain this?

Use after page 350.
Why do you breathe more rapidly when you are exercising than when you are sleeping?

Use after page 355.
In an adult, the kidneys filter about 180 L of blood each day. But there are only about 6 L of blood in an adult's body. Where do the other 172 L come from?

Reading a Line Graph

This line graph shows the pulse rate of a person over a period of time. Use the graph to answer the following questions.

1. At which point (indicated by a letter) is the pulse rate the highest?

2. At which point is it the lowest?
3. At which point did the person probably start exercising?
4. At which point was the person sleeping?

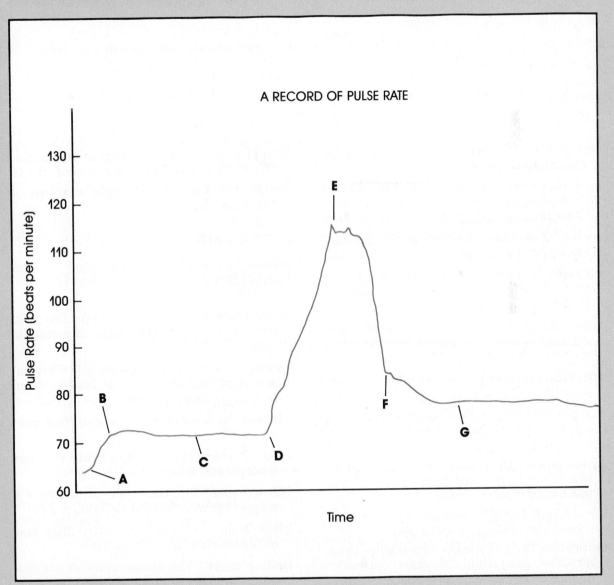

A RECORD OF PULSE RATE

Glossary

Key to Pronunciation

a apple, bat	i if, pig	sh she, wish	ə stands for:
ā ate, page	ī idea, fine	th think, moth	a in asleep
ã air, care	ng ring, sink	ŦH the, bathe	e in garden
ä father, star	o ox, top	u uncle, sun	i in pencil
ch chest, such	ō owe, no	ù pull, foot	o in button
e egg, bed	ô orbit, saw	ü glue, boot	u in circus
ē even, me	oi oil, joy	zh usual, vision	
ėr earn, bird	ou out, mouse		

This Key to Pronunciation is adapted from *Scott, Foresman Intermediate Dictionary*, by E. L. Thorndike and Clarence L. Barnhart. Copyright © 1983 by Scott, Foresman and Company. Reprinted by permission.

abdomen (ab′də mən)   The rear part of an insect's body. *p. 48*

acid rain   Weak acids that fall in rain or snow. Acid rain can kill living things and damage structures. *p. 241*

agents of erosion   Moving water, moving ice, and wind. *p. 220*

air mass   A large body of air that has about the same temperature and moisture throughout. *p. 269*

amphibian (am fib′ē ən)   A cold-blooded vertebrate that lives part of its life in water and part on land. *p. 61*

antennae (an ten′ē)   The two feelers on the head of an insect. *p. 49*

artery (är′tər ē)   A thick-walled blood vessel that carries blood away from the heart. *p. 339*

arthropod (är′thrə pod)   An invertebrate that has a segmented body, jointed legs, and a hard outer covering. *p. 45*

astronomer (ə stron′ə mər)   A scientist who studies the universe. *p. 286*

astronomy (ə stron′ə mē)   The science that includes the study of stars, planets, moons, and other objects in space. *p. 286*

atom (at′əm)   The basic unit of all matter; the smallest particle of an element. *p. 116*

atrium (ā′trē əm)   The upper chamber of the heart. *p. 339*

ball-and-socket joint   The kind of joint that allows the most movement of bones. *p. 319*

bioconversion (bī ō kən vėr′zhən)   The process of changing biomass into usable energy. *p. 201*

biodegradable (bī ō di grā′də bəl) **material**   Material that decays, or is broken down by living things. *p. 254*

biomass (bī′ō mas)   Plant and animal matter. *p. 201*

bird   A warm-blooded vertebrate that has feathers and wings. *p. 67*

black dwarf   The last stage in the life of a star; a star with no heat or light. *p. 294*

black hole   A region in space that was once occupied by a star. *p. 295*

boiling point   The temperature at which a liquid changes to a gas. *p. 140*

bone marrow   A soft material inside the long bones of the arms and legs. Old blood cells are repaired and new blood cells are made in the bone marrow. *p. 317*

bristles (bris′əlz)   The stiff, strong hairs on an earthworm that are used for moving and clinging. *p. 37*

bronchial (brong′kē əl) **tubes**   The two tubes into which the trachea branches. *p. 347*

bronchitis (brong kī′tis)   A respiratory disease in which the bronchial tubes become red and swollen. *p. 352*

canyon   A deep valley with deep sides. *p. 222*

capillary (kap′ə ler ē)   A tiny blood vessel that connects an artery and a vein. *p. 339*

cartilage (kär′tə lij)   A soft, bonelike material that bends; it makes up the skeleton of some fish, such as sharks. *p. 58*   In people, a soft, bonelike material in the tip of the nose, the ears, and between the small bones that make up the backbone. *p. 318*

cell   The basic unit of all living things. *p. 4*

chemical change   A change in matter in which one or more different kinds of matter form. *p. 149*

chemical weathering   All the processes that break apart rock by changing its chemical makeup. *p. 218*

chlorophyll (klôr′ə fil)   Green-colored material in plant cells needed by a plant to make food. *p. 13*

chloroplast (klôr′ə plast)   A small green body in plant cells. *p. 12*

circuit (sėr′kit)   The path on which electrons move. *p. 163*

circuit breaker   A safety device with a switch that turns off to break the flow of electricity when wires become too hot. *p. 175*

circulatory (sėr′kyə lə tôr ē) **system**   One of the transport systems of the body. It carries food and oxygen to the cells and carries away waste products from the cells. *p. 336*

cirrus (sir′əs) **clouds**   Thin, wispy clouds that look like feathers or curls of hair. Cirrus clouds form high in the sky and are often a sign that a warm front is moving in. *p. 276*

classify (klas′ə fī)   To arrange in groups by features that are alike. *p. 28*

climax (klī′maks) **stage**   The last stage in the process of succession. *p. 99*

cold front   The place where a moving cold air mass meets a warmer air mass. *p. 271*

cold-blooded animal   An animal whose body temperature changes with the temperature of the water or air around it. *p. 58*

combustion (kəm bus′chən)   The process by which oxygen from the air combines with a fuel, producing heat and light. *p. 184*

community (kə myü′nə tē)   All the plants and animals that live and interact with each other in a place. *p. 84*

compound (kom′pound)   A new substance that forms when atoms of different elements combine. *p. 122*

compound fracture   A break in a bone in which the broken end of the bone pushes through the muscle and skin. *p. 327*

conductor (kən duk′tər)   Matter through which electrons move easily. *p. 160*

constellation (kon stə lā′shən)   A group of stars that seems to form a pattern. *p. 301*

cramp   A sudden strong contraction of a muscle. *p. 328*

crude oil   Oil that has not been refined; oil that is taken from the earth. *p. 183*

crustacean (krus tā′shən)   One of a group of arthropods that includes animals such as shrimps, lobsters, and crayfish. *p. 47*

cumulus (kyü′myə ləs) **clouds**   Large fluffy white clouds that are often seen during fair weather. *p. 276*

current electricity   The movement of electrons from one place to another. *p. 160*

delta   A fan-shaped landmass formed by sediments deposited at the mouth of a river. *p. 225*

deposition (dep ə zish′ən)   The dropping of sediments by the agents of erosion. *p. 223*

diaphragm (dī′ə fram)   A thick sheet of muscle at the bottom of the chest cavity. *p. 348*

down   Small fluffy feathers near a bird's body that trap air and help to keep the bird warm. *p. 68*

dry cell   A type of electric cell that uses a chemical paste and two kinds of metal to produce a flow of electrons. *p. 170*

echinoderm (i kī′nə dėrm)   A spiny-skinned invertebrate that lives in the ocean. *p. 39*

ecology (ē kol′ə jē)   The study of how living and nonliving things affect each other. *p. 82*

ecosystem (ē′kə sis təm)   A group of living things and their nonliving environment. *p. 83*

electric cell   A device that changes chemical energy to electrical energy. *p. 169*

electric discharge (dis′chärj)   The movement of extra electrons. *p. 160*

electric motor   A machine that changes electrical energy to mechanical energy. *p. 172*

electron (i lek′tron)   A tiny, negatively charged particle that travels around the nucleus of an atom. *p. 117*

element (el′ə mənt)   Matter that is made up of only one kind of atom. *p. 118*

elliptical (i lip′tə kəl) **galaxy**   A galaxy shaped like a flat disk. *p. 298*

embryo (em′brē ō)   The tiny young plant in a seed. *p. 22*

environment (en vī′rən mənt)   Everything that surrounds and affects a living thing. *p. 82*

erosion (i rō′zhən)   The movement of weathered rock and soil from one place to another. *p. 220*

excretory (eks′krə tôr ē) **system**   The transport system that removes waste products from the body. *p. 353*

exhaling (eks hāl′ing)   The process of breathing out, during which air leaves the lungs. *p. 349*

exoskeleton (ek sō skel′ə tən)   A hard outer covering that is like a skeleton on the outside of an animal's body. *p. 45*

femur (fē′mər)   The long bone in the thigh; it is the longest and heaviest bone in the human body. *p. 317*

fertilization (fėr tə lə zā′shən)   The joining of male and female reproductive cells. *p. 22*

fertilizer (fėr´tə lī zər)   A substance that helps plants grow. *p. 247*

filament (fil´ə mənt)   A thin coil of wire. *p. 172*

fin   A structure on a fish that helps it move through the water. *p. 58*

fish   A cold-blooded vertebrate with fins. *p. 58*

fixed joint   The kind of joint between bones that cannot move. *p. 320*

formula (fôr´myə lə)   A group of symbols and numbers that stands for a compound. *p. 128*

fossil fuel   A fuel that forms from the remains of dead plants and animals. Coal, oil, and natural gas are fossil fuels. *p. 182*

fracture (frak´chər)   A crack or a break in a bone. *p. 327*

front   The place where two air masses meet. *p. 271*

frost action   A kind of physical weathering in which large rocks are broken apart by the freezing and melting of water in cracks of the rock. *p. 215*

fuse (fyüz)   A safety device with a metal strip that melts to break the flow of electricity when wires become too hot. *p. 175*

galaxy (gal´ək sē)   A large group of stars and other bodies in space. *p. 296*

generator (jen´ə rā tər)   A machine that changes energy of motion into electrical energy. *p. 168*

geothermal (jē ə thėr´məl) **energy**   Energy from natural heat trapped beneath the earth's surface. *p. 197*

germination (jėr mə nā´shən)   The growth of a plant embryo from a seed. *p. 22*

gills   Thin, feathery structures filled with blood and used for breathing by some animals that live in water. *p. 59*

glacier (glā´shər)   A slow-moving mass of ice on land. *p. 227*

greenhouse effect   The buildup of heat that occurs when solar energy strikes material and is trapped. *p. 190*

habitat (hab´ə tat)   The special place in a community in which a plant or animal lives. *p. 87*

heart muscle   A special kind of involuntary muscle that makes up the heart. *p. 326*

hinge joint   The kind of joint that allows bones to move back and forth. *p. 320*

host   The animal or plant in or on which a parasite lives. *p. 35*

hot spot   An area of geothermal energy; an area beneath the earth's surface in which magma collects. *p. 197*

hydroelectric (hī drō i lek´tric) **power plant**   A place in which the energy of moving water turns turbines attached to generators that produce electricity. *p. 195*

hypothesis (hī poth´ə sis)   A logical guess based on direct and indirect evidence. *p. 114*

indirect evidence (in də rekt´ ev´ə dəns)   A set of clues that scientists use to make logical guesses about things they cannot see or test directly. *p. 114*

inhaling (in hāl´ing)   The process of breathing in, during which air enters the lungs. *p. 349*

insulator (in′sə lā tər)   Matter through which electrons do not move easily; matter that is not a good conductor. *p. 161*

invertebrate (in vėr′tə brit)   An animal without a backbone. *p. 29*

involuntary (in vol′ən ter ē) **muscles**   The group of muscles that cannot be controlled. *p. 325*

irregular (i reg′yə lər) **galaxy**   A galaxy that does not have a definite shape or size. *p. 298*

joint   The place where two or more bones are joined together. *p. 319*

kilowatt (kil′ə wot)   A unit of measure of large amounts of electric power. A kilowatt is 1,000 watts. *p. 173*

kilowatt-hour   A unit equal to 1,000 watts of electricity used for 1 hour. *p. 174*

land breeze   The movement of air from land to water. *p. 267*

larynx (lar′ingks)   The voice box. *p. 347*

life processes   The activities that keep living things alive. *p. 5*

ligament (lig′ə mənt)   A strong cord of tissue that holds bones together at a joint. *p. 319*

light-year   The distance that light travels in 1 year. *p. 288*

lungs   Organs through which animals get oxygen from the air. *p. 62*

magma (mag′mə)   Melted rock inside the earth. *p. 197*

magnitude (mag′nə tüd)   The measure of the brightness of a star as seen from the earth. *p. 289*

mammal   A warm-blooded vertebrate that is usually covered with fur or hair and whose young are fed from the female's milk glands. *p. 72*

mass   A measure of the amount of matter in an object. *p. 112*

matter   Anything that has mass and takes up space. *p. 112*

mechanical (mə kan′ə kəl) **energy**   Energy of moving machine parts. *p. 172*

melting point   The temperature at which a solid changes to a liquid. *p. 140*

mixture (miks′chər)   A material formed by the physical combining of two or more different materials. *p. 142*

molecule (mol′ə kyül)   The simplest particle of many compounds. *p. 122*

mollusk (mol′əsk)   An invertebrate with a soft body. Some have two outer shells; some live in a one-piece shell; others have no shell at all. *p. 41*

molt (mōlt)   To shed an outer covering. *p. 52*

natural resource   A useful material found in or on the earth. *p. 238*

nebula (neb′yə lə)   A cloud of dust and gas found in space. *p. 292*

neutron (nü′tron)   A particle in the nucleus of an atom. *p. 117*

neutron star   A very dense star; what remains after a supernova collapses. *p. 295*

niche (nich)   The role that each living thing plays in a habitat. *p. 89*

nonbiodegradable (non bī ō di grā′də bəl) **material** Material that cannot be broken down by living things. *p. 254*

nova An exploding star. *p. 294*

nuclear (nü′klē ər) **energy** The energy stored in the nucleus of an atom. *p. 186*

nuclear fission (fish′ən) The process by which the nucleus of an atom is split, releasing energy. *p. 186*

nuclear fusion (fyü′zhən) The process by which the nuclei (nü′klē ī) of atoms are combined, releasing energy. *p. 187*

nuclear reactor A special structure in which fission takes place. *p. 187*

nucleus (nü′klē əs) The central part of an atom. *p. 117*

organ A body part that does a certain job. *p. 34*

ovary (ō′vər ē) The bottom part of the pistil which contains the ovules. *p. 19*

ovule (ō′vyül) A small round body in a flower that contains the female reproductive cell. Ovules grow into seeds. *p. 19*

parallel (par′ə lel) **circuit** A circuit in which electrons can follow more than one path. *p. 165*

parasite (par′ə sīt) An animal or plant that depends on and harms another animal or plant. *p. 35*

petals The leaflike outer parts of a flower that protect the inner reproductive parts. *p. 19*

photosynthesis (fō tə sin′thə sis) The process by which green plants make food. *p. 12*

physical change A change in the size, shape, or state of matter. *p. 136*

physical property A property that can be used to identify matter. Color, shape, and hardness are physical properties. *p. 134*

physical weathering All the processes that break apart rock without changing its chemical makeup. *p. 215*

pioneer (pī ə nir′) **stage** The first stage in the process of succession. *p. 99*

pistil The female reproductive part of a flower. *p. 19*

pivot joint The kind of joint that allows bones to move from side to side. *p. 320*

planarian (plə när′ē ən) A common flatworm found in fresh water. *p. 34*

plasma (plaz′mə) The yellowish, liquid part of the blood. *p. 336*

platelet (plāt′lit) A solid part of the blood that controls bleeding. *p. 337*

pollen (pol′ən) **grain** A tiny body in a flower which contains the male reproductive cell. *p. 19*

pollination (pol ə nā′shən) The process by which pollen grains move from the stamen to the pistil of a flower. *p. 21*

pollutant (pə lü′tənt) A substance that causes pollution. *p. 239*

pollution (pə lü′shən) The presence of waste or other unwanted materials in a resource. *p. 239*

population (pop yə lā′shən) A group of the same kind of living thing in a community. *p. 84*

pores The small holes in the body of a sponge. *p. 30*

power The amount of work done in a certain period of time. *p. 173*

predator (pred′ə tər) An animal that hunts other animals for food. *p. 93*

prey (prā)   An animal that is hunted by a predator. *p. 93*

proton (prō'ton)   A positively charged particle in the nucleus of an atom. *p. 117*

red blood cell   A solid part of the blood; it carries oxygen to all the other cells of the body. *p. 336*

red giant   One of the stages in the life of a star. During this stage a star expands and is many times larger than the sun. *p. 293*

refinery (ri fī' nər ē)   A place where crude oil is changed to useful products. *p. 183*

regenerate (ri jen'ə rāt)   To regrow. *p. 35*

renewable (ri nü'ə bəl) **resource**   A resource that can be replaced. *p. 239*

reproduction (rē prə duk'shən)   The process by which living things produce new living things of the same kind. *p. 18*

reptile (rep'tīl)   A cold-blooded vertebrate that has lungs and dry skin. *p. 63*

respiration (res pə rā'shən)   The process by which living things use oxygen to release energy in food. *pp. 16, 346*

respiratory (res'pər ə tôr ē) **system**   One of the transport systems of the body. It works closely with the circulatory system to put to use oxygen that is taken in during breathing. *p. 346*

root hair   In a plant, the part of a single cell that grows from a root into the soil. *p. 7*

roundworm   A worm that has a long tube-shaped body with a digestive system. *p. 36*

runoff   Water from rain and melting snow that flows over the earth's surface. *p. 220*

sand dune   A pile of sand formed by the deposition of wind-carried sand. *p. 231*

sea breeze   The movement of air from water to land. *p. 267*

sediments (sed'ə mənts)   The materials carried by the agents of erosion. Sediments include sand, soil, and rock. *p. 223*

seed   A tiny young plant and its stored food. *p. 22*

segmented worm   A worm whose body is divided into segments, or sections. *p. 36*

series (sir'ēz) **circuit**   A circuit in which electrons can follow only one path. *p. 164*

simple fracture   A break in a bone in which the bone does not push through the muscle and skin. *p. 327*

skeletal muscles   Voluntary muscles that move bones. Skeletal muscles are made of long fibers. *p. 326*

skeleton (skel'ə tən)   The system of bones that supports and protects the body and the organs inside it. The skeleton is also called the skeletal (skel'ə təl) system. *p. 314*

skull   The bones of the face joined together with the bones that protect the brain. *p. 315*

smog   A mixture of smoke and fog. *p. 242*

smooth muscles   Involuntary muscles that make up the blood vessels, stomach, intestine, and other organs. *p. 326*

solar (sō'lər) **cell**   A device that changes solar energy into electrical energy. *p. 192*

solar collector   A device that collects sunlight and changes it to another form of energy. *p. 191*

solar energy   Energy from the sun. *p. 190*

solute (sol'yüt)   The substance in a solution that dissolves. *p. 146*

solution (sə lü′shən) A mixture that forms when one substance dissolves in another. *p. 145*

solvent (sol′vənt) The substance in a solution that does the dissolving. *p. 146*

space probe (spās′ prōb′) Unmanned spacecraft that collects information about planets and stars. *p. 284*

spiral (spī′rəl) **galaxy** A galaxy shaped like a flat disk, or wheel, with curved arms coming out from the center. *p. 296*

sponge An invertebrate with a simple body that contains many small holes. *p. 30*

sprain An injury in which a ligament is stretched or torn. *p. 328*

stamen (stā′mən) The male reproductive part of a flower. *p. 19*

static (stat′ik) **electricity** Buildup of electrons on an object. *p. 159*

stinging cell A special structure used to capture food. Jellyfish and hydras have stinging cells. *p. 32*

stomata (stō′mə tə) The openings in a leaf through which air enters the leaf. *p. 10*

strain An injury caused by overstretching a muscle or a tendon. *p. 328*

stratus (strā′təs) **clouds** Thick low clouds that cover the sky. Stratus clouds are a sign of rainy weather. *p. 277*

succession (sək sesh′ən) The series of changes in the communities of an ecosystem. *p. 98*

supernova A large star that has exploded violently. *p. 294*

suspension (sə spen′shən) A mixture in which particles of a substance do not dissolve in another substance. *p. 148*

symbol A short way to write the name of an element. *p. 119*

tadpole The fishlike stage in the life of the frog. *p. 62*

tendon (ten′dən) A tough cord that attaches muscle to bone. *p. 322*

tentacle (ten′tə kəl) A long, armlike part of an animal with stinging cells. *p. 32*

thermal (thėr′məl) **pollution** The dumping of heated materials into water. *p. 249*

thorax (thôr′aks) The middle part of an insect's body. *p. 48*

tidal (tī′dəl) **energy** The energy of rising and falling tides. Tidal energy can be used to produce electricity. *p. 196*

tides The daily movements of the water level along the shore. *p. 196*

toxic (tok′sik) **wastes** Waste materials that are poisonous. *p. 253*

trachea (trā′kē ə) The windpipe. *p. 347*

tube foot A hollow structure with a sucker at the end. Most echinoderms have tube feet. *p. 39*

turbine (tėr′bin) A device that is made up of a wheel and blades. *p. 169*

universe (yü′nə vers) All of space and all the matter and energy in it. *p. 286*

urine (yür′ən) Water with body wastes and salts dissolved in it. *p. 354*

vein (vān) A small thin tube in a leaf that carries water and food to and from leaf cells. *p. 10* A blood vessel that carries blood back to the heart from the body cells. *p. 339*

ventricle (ven′trə kəl) Lower chamber of the heart. *p. 339*

vertebrae (vėr′tə brā) The small bones linked together to form the backbone. *p. 29*

vertebrate (vėr′tə brit) An animal with a backbone. *p. 29*

voluntary (vol′ən ter ē) **muscles** The group of muscles that can be controlled. *p. 325*

warm front The place where a moving warm air mass meets a colder air mass. *p. 273*

warm-blooded animal An animal whose body temperature stays the same even when the temperature of the air or water

around it changes. *p. 67*

watt (wot) A unit of measure of small amounts of electric power. *p. 173*

weathering All the processes that break rock into smaller pieces. *p. 214*

wet cell A type of electric cell that uses acid and water; the acid reacts with metal plates to produce a flow of electrons. *p. 170*

white blood cell A solid part of the blood; it helps the body fight infection. *p. 337*

white dwarf One of the stages in the life of a star; a hot white star about the size of the earth. *p. 294*

windbreak Something that blocks the force of the wind. *p. 233*

Index

Abalone, 44
Acid rain, 241–242
Active solar heating, 191
Agents of erosion, 220
Air, 260–273
Air masses, 269–270
    meeting of, 271–274
Air pollution, 240–244
    acid rain as, 241
    causes of, 240–242
    cleaning up, 242–243
    smog as, 242
Air pressure, 265–268
Airplane, solar-powered, 193
Alcohol as an energy source,
    202–203
Algae, 247
Allergies, 351
Alligators, 63, 64
Alloys, 144
Altocumulus clouds, 278
Aluminum, 141
Ammonia, 125
Amphibians, 61–62
    frogs, 61
    salamanders, 61
    toads, 61
Animal keeper, career as an,
    104
Animals
    with backbones, 29, 56–77
    without backbones, 26–53
    cold-blooded, 58–66
    in communities, 80–102
    with jointed legs, 45–53
    with a soft body, 41–44
    with spiny skin, 39–40
    with stinging cells, 32–33
    warm-blooded, 67–75
Antennae (of an insect), 49
Ants, 45
Architect, career as an, 206

Arteries, 339–340, 343, 344
    clogged, 343–344
Arthropods, 45–53
    ants, 45
    centipedes, 46
    crustaceans, 46–47
    groups of, 46–48
    insects, 48–53
    millipedes, 46
    mites, 47–48
    spiders, 47–48
    ticks, 47–48
Arthroscope, 318
Arthroscopic surgery, 318
Artificial hearts, 338
Astronomer, 286, 287, 288,
    297
    career as an, 306
Astronomy, 286
Athletes, training of, 161
Atmosphere, 259, 260–263
Atom, 116–119, 122, 124,
    127–129, 156–158
    electrons of, 117, 157–161,
        163–165, 167–168, 170
    energy from the, 186
    model of, 116–117
    neutral, 157, 160
    neutrons of, 117
    nucleus of, 117, 156
    protons of, 117, 157
Atrium, 339, 340

Bacteria in bioconversion,
    202
Ball-and-socket joint, 319
Battery, 169–170
    dry cell, 163, 170
    wet cell, 170
Beavers, 90

Big Dipper, 301
Bioconversion, 201–203
Biodegradable materials, 254
Biomass, 201, 202
Birds, 67–71, 90
    flamingoes, 69
    pigeons, 70
    weaverbirds, 70
Birth rate in animal
    populations, 91–93
Black dwarf, 293, 294
Black hole, 295
Bladder, 354
Bleeding, 342
Blizzard, 273
Blood, 335, 336–338
    plasma in, 336
    platelets in, 337–338
    red blood cells in, 334–335,
        336
    white blood cells in, 337
Blood circulation, 339–341
Blood pressure, 343–344
Blood system in mollusks, 41
Blood vessels, 310–311, 335,
    336, 337, 339–341, 343,
    344
    arteries, 339, 343, 344
    capillaries, 339–341, 348
    veins, 339–341
Boiling point, 140, 141
Bone marrow, 317
Bones
    care of, 329
    injuries to, 318, 327
    muscles and, 321–323
    number of, 315
    of skeleton, 314–318
Botanist, career as a, 104
Brain (of a flatworm), 34
Bristle, 37
Bronchial tubes, 347

Bronchitis, 352
Bryce Canyon, 212–213

Calculator, solar-powered,
193
Cancer, lung, 352
Canyon, 222
Capillaries, 339–341, 348
Carbon dioxide
in the blood, 336
and plants, 10–15, 17, 83
in respiration, 59, 346, 353
in weathering, 218
Carbonic acid, 218
Carson, Rachel, 307
Cartilage, 58, 318
Centipedes, 46
Ceramics, 144
Chameleons, 66
Charge, negative and
positive, 156–157, 170
Chemical change, 149–150
Chemical energy, 169
Chemical sprays, 247, 248
Chemical weathering,
218–219
Chemicals, dangerous, 127
Chemist, career as a, 206
Chlorine, 246
Chlorophyll, 13, 14
Chloroplast, 12–13
Circuit, 163–166, 175
complete, 163
closed, 163
incomplete, 163
open, 163
parallel, 164–165
series, 164
Circuit breaker, 175
Circulatory system, 336–344
diseases and care of,
342–344
path of blood in, 339–341
Cirrus clouds, 276

Clams, 41–42
Clark, Barney, 338
Classification of animals, 28,
29, 57, 73
Clean Air Act, 243
Climax stage, 99
Closed circuit, 163
Clouds, 271–279
altocumulus, 278
cirrus, 276–277
cumulus, 276
fog, 242, 277
nimbostratus, 279
nimbus, 278
stratocumulus, 278
stratus, 277
Coal, 182, 184, 185, 240–241
Cold front, 271–273
Cold-blooded animals, 56–66
Colds, 351
Color, 134
Combustion, 184
Community, 84–85, 87, 91,
95–101
changes in a, 95–101
Complete circuits, 163
Compound, 122–129, 142,
150
ammonia, 125
sugar, 124–125
table salt, 124–125
water, 125–128
Compound fracture, 327
Computers, 127, 161, 274,
297
Conductor, 161–163
Conservation in the home,
185, 208–209
Constellations, 301–302
Crab Nebula, 294
Cramp, muscle, 328
Crocodiles, 63, 64
Crude oil, 183, 185
Crustaceans, 46–47
Cultured pearl, 44
Cumulonimbus clouds, 278

Cumulus clouds, 276
Current electricity, 160–176

DDT, 307
Death rate in animal
populations, 91, 92
Deer, 92, 94
Density, 135
Deposition, 223–225
flooding and, 224
Desert, 80–81, 87
Desert pavement, 231
DeVries, William, 359
Diaphragm, 348–349, 352
Diet, 329, 344, 355
bread and cereals in, 329
dairy foods in, 329
fats in, 344
fruits and vegetables in,
329, 355
protein foods in, 329
Dietician, career as a, 358
Digestive system in worms,
35–37
Dolphins, 73
Down (feathers), 68
Drought, 232
Dry cell, 163, 170
Duck-billed platypus, 73
Dust Bowl, 232
Dust storm, 232

Earth, changes in the,
212–233
Earthworms, 36–37
Echinoderms, 39–40
starfish, 39–40
Ecologists, 82, 91
Ecology, 81–101
Ecosystem, 82–101
community in an, 84–85,
87, 95–101
habitat in an, 87–90

population in an, 84–87, 90–94
succession in an, 98–101
Eggs, 62, 63, 67
Electric cell, 169–170
 dry cell, 163, 170
 wet cell, 170
Electric circuits, 163–166, 175
Electric discharge, 160
Electric meter, 173, 174
Electric motor, 172
Electrical energy, 156–177
Electricity, 154–177
 current, 160–176
 definition of, 156–158
 kinds of, 159–161
 measuring, 173–174
 producing, 167–170, 184, 187, 192, 193, 195–199, 202
 safety and, 175–176
 sources of, 184, 187, 192, 193, 195–199, 201–203
 static, 159–160
 using, 171–172, 184–185
Electromagnet, 171
Electrons, 117, 157–161, 163–165, 167–168, 170
Element, 118–121, 122, 124–127, 144
Elliptical galaxy, 298
Embryo, plant, 22
Emergency medical technician, career as an, 358
Energy, 156, 171–172, 181–203, 260–263
 alcohol as a source of, 202–203
 bioconversion as a source of, 201–203
 chemical, 170
 conserving, 185, 208–209
 electrical, 156–177
 fossil fuels as a source of,

182–185, 240–241
 geothermal, 197–198
 heat, 140, 141, 172, 201–202, 260–264
 hydroelectric, 195
 light, 172
 mechanical, 168, 172
 nuclear, 186–189
 and physical change, 139–141
 solar, 180–181, 190–193, 260–263
 sources of, 180–203
 tidal, 196
 from water, 168–169, 195–196
 wind, 199
Environment, 82, 97
Equator, 261
Erosion, 220–233
 agents of, 220
 and gravity, 220
 ice and, 227–229
 water and, 215–225
 wind and, 231–233
Evidence
 direct, 113
 indirect, 114, 115
Excretory system, 353–355
 bladder, 354
 kidneys, 353, 354
 lungs, 353
 skin, 353
 sweat glands, 353
 urine, 354
Exercise, 331, 344, 345, 352
 circulation and, 344
 muscles and, 331
 respiration and, 352
Exhaling, 349, 353
Exoskeleton, 45, 52
Eyelid muscles, 326
Eyes, 41
 compound, 49
Eyespots, 34

Faraday, Michael, 167–168
Feathers, 67, 68, 71
Femur, 317
Fertilization in flowers, 22
Fertilizer, 247
Filament, 172
Fin, 58–59
Fish, 58–60
 fossils of, 114
Fission, nuclear, 186–187
Fixed joint, 320
Flamingoes, 69
Flatworms, 34–35
 planarians, 34–35
 tapeworms, 35
Flooding, 224–225
Floral designer, career as a, 104
Flower, 18–22
 ovule in a, 19, 22
 petals of a, 18, 19
 pistil of a, 18, 19, 21–22
 pollen grains in a, 19, 21–22
 pollination in a, 21–22
 stamen, 18, 19, 21
Fog, 242, 276
Food groups, 329
Foot (of a snail), 42
Formula, chemical, 128–129
Fossil fuels, 182–185, 240–241
 coal, 182–183, 185, 240–241
 natural gas, 183, 185
 oil, 183, 185
 as pollutants, 240–243
Fossils, 114
Fracture of a bone, 327
 compound, 327
 simple, 327
Frogs, 61, 62
Front (weather), 271–274
 cold, 271–273
 warm, 273–274

Frost action, 215–216
Fuels, fossil, 182–185,
    240–241
Fur, 72
Fuse, 175
Fusion, nuclear, 186–187

Galaxy, 296–300
    elliptical, 298
    irregular, 298
    spiral, 296
Gas (state of matter),
    137–141
Gas, natural, 183, 185
Gasohol, 202
Geese, 85
Generators, 168–169, 184,
    187, 192, 195, 196, 198,
    199, 202
Geothermal energy, 197–198
Geothermal power plant, 198
Germination, 22–23
Geyser, 198
Gills, 59, 62
Glaciers, 227–229
Global winds, 268
Grand Canyon, 222
Gravity and erosion, 220
Greenhouse effect, 190–191,
    263

Habitat, 87–90
Hair, 72
Hardness, 134
Heart, 335, 336, 338,
    339–341
    artificial, 338, 359
    atrium of, 339
    disease, 343–344
    of earthworm, 36
    ventricle of, 339
Heart muscle, 326

Heat energy, 140, 141, 172,
    197, 201–202, 260–264
Helium, 117
Hemoglobin, 336
High blood pressure,
    343–344
Hinge joint, 320
Host, 35
Hot spot, 197
Human body
    care of, 329–331
    circulatory system,
        336–345
    excretory system,
        353–355
    joints, 319–320
    muscles, 321–328
    respiratory system,
        346–352
    skeletal system, 314–318
Humans, 74
Hurricane Gloria, 274
Hydra, 32–33
Hydroelectric power plant,
    168–169, 195
Hydrogen, 14, 126–129
Hyman, Libbie, 105
Hypothesis, 114

Ice, 132–133, 135, 137, 140
    as agent of erosion,
        227–229
Ice sheets, 229
Incomplete circuit, 163
Indirect evidence, 114
Inhaling, 349
Insects, 48–53
    body segments of, 48
    as food for plants, 9
    mouth parts of, 45, 51
Insulator, 161
Invertebrates, 26–53
    arthropods, 45–53

echinoderms, 39–40
mollusks, 41–44
sponges, 30–31
with stinging cells, 32–33
worms, 34–37
Involuntary muscles, 325,
    326
Iron, 219
Iron oxide, 219
Irregular galaxy, 298

Jarvik, Robert, 338
Jarvik-7, artificial heart, 338
Jellyfish, 32–33
Jointed legs, animals with,
    45–53
Joints, 319–320
    ball-and-socket, 319
    fixed, 320
    hinge, 320
    pivot, 320
Julian, Percy, 207

Kangaroos, 75
Kidneys, 353, 354
Kilowatt, 173–174
Kilowatt-hour, 174
Knee, surgery on, 318
Koalas, 88

Laboratory, robots in, 127
Land breeze, 267–268
Land pollution, 253–255
Larynx, 347
Leaves
    photosynthesis in, 12–15,
        17, 23
    stomata in, 10–11, 13
    veins in, 10, 13, 17

Lichens, weathering effects of, 219
Life processes, 5
    energy release, 5, 16–17, 346
    food needed for, 5, 12–17
    growth, 5, 22–23
    reproduction, 5, 18–22
    waste removal, 5, 17, 353–355
Ligaments, 319, 328
Light, speed of, 287
Light bulb, 172
    filament of, 172
Light energy, 172
    and plants, 10–12, 14–15
Lightning, 160
Light-year, 288, 297
Limestone, 218
Limestone caves, 218
Limpets, 43
Liquid (state of matter), 137–141
Litter (pollution), 254–255
Living things
    classification of, 28–29
    groups of, 28–29
    life processes of, 5
    likenesses among, 4–5
Lizards, 63, 65–66
Local winds, 266, 268
Lung cancer, 352
Lungs, 62, 67, 340–341, 347–350, 353
Lynx, 93

Magma, 197
Magnet, 167, 168, 169
Magnetic lines of force, 167
Magnitude, 289–290
Mammals, 72–75
    dolphins, 73
    humans, 74
    kangaroos, 75

opossums, 75
platypuses, 73
whales, 56–57, 73
Mass, 112, 135, 265
Matter, 111–129, 133–151, 156
    atoms in, 116–119, 122, 124, 127–129, 156–157
    changes in, 132–151
    chemical changes in, 149–150
    elements of, 118–119, 122, 124–127
    molecules and compounds of, 122–129, 142, 150
    physical changes in, 136–141
    physical properties of, 134–135, 141
    states of, 137–141
    studying, 112–114
Mechanical energy, 168, 172
Melting point, 140, 141, 153
Metals, 120, 144
Meter, electric, 173, 174
Methane gas, 202
Mice, 88
Microscope, 112–113
Milk, glands of mammals, 72, 73, 74
Milky Way, 296–297
Millipedes, 46
Minerals in plants, 9, 10
Mississippi River Delta, 225
Mites, 47–48
Mixtures, 142–148
    solutions, 145–147
    suspensions, 148
Model of an atom, 116–117
Molecule, 122, 126–129
    oxygen, 122
    sugar, 128–129, 145–146, 148
    water, 126–128, 145–146
Mollusks, 41–44
abalone, 44

clams, 41–42
limpets, 43
octopus, 41, 43–44
oysters, 42, 44
periwinkles, 43
scallops, 41, 42, 44
slugs, 42
snails, 42
squids, 43, 44
Molting
    in birds, 68
    in invertebrates, 52
Mosses, weathering effects of, 219
Mother-of-pearl, 44
Motor, electric, 172
Mount St. Helens, 95–96, 99
Mountain glaciers, 229
Muscles
    bones and, 321–323
    care of, 329, 331
    groups of, 325–326
    heart, 326
    injuries to, 328
    skeletal, 321–323, 326
    smooth, 326

Nacre, 44
Natural gas, 183, 185
Natural resources, 238–239, 245
Nebula, 292
Negative charge, 157, 158, 159, 170
Neutral atoms, 157
Neutron star, 295
Neutrons, 117
Niche, 89–90
Nimbostratus clouds, 279
Nimbus clouds, 278
Nonbiodegradable materials, 254
Nonmetals, 120
Nova, 294

Nuclear energy, 186–189
Nuclear fission, 186–187
Nuclear fusion, 187–188
Nuclear fusion test reactor, 188
Nuclear reactor, 187
Nucleus of an atom, 117, 156

Octopus, 41, 43–44
Odor, 134
Oil spills, pollution from, 250, 251
Open circuit, 163
Opossums, 75
Organ, 34
Owls, 87
Oxygen, 14–15, 17, 59, 62, 83, 122, 126, 339–340, 346–348
  in blood, 339–340, 335, 336
  molecule, 122
  in respiration, 59, 346–348
  in weathering, 219
Oysters, 42, 44

Panda, 88
Parallel circuit, 164–165
Parasite, 35, 36
Passive solar heating, 191
Pearl, formation of, 44
Pennsylvania State artificial heart, 338
Periwinkles, 43
Petroleum geologist, career as a, 306
Photosynthesis, 12–15, 17, 23
Physical change, 136–141
  energy and, 139–140
Physical property, 134–135, 141
  boiling point as a, 140, 141

color as a, 134
density as a, 135
hardness as a, 134
melting point as a, 140, 141
odor as a, 134
shape as a, 134
Physical therapist, career as a, 358
Physical weathering, 215–217, 219
Pigeons, 70
Pioneer stage, 99
Pioneer 10, 285
Pivot joint, 320
Planarians, 34–35
Plants
  activities of, 2–25
  to control sand dunes, 232
  food production in, 6, 9–11, 12–15, 112–113
  insect-eating, 9
  needs of, 5–6
  photosynthesis in, 12–15, 17, 23
  reproduction in, 18–22
  respiration in, 16–17
  transportation in, 6–10, 11
Plasma, 336
Platelets, 337–338
Platypus, 73
Poles, North and South, 261
Pollination, 21–22
Pollutants, 189, 239
Pollution, 189, 239–255, 307
  air, 240–244
  land, 241, 253–255
  radioactive, 189
  thermal, 249–250
  water, 236–237, 241–242, 245–250
Population, 84–87, 90–94
  changes in a, 91–94
Pores (of a sponge), 30
Portuguese man-of-war, 33
Positive charge, 156–157, 158, 170

Power (electric), 168–169, 173
Power plant, 168–169, 184, 187, 192, 195–198, 202, 241
Power station, 169
Predator, 93
Prey, 93
Protons, 117, 119, 156–158
Proxima Centauri, 285, 288
Pulsar, 297
Pulse rate and exercise, 345

Quasar, 297

Rabbit, snowshoe, 93
Radar, Doppler, 274
Radiation, 127, 189
Radio telescope, 297
Red blood cells, 334–335, 336
Red giant, 293
Refinery, 183
Reflection and solar energy, 262–263
Regeneration, 35, 40
Renewable resources, 239
Reproduction in flowering plants, 18–22
Reptiles, 63–66
  alligators, 63, 64
  crocodiles, 63, 64
  lizards, 63, 65–66
  snakes, 63, 64–65
  turtles, 63, 66
Respiration
  in humans, 346, 348
  in plants, 16–17
Respiratory system, 346–352
  bronchial tubes, 347
  diseases and care of, 351–352
  larynx, 347

lungs, 347–350
  trachea, 347
Rest, muscles and, 331
Riverbed, 222
Robots, 127
Root hairs, 6, 7
Roots, 6–9
Roundworms, 34, 36
Runners, 161
Runoff, 220

Salamanders, 61
Salt, 124–125
Sand dunes, 231, 232
Sandbar, 225
Satellites, 193, 274
Scales, 58, 63, 65
Scallops, 41, 42, 44
Scientists, gathering
    information, 91, 112–
    115, 116–117, 118, 306
Sea anemone, 32, 33
Sea breeze, 266–268
Sediments, 223–225
Segmented worms, 34,
    36–37
  earthworms, 36–37
Sense organs of arthropods,
    45
Series circuit, 164
Sewage-treatment plant,
    236–237, 246
Shape, 134
Shark, 58
Simple fracture, 327
Skeletal muscle, 321–323,
    326
Skeletal system, 314–318
Skeleton, 314–318
Skin, 353
Skull, 315, 320
Slugs, 42
Smog, 242
Smooth muscle, 326

Snails, 42
Snakes, 63, 64–65
Soft body, animals with a,
    41–44
Soil, 219
  pollution of, 253–255
Soil conservationist, career as
    a, 306
Soil erosion, 220–223, 253
Solar cell, 192, 193
Solar Challenger, 193
Solar collector, 191, 192
Solar energy, 180–181,
    190–193, 260–263
  and reflection, 262–263
Solar heating
  active, 191
  passive, 191
Solar power tower, 180–181
Solar system, 284–285
Solid (state of matter), 137,
    138, 140, 141
Solute, 146–147
Solution, 145–147
Solvent, 146
Space, 144, 282–302
  distances in, 284–288
Space probes, 284, 285
Space Shuttle, 144
Spiders, 26–27, 47–48
Spiny skin, animals with,
    39–40
Spiral galaxy, 296
Sponges, 30–31
  pores of, 30
Sprain, ligament, 328
Squid, 43, 44
Squirrels, 87, 88, 89
Starch, 15
Starfish, 39–40
Stars, 113, 282–303
  characteristics of, 289–290
  in constellations, 301–302
  galaxies of, 296–299
  life stages of, 292–295
  magnitude of, 289–290

patterns of, 301–302
  size of, 290
  temperature of, 290
States of matter, 137–141
  gas, 137–141
  liquid, 137, 138–141
  solid, 137, 138, 140, 141
Static electricity, 159–160
Stems, 6, 9, 11, 17
Stinging cells, animals with,
    32–33
  hydra, 32–33
  jellyfish, 32–33
  sea anemone, 32–33
Stingray, 58
Stomata, 10–11, 13
Storms, 274
Strain, muscle, 328
Stratocumulus clouds, 278
Stratus clouds, 277
Succession, 98–101
  climax stage, 99
  pioneer stage, 99
Sugar, 14–15, 17, 124–125,
    128–129
  molecule of, 128–129,
    145–146
  solution, 145–146
Sun, as source of energy, 193
Supernova, 294
Suspension, 148
Sweat glands, 353
Switch, electric, 163–165,
    175
Symbol, chemical, 119–121,
    126–129

Table salt, 124–125
Tadpoles, 62
Tapeworms, 35
Telephone cable worker,
    career as a, 206
Telescope, 113, 297

Temperature, effect on
    matter, 140, 141, 146,
    265–266
Tendons, 322
Tentacles, 32–33, 43
Thermal pollution, 249–250
Thunderstorm, 272
Ticks, 47–48
Tidal energy, 196
Tidal power plant, 196
Tides, 196
Toads, 61, 62
Tornado, 272–273
Toxic wastes, 253
Trachea, 347
Tropical rain forest, 89
Tube foot, 39–40
Tungsten, 119
Turbines, 168–169, 184, 187,
    192, 195, 198, 199
Turtles, 63, 66

Universe, 286, 299
Uranium, 186, 189
Urine, 354

Veins
    of human body, 339–341
    of leaves, 10, 13, 17
Ventricle, 339, 340
Venus's-flytrap, 9
Vertebrae, 29, 316
Vertebrates, 29, 56–57
    amphibians, 61–62
    birds, 67–71

fish, 58–60
    mammals, 72–75
    reptiles, 63–66
Veterinarian, career as a, 104
Volcano, 95
Volume, 135, 139
Voluntary muscles, 325, 326
Voyager 2, 284

Warm front, 273–274
Warm-blooded animals,
    67–75
Waste-treatment plant,
    236–237, 246, 249
Water, 126–128, 132–133,
    139, 140, 236–237
    as agent of erosion,
        215–226
    as body fluid, 355
    flooding, 224–225
    frost action and, 215–216
    heat absorption and, 263
    molecule of, 126–128,
        145–146
    physical changes in,
        132–133, 137, 139, 140
    in plants, 6–15
    as source of power,
        195–196
Water pollution, 236–237,
    241–242, 245–252
    from farming, 247–248
    from industry, 240–241,
        249–250
    from oil spills, 250–251
    sewage as, 236–237, 246
Watt, 173–174

Weather, 258–279
    air masses and, 269–270,
        271–274
    air pressure and winds,
        265–268
    beginning of, 260–264
    clouds and, 271–279
    forecasting, 274
Weathering, 214–219,
    227–230, 231
    chemical, 218–219
    by ice, 227–230
    physical, 215–217, 219,
        227–230, 231
    by water, 215–225
Weaverbirds, 70
Wet cell, 170
Whales, 56–57, 73
White blood cells, 337
White dwarf, 293, 294
Wind energy, 199
Wind turbine, 199
Windbreak, 233
Windmills, 199
Winds, 265–268, 272, 274
    as agent of erosion,
        231–233
    global, 266, 268
    land breeze, 267–268
    local, 268
    sea breeze, 266–268
Westerlies, 268
Wolfram, 119
Worms, 34–37
    flat, 34–35
    round, 34, 36
    segmented, 34, 36–37

Yeast, 203

Credits

Chapter 10 236–237: Runk/Schoenberger/Grant Heilman Photography. 239: *l.* Keith Gunnar/Bruce Coleman; *r.* © Harald Sund. 240: Tom Tracy/The Stock Shop. 241: John Zoiner/Peter Arnold, Inc. 242: *t.* Gary Milburn/Tom Stack & Associates; *b.l., b.r.* D. Brewster/Bruce Coleman. 243: *t.l.* Donald Dietz/Stock, Boston; *t.r.* Silver Burdett & Ginn; *b.r.* Dave Davidson/Tom Stack & Associates. 244: Silver Burdett & Ginn. 245: *l.* Jan Comprecht/Tom Stack & Associates; *t.r.* Mike Mazzaschi/Stock, Boston; *b.r.* Bruce Coleman. 246: Silver Burdett & Ginn. 247: E.R. Degginger. 249: © Tom McHugh/Photo Researchers, Inc. 250: *m.l.* © Earl Roberge/Photo Researchers, Inc.; *b.l.* Jeff Foott/Bruce Coleman; *b.r.* Ted Gruen/Bruce Coleman. 251: Larry LeFever/Grant Heilman Photography. 252: Silver Burdett & Ginn. 253: *t.* Grant Heilman Photography; *l.* David M. Doody/Black Star; *r.* Aronson Photo/Stock, Boston. 254: *t.* Silver Burdett & Ginn; *b.* Dan De Wilde for Silver Burdett & Ginn.

Chapter 11 258–259: © Georg Gerster/Photo Researchers, Inc. 260: Bill Brooks/Bruce Coleman. 262: *t.l.* Ron Sanford/Black Star; *b.l.* Ron Watts/Black Star. 263: Fred Bavendam/Peter Arnold, Inc. 269: *l.* Bob and Clara Calhoun/Bruce Coleman; *r.* Vic Cox/Peter Arnold, Inc. 270: *l.* Diane M. Lowe/Stock, Boston; *r.* © 1987 Michael Friedal/Woodfin Camp & Associates. 272: *l.* E.R. Degginger/Bruce Coleman; *r.* © Jerry L. Ferrara/Photo Researchers, Inc. 273: D. Franken/Sygma. 274: *t.* NASA; *m.* Herbert Wagner/Phototake; *b.* E.R. Degginger. 275: Hickson-Bender for Silver Burdett & Ginn. 276: *l.* Grant Heilman Photography; *r.* S.J. Krasemann/Peter Arnold, Inc. 277: E.R. Degginger. 278: *t.l., r.* Grant Heilman Photography; *b.l.* Salvatore Giordano, III. 279: © Van Bucher/Photo Researchers, Inc.

Chapter 12 282–283: © California Institute of Technology and the Carnegie Institution of Washington. 284: NASA. 286: The Bettman Archive. 287: Ron Dillow/Tom Stack & Associates. 289: James Lowenthal/Bruce Coleman. 291: Silver Burdett & Ginn. 292: California Institute of Technology and the Carnegie Institution of Washington. 297: *l.* © Steve Northup/Black Star; *r.* Dick George/Tom Stack & Associates. 299: California Institute of Technology and the Carnegie Institution of Washington. 300–301: Silver Burdett & Ginn. 306: *l.* John Colwell/Grant Heilman Photography; *r.* Douglas Kirkland/Contact Press. 307: Robert Pelham/Bruce Coleman.

Unit Four 310–311: Lester V. Bergman & Associates. 310: *l.* © Joseph Nettis/Photo Researchers, Inc. 311: *t.* Manfred Kage/Peter Arnold, Inc.; *b.* Lester V. Bergman & Associates.

Chapter 13 312–313: Dan De Wilde for Silver Burdett & Ginn. 314: Runk/Schoenberger/Grant Heilman Photography. 315: © Karen Bussolini/Photo Researchers, Inc. 318: David Madison/Bruce Coleman. 319–320: Victoria Beller-Smith for Silver Burdett & Ginn. 321: © Stan Pantovic/Photo Researchers, Inc. 324: Silver Burdett & Ginn. 325: *l.* Pam Hasegawa/Taurus Photos; *t.r.* Edward Slater/The Stock Shop; *b.r.* Menscher Freund/Taurus Photos. 326: *t.l.* Dan De Wilde for Silver Burdett & Ginn; *m.* Tom Stack/Tom Stack & Associates; *m.l., b.l.* Martin M. Rotker/Taurus Photos. 327: Salvatore Giordano, III. 328: *t.* 328: *t.* Jeffrey E. Blackman/Medichrome/The Stock Shop; *m., b.* Silver Burdett & Ginn. 329–331: Silver Burdett & Ginn.

Chapter 14 334–335: © Dr. Tony Brain/Science Photo Library/Photo Researchers, Inc. 336: *t.* © Grace Moore; *b.* © Russ Kinne/Photo Researchers, Inc. 337: © M. Abby/Photo Researchers, Inc. 338: *l.* Alfred Owczarzak/Taurus Photos; *r.* Tim Kelly/Black Star. 342: *l.* Salvatore Giordano, III; *r.* Silver Burdett & Ginn. 343: *t.* Manfred Kage/Peter Arnold, Inc.; *m.* Lester V. Bergman & Associates; *b.* © Grace Moore. 344: *t.l.* B.L. Ullmann/Taurus Photos; *b.l.* New York Heart Association; *r.* Phil Degginger. 345: Dan De Wilde for Silver Burdett & Ginn. 346: © Grace Moore. 349–350: Silver Burdett & Ginn. 351: Grant Heilman Photography. 352: *t.l.* Silver Burdett & Ginn; *b.l.* S.L. Craig, Jr./Bruce Coleman; *m., r.* Martin M. Rotker/Taurus Photos. 353: Owen Franken/Stock, Boston. 354: *t.* Lester V. Bergman & Associates; *b.* Tom Tracy/Medichrome/The Stock Shop. 358: *l.* Michal Heron; *r.* © Grace Moore. 359: Sygma.